BLACK AMERICANS

IN

VICTORIAN BRITAIN

This study is dedicated to David Killingray who knows why; and to Adam David Greiff and Oliver George Greiff who may get to understand their grandfather.

BLACK AMERICANS
IN
VICTORIAN BRITAIN

Jeffrey Green

PEN & SWORD
HISTORY

First published in Great Britain in 2018 by
PEN AND SWORD HISTORY
an imprint of
Pen and Sword Books Ltd
47 Church Street
Barnsley
South Yorkshire S70 2AS

ISBN 978 1 52673 759 5

Printed and bound in the UK by TJ International, Padstow, Cornwall

Typeset in Times New Roman 11/13.5 by
Aura Technology and Software Services, India

Pen & Sword Books Ltd incorporates the imprints of Pen & Sword
Archaeology, Atlas, Aviation, Battleground, Discovery,
Family History, History, Maritime, Military, Naval, Politics, Railways,
Select, Social History, Transport, True Crime, Claymore Press,
Frontline Books, Leo Cooper, Praetorian Press, Remember When,
Seaforth Publishing and Wharncliffe.

For a complete list of Pen and Sword titles please contact
Pen and Sword Books Limited
47 Church Street, Barnsley, South Yorkshire, S70 2AS, England
E-mail: enquiries@pen-and-sword.co.uk
Website: www.pen-and-sword.co.uk

Contents

Acknowledgements

Evidence of people's lives – history – is scattered. Librarians and archivists have been very helpful and the elderly documents they care for have provided valuable evidence. Their role is easy to overlook when resources have been digitized. To sit in England and check lists of prisoners disembarking in Australia in the 1830s, to read copies of slave narratives from the 1840s and to search numerous newspapers, all online are wonderful facilities. But the help of descendants of the Victorians, family historians, and the downright curious has been essential.

My website www.jeffreygreen.co.uk started in 2009 and has encouraged contacts by individuals, including Geoffrey Gillon who alerted me to his discovery of the 1875 grave of Joseph Freeman, and Chris Clark who shared his interest in his ancestors Ellen and William Craft who escaped slavery in Georgia in 1848 and had six children in England.

Help from the following is acknowledged with many thanks:

Susanna Ashton * Anita Bateson * Richard Blackett * Jenni Blair * Stephen Bourne * Caroline Bressey * Ed Bristow * John Burton * Kathy Chater * Chris Clark * Sean Creighton * Emily DeCosta * Bill Egan * Marjorie Evans * Helen Franklin * Geoffrey Gillon * Harlan Greene * Kyra Hicks * Rita Hughes * Jess Jenkins * David Killingray * Bernth Lindfors * Fay Lock * Rainer Lotz * Greta Morton-Elangué * Hannah Murray * Jill Newmark * John Rogan * Mark Rollason * L. David Roper * Lesley Russell * Howard Rye * Elizabeth Stacey * Beverly Tetterton * Andrew Ward * Mary Watson.

Introduction

In 1986, marking the centennial of New York's Statue of Liberty, an exhibition noted 'For most Afro-Americans, the Statue of Liberty is of minor importance except as a symbol of their unfulfilled dreams.'[1] Certainly the huddled masses of Africans who had crossed the Atlantic in the centuries of the slave trade were not included in the thinking behind the monument. They and their ancestors had been shipped from Africa: the last landing in Mobile, Alabama in 1860.[2] At the time of the statue's construction, adult Americans of African descent had first-hand knowledge of slavery.

Enslaved black men, women and children were vital to the economic growth of what became the United States of America. The world they created and the hardships they experienced have rightly dominated studies of African American life. They were kept in ignorance and were lacking education, and few had knowledge of anywhere other than their immediate district although African words, social practices and crafts survived in isolation.

There has been much interest in those who, despite so many disadvantages, escaped from servitude in the Southern states. Those who ran to freedom were both a drain on the Southern economy and a political irritation.[3] Southern slave states had white patrols which were ubiquitous: they and their dogs sought unauthorized travellers and created fear among the masses. Some have seen runaways as 'a safety valve for slavery by drawing off those who might have led insurrections'.[4] Reaching the less restrictive Northern states did not end the risk of recapture nor provide the freedom that many sought, so fugitives went further north into British North America (Canada). Some went to Africa, some to the Caribbean, others to the west including California.

This study is focussed on the east-bound migration to Britain. British attitudes were affected by the testimony of these black witnesses who informed the British and Irish about life in the United States. Individuals made their homes in Britain and married British people to an extent which might have surprised historian Benjamin Quarles who commented in 1969: 'they posed no threat to the laboring man or to the purity of the national blood stream. Hence they received that heartiest of welcomes that comes from a love of virtue combined with an absence of apprehension'.[5]

Some individuals such as New York-born actor Ira Aldridge, absent from America for forty years, have been studied.[6] Ezra Greenspan's study of William Wells Brown, who lived in Britain from 1849 to 1854 and made a visit in 1877, documents this prolific journalist and author, and his daughter Clarissa who died in Leeds in 1874 having lived in Britain for twenty years.[7] Richard Blackett has examined others who were prominent in articulating black ambitions in Victorian Britain.[8] Frederick Douglass, who toured Britain and Ireland from the 1840s, is well documented.[9] Henry 'Box' Brown, refugee then entertainer in Britain for twenty years, has been detailed by Jeffrey Ruggles.[10]

Some refugees did not return after slavery was abolished and the Confederacy defeated. Sarah Parker Remond, whose brother Charles Remond had been in England in the 1840s, applied to become a British citizen in 1865 and testified that she had been living in Britain for over six years. Citizenship was granted. She studied medicine in Rome, married an Italian, and died there in 1894.[11] Nelson Countee, a slave in Virginia, lived in the English Midlands from the mid-1860s where the British census of 1871 lists him as a cooper (barrel maker) and local Methodist preacher. He married a Londoner and died in 1886 aged 53.[12] Descendants live in the Leicester area and California. Thomas Lewis Johnson lived in London then Bournemouth in the 1890s, and his *Twenty-Eight Years a Slave* was published in Bournemouth in 1909 where he died in 1921, aged 85. Lewis Charlton, recorded as a free man in the US census of Maryland in 1870, toured Britain from 1881 and died in Sheffield in 1888, aged 74. British newspapers, used extensively in this research, reported on the activities of ex-slaves for decades after American slavery had ended.

Many of the newcomers were active in entertainment.[13] We know three members of the Fisk Singers settled in Britain: Isaac Dickerson died in Plumstead, south-east London, in 1900; his colleague Thomas Rutling died in Harrogate, Yorkshire, in 1915; Mattie Lawrence married an Englishman in Croydon in 1890 and died there in 1907. Isaac Cisco of the Wilmington Singers lived in Lancashire from 1878 and died in Bolton in 1905. His son served in the Loyal North Lancashire Regiment from 1917 to 1919, and died in Bolton in 1935.

Others were conducting campaigns against lynching, notably Ida B. Wells from Mississippi who toured in 1893 and 1894.[14] And, as with Wells Brown,

Charlton and Countee, African Americans campaigned against alcohol. All had an impact on the people of the British Isles who attended their lectures, purchased autobiographies, heard their songs and their sermons, and worked alongside them in factories, on ships, and in domestic service.

Moses Roper escaped from slavery in Georgia to reach New England where to avoid recapture he signed on the *Napoleon* bound for Britain. Aged 20 he arrived in Liverpool in November 1835.[15] He could never have imagined that he would marry a British woman or that their daughters would settle in Australia, Canada and Egypt. Harriet Ann Jacobs who wrote *Incidents in the Life of a Slave Girl* published in 1861 spent much of 1845 as a nursemaid for an American in the village of Steventon, on the Berkshire-Oxfordshire border.[16] Christian evangelist Zilpha Elaw lived in Britain from 1840. She married in London in 1850 and died there in 1873.

William Peter Powell studied in Dublin and Liverpool and qualified as a doctor in 1857, working in Liverpool hospitals until, with his parents and siblings, he returned to New York and served in the Union Army in the Civil War. He died in Liverpool in 1916. George Rice qualified in medicine in Edinburgh in 1874 and worked in the London area into the 1930s. Philadelphia-born Samuel Morgan Smith an actor in provincial England died in Sheffield in 1882. James Cooney was born in Virginia and died in Morecambe, Lancashire aged 67, in 1932. He had been a valet in Ireland, a sailor in the South Atlantic, a migrant to Sierra Leone, and worked in a circus, with the Bohee Brothers showmen in Britain, as a fairground boxer, and as a comedian-entertainer.[17]

These and other experiences of African Americans in nineteenth-century Britain reveal overlooked elements in the history of the American people and aspects of the nature of Victorian Britain. Uncovered fragments are part of a mosaic, sometimes with only one piece discovered. This study sometimes has just a name, whilst others have been traced in more detail. The individuals were of African descent, but widely different activities and achievements make it unwise to invent categories. Reuben Nixon established a hairdresser's shop in Southsea in 1856 – customers would have trusted him.[18] The illiterate Lewis Charlton ordered leaflets from a Bristol printer in 1885.[19] Joseph Freeman worked alongside his son in a Chelmsford foundry according to the 1871 census, and Nelson Countee made barrels.[20] Henry Lewis, of Virginian descent and born around 1818 in St John, New Brunswick, was a mesmerist in the 1850s.[21]

Individuals who had lived in the United States but had been raised in Canada or the Caribbean were often regarded as African Americans, as were those who settled in Liberia. I have followed this for allocating a nationality can restrict our understanding of individuals, as with the Revd Thomas Pinckney. Born in South Carolina, 'a clergyman of colour' trained in England, he worked in Liberia in the 1850s and then in Canada. He married an Englishwoman in Canada and they moved to Southampton where they are listed in the 1871 census. He died there in 1887, aged 70.

And there is the question of the children. In 1892 an *Uncle Tom's Cabin* show reached Birmingham's Theatre Royal and a locally-born woman, 21-year-old Esther Ann 'Hettie' Johnson joined. She was the daughter of an African American singer named John Alexander Johnson who had settled in Birmingham where he was listed in the 1871 census, living with Hannah Greaves. Weeks later on 16 August their daughter Esther Johnson was born. She had an older brother (John Albert Johnson) and Charles Albert Johnson was seven years younger according to the 1881 census. By 1889 their parents had died and in 1891 Hettie was listed as a machine-press operator. In 1901 she married an African American entertainer. She had a career as an actress and died in Fareham in 1973, aged 102.[22] Her brothers are untraced.

Escaped slaves Ellen and William Craft lived in Britain from 1850 to 1869, and had six children. The second son, William Ivens Craft, returned to England where in 1884 he married in London and had four children. Like Ira Aldridge's daughters (who died in London in 1932 and 1956), the nationality of these children is not clear. But official nationality did not really matter in Victorian Britain. After all, no passports were required to enter or leave the United Kingdom – those documents were for other countries – and even destitute aliens could not be expelled.[23] Exposing the hypocrisy of the Statue of Liberty, west-bound migrants 'always had the thought at the back of their minds that if they were denied entry to America they could return to England and settle there'.[24]

In naming individuals of African descent in Victorian Britain and Ireland this project hopes to encourage detailed research, whilst acknowledging the testimony of witnesses is sparse and sometimes unreliable. Fugitives, reformists, temperance advocates and associates of abolitionists were unlikely to express their true opinions of Britain, the British and British society, for where else could they run to? Those who communicated with the old folks at home – as several Fisk singers did – would be unlikely to admit major problems and failure.

Having crossed the Atlantic towards the rising sun, they had rejected the United States of America. A number went further east by migrating to Australia and New Zealand suggesting their ambitions had not been satisfied by life in Britain. Thousands of British people migrated to the Antipodes, so we cannot be sure what had encouraged that secondary black migration which like the African American presence in Victorian Britain, is under-researched.

The often superficial nature of newspaper reports and inconsistencies in official documents with the spelling of names (Johnson/Johnston; Lewis/Louis; Countee/County; Pinckney/Pinkney; Lawrence/Lawrance) is one difficulty but the almost total absence of 'race' as a concept is a major problem. No British birth, marriage or death registrations indicate 'race' or 'color' as American documents did. Schools, colleges, churches, chapels, graveyards, and street directories do not distinguish between the people they listed. For migrant African Americans, whose entire lives had been defined by the colour of their skin, this official blindness and its apparent recognition by the majority of Britons was so different to their natal land.

African Americans who had lived in Victorian Britain had an impact on kinfolk in the United States. They influenced the British. It is hoped that this book will encourage others to examine this phenomenon and, whilst not anticipating the Statue of Liberty will be modified to have her waving a handkerchief in farewell to those who sailed east, this black presence at the time of the ever-expanding imperialist Britain will improve our understanding of the era and the men, women and children who turned their backs on America to face the future in a new land.

Chapter 1

Escape from these Regions
of Wickedness

Moses Roper escaped from slavery in Georgia to New York where 'I thought I was free; but learned I was not: and could be taken there.'[1] In November 1835 he sailed to Liverpool, with letters of introduction to sympathizers in London. He spent six months 'going through the rudiments of an English education' in Hackney, London and then went 'to another boarding-school at Wallingford' in Oxfordshire. He started at University College London but ill-health prevented further education. He lectured all around Britain, and his *Narrative of the Adventures and Escape of Moses Roper from American Slavery* was published in 1837: it provides these details. He wrote 'he has hitherto been supported by a few ministers and gentlemen; his object in visiting some of the principal towns now, is to sell a sufficient number of his books to educate himself; which will enable him fully to carry out the object he contemplates, that of being qualified to labor amongst the children of Africa. And he hopes that he may in time be a humble instrument in liberating his mother, brothers and sisters from slavery.'

In December 1839 he married Ann Stephen Price in Bristol. His narrative had five English editions by 1843 and was published in Welsh in 1841, and another was printed in Berwick on Tweed in 1848, which stated sales had been 36,000. Several pages list locations (almost all Nonconformist) in Wales, Scotland and England where he spoke, and they include Oswaldtwistle (Lancashire), Leominster (Herts), Yeovil (Somerset), Axminster, Dorking and Towcester. Roper had told his tale widely. After twelve years the public appearances of this 'nearly white' escaped slave still drew crowds. His *Narrative* had helped finance his education.[2] Roper was a dramatic speaker, showing his audiences 'several instruments of torture'. His height (he was 6ft 5in – over 2 metres) added to his appeal.

Scrutiny of the places named reveals many were villages, even hamlets, with fewer than 1,000 inhabitants and less than 200 houses. Although

Britain's rail network was substantial and expanding, the modern mind is struck by the isolation of some venues. Croyde in North Devon is on the coast, 10 miles (16km) from Barnstaple, and both Mursley in Buckinghamshire and Bluntisham in Huntingdon are hamlets, as was Loscoe in Derbyshire although Roper could have walked there from the nearest rail station. Steventon in Bedfordshire is better known as Stevington, and was 5 miles (8km) from the centre of Bedford. The *Imperial Gazetteer* of the 1870s indicates that it had 148 houses with 606 residents. One of his lectures was in Barton-le-Clay near Luton on 17 August 1860.[3]

Where did he stay, who came to hear him, who purchased his *Narrative*? His appearance at the Bible Christian chapel in Wroxall on the Isle of Wight was in a village with no church. His list indicates he also spoke at town halls and in school rooms of the Church of England, and some locations suggest a planned tour. Perhaps pamphlets announcing his programme will be traced in libraries and at ephemera fairs.

Writing from Daventry in May 1844 he informed the committee of the British and Foreign Anti-Slavery Society in London of his eight years in Britain, sometimes lecturing twice a day and visiting 2,000 places. He had accumulated £80 which would take him, his wife and his child (that child seems to have died young) to settle in South Africa but then they would have no funds left. He requested a loan, promising to use his knowledge of cotton, tobacco and maize which he was sure grew in the Cape region. There was enough for the Ropers to go to Canada in the mid-1840s (their daughter Annie was born on the voyage). He had returned by mid-1855 when he spoke in Hereford (the newspaper noted his style had improved since he was last in the town, seventeen years before). A collection helped towards his costs. He was noted by a Guildford newspaper in October 1855.[4]

The Ropers had four daughters. They and their mother were listed in the 1861 census in Merthyr Tydfil, Wales when he was in Cambridge where he was living in a working-class area of the city and described as a 'Lecturer on Slavery, U. States'. That census shows his family in the house of William Price, the father-in-law of Roper, a Welsh-born widowed tailor, aged 76. Price's daughter Ann, born in 1819, was described as a teacher in a private school. Roper's oldest daughter Annie had been born in 1846, and was working as an assistant teacher. Her birthplace was stated to be 'on the Atlantic Ocean'. Three girls were still at school: Maria was aged 11, Ada Victoria was 9, and May Alice (also known as Alice Maud Mary) was 7. They had been born in Canada. Ada had been born in Lower Canada (Quebec) and May in Nova Scotia.[5] All four daughters were British subjects.

ESCAPE FROM THESE REGIONS OF WICKEDNESS

In 1867 Annie sailed on the *Atlanta* to Australia, to work as a governess.[6] There she married Thomas Edward Donehue in 1871. He died in 1886: she died in 1927. In 1883 Alice Maud Mary Roper, aged 26, who declared her 'Baptist missionary' father to be dead, married Youhannah El Karey – a Baptist missionary in Palestine – in a chapel in Newport, South Wales, with her sister Victoria Ada Roper (*sic*) as a witness.[7] Moses Roper died, a pauper, in America in 1891.[8]

Education, independence, marriage, children, were all aspirations that were often dreams for African Americans in the United States. Running from servitude could take them to Canada, to the apparently friendly Northern states, out west to California, across the Atlantic to Britain, or to the islands notably Jamaica and the Bahamas. Slave catchers anxious to receive rewards for the capture of fugitives had widespread support. American laws regarded the escapees as thieves – they had stolen themselves (the property of others) and also the clothes they wore (likewise, the property of others), and any boat or horse used in the escape. The small minority of African descent Americans who were 'free people of color' were constrained and restricted, excluded from white-run activities other than as menials.

Their leaders were often active in Christian churches, independent from whites. The Christian message of redemption and salvation provided comfort. They could worship in a manner compatible to their circumstances, organized outside white ecclesiastical structures. The black-led churches and their ministers had an obligation to represent African Americans.

British reformers and social agitators often had strong Christian beliefs, and the horrors faced by African Americans were not acceptable to many of them. British chapels and churches became places for meetings and lectures on slavery, and Roper was followed by dozens of others, who spread news of American life around Victorian Britain and Ireland.

There was Zilpha Elaw, a Methodist evangelist born in Pennsylvania who was active in Britain from the 1840s, who published her *Memoirs of the Life, Religious Experience, and Ministerial Travels and Labours of Mrs. Zilpha Elaw, an American Female of Colour* in London in 1846. The book's dedication suggests that she was about to return to America. She thought that there was a 'weakness of faith' in Britain. She had travelled into the slave states which she called 'these regions of wickedness'.[9] She wrote of giving over 1,000 sermons around Britain. She had left her daughter and grandchildren in America (her husband had died in 1823). A dispute led to letters in the *Kendal Mercury* in 1847, when she was supported and praised by her host in the Lake District town of Sedbergh.[10] The *Watchman and Wesleyan Advertiser* of 15 January 1851 reported that she had married Ralph Bressey Shum in Poplar, east London, towards the end of 1850.[11] Their marriage registration at the parish church in Bow Road on 9 December 1850 states that she was a widow and he a widower. Their fathers (her father was Sancho Pancost) had been butchers. Shum died in 1854 and she died in London in 1873. She is listed in the 1871 census at 33 Turner Street close by the London Hospital. Her book, with her portrait, which may have been reissued in 1849, says she arrived in London in July 1840 and mentions locations where she preached and attended Christian services. She gives no names in full, just the initial of the surname.[12]

Her *Memoirs*, which plod on with few useful details, and indicate she had visions and was often incapacitated, state that she first lived in Wellclose Square near the Tower of London, and toured in Kent and Yorkshire.[13] A feel for the style might be seen in this: 'In the year 1808, I united myself in the fellowship of the saints with the militant church of Jesus on earth.'[14] As a professional preacher she had to fight widespread prejudice against women. It is probable that donations and collections financed her life. It has been assumed that she died soon after her *Memoirs* were published. Failures by historians condemned this African American into near-invisibility despite her thirty-three years in England.

It is not rare for accounts of Americans (of all origins) in Europe to note their associations with aristocrats and monarchs, although evidence is sometimes elusive. Frank Johnson, a band leader from Philadelphia, was in Britain from late 1837. His quintet was announced in the London press: 'The American minstrels, self-taught men of colour from Philadelphia, have the honour to announce their intention of giving a series of Morning Concerts.' Johnson was later said to have given a command performance for Victoria at Windsor, and to have received a silver bugle from the monarch. Victoria had become Queen in June 1837, aged 18. The most likely time was in April 1838: but there is no evidence. Johnson was said to have been born in Martinique around 1792, which seems unlikely. We will see others born and raised outside the U.S.A. who were regarded as African Americans.

· In February 1840 Victoria married her German cousin, Prince Albert of Saxe-Coburg and Gotha. He busied himself with civic affairs, including presiding over the African Civilization Society which was concerned in the suppression of the West African slave trade, trying to replace it with legitimate commerce. It was Albert's first appearance chairing a public meeting.[15] In 1841 three ships sailed off to the River Niger where it was planned to move up the river and form a settlement in the interior. Disease decimated the people and the project failed.

That royal involvement in actions to affect the lives of black people was not the only participation by members of Britain's ruling elite. An Anti-Slavery Convention was held in London in June 1840. Benjamin Robert Haydon's massive painting shows five African-descent men present. Three were from Jamaica, and there was a Haitian named L'Instant and Samuel Prescod, a journalist from Barbados.[16] In September 1841 Prescod was in a deputation of the British and Foreign Anti-Slavery Society to Downing Street, and met Prime Minister Robert Peel. This concerned slavery in India.[17] We know of one African American involved in the 1840 convention: Charles Lenox Remond was a free black, born in Massachusetts of a Bostonian mother and a hairdresser from Curacao (Dutch West Indies) in 1810. An excellent public speaker, he was a member of the American Anti-Slavery Society's delegation to London's Anti-Slavery Convention of 1840.

Remond went on to speak in Manchester and in Glasgow. In the former city he 'traced the effect which the cultivation of cotton in India must have in abolishing American slavery'.[18] Remond and others were aware America's slave-produced cotton was crucial to the textile industries of Britain (visible in the mill towns of Lancashire) and sought to have a less-tainted source to replace it. He continued speaking around the British Isles, appearing in Cork in late 1841 when his lectures were described as being 'productive of much good no one could listen unmoved to his appeals on behalf of the suffering and oppressed'. He was 'eloquent' and had 'good manners – then because he is young, handsome, and interesting. He had great tact and discretion'. Nearly twenty years later his sister Sarah Parker Remond came to Britain and was very busy on the lecture circuit, as we will see.

In 1842 Moses Grandy was in Britain and his *Narrative of the Life of Moses Grandy; Late a Slave in the United States of America* was published in London. It had seventy-two pages, and its introduction by British abolitionist George Thompson was dated 18 October 1842, two months after the North Carolinian arrived in Liverpool, aged 50. Thompson has been described as the 'one Englishman above all others to whom the visiting blacks were indebted', doing 'all that he could for the visitors'.

The leading Irish abolitionist Richard Webb published it in Dublin in 1843. It was also published in Boston, Massachusetts in 1844, and 'sold for the benefit of his relations still in slavery'. Grandy had 'lived in Boston ever since I bought my freedom'. It has a note 'It is not improbable that some of the proper names in the following pages are incorrectly spelled.

M.G., owing to the laws of the slave states, being perfectly illiterate, his pronunciation is the only guide.' Grandy had been a sailor and had travelled to the Mediterranean and the East Indies. He used his earnings to purchase his freedom, and that of relatives. He states he paid $1,850 for his freedom, $300 for his wife, $450 for his son, $400 for the grandson, and $60 to redeem his kidnapped son. He was seeking $100, the agreed price to buy his sister Mary in North Carolina.

Jacob Walker had been a slave to a Virginia family. George Long was a professor of ancient languages at Charlottesville and in 1828 became a professor of Greek in London. His wife, Harriet, the children and their slave Jacob Walker came too, and settled in Hornsey in north London. Harriet Long died in June 1841 and Walker in August 1841, aged 40. He had died from smallpox. They were buried together. Their slate gravestone at St Mary's parish church states Walker had been 'In America the faithful slave, in England the faithful servant.' The 1841 census declared him to be a servant.

Walker was brought across the Atlantic, Grandy and Roper had worked their way to Britain, Remond was a delegate attending an international meeting, Johnson and his colleagues were a commercial venture, Elaw was a reformist.

James Pennington came to Britain in 1843. Born in Maryland in 1807 he escaped in 1827 and reached New York City in 1828. A skilled artisan, a blacksmith and with other skills, he had acquired literacy when hidden by a Quaker family. Adding Greek and Latin, he took leading roles in black church organizations, became a minister in Hartford, Connecticut, and wrote *A Text Book on the Origin and History of the Colored People* in 1841. In 1843 he was sent by the Connecticut State Anti-Slavery Society to attend the World Anti-Slavery Convention in London.

Britain's elite continued to be named in reports on the Anti-Slavery Society and the African Civilisation Society, with members of both houses of parliament, clergy and a scattering of bishops reported at their annual meetings in London in 1842.[19] At the Anti-Slavery Society's annual meeting in 1843 the audience heard Pennington 'a black gentleman' speak 'with some effect'.[20] Grandy was present. Pennington met various activists in Britain's anti-slavery circles, visiting Worcester, Leeds and Birmingham as well as London. 'For the first time in his life he was cordially received by all, welcomed into their homes and churches, and he travelled freely, encountering no nagging racial restrictions.' He was legally owned in Maryland and negotiations to buy the freedom of Pennington and members of his family continued. Back in America Pennington faced the problem that his fame had drawn attention to his status as an escaped slave. Slave catchers were active and would obtain payment if they snared him and returned him to his owner. He moved to Jamaica, away from slave catchers, for two years.

He was convinced African Americans were suited to be Christian missionaries in Jamaica, and when he made a second visit to Britain in 1849 he met with the missionary wing of the United Presbyterian Church of Scotland. His *The Fugitive Blacksmith* was published in London in 1849 and went into further editions selling 6,000 copies. It has ninety pages. His preface dated 15 August 1849 was written at 13 Princes Square, London. The Presbyterians of Berwickshire, notably in the small town of Duns (or Dunse) supported Pennington, the town's £60 helping purchase his freedom from his Maryland owner.[21] In Kelso in Berwickshire he proposed relocating ex-slaves from Canada to Jamaica. Pennington was linked to the Free Produce Association, which supported a boycott of slave-produced sugar and cotton, promoting the idea that the produce of free labour was fairer. Awarded an honorary degree by the University of Heidelberg in 1849 the now Dr Pennington became well-known in England and Scotland. He left for the U.S.A. via Edinburgh in July 1851.

The British listened, and read the slavery narratives. British newspapers reported on incidents such as the seizure of the *Creole* by nineteen slaves, part of a human cargo numbering 135 being shipped from Virginia to New Orleans, and its arrival in Nassau in the British Bahamas in November 1841. This led to a dispute between the British and American governments, the latter seeking the return of property and the British regarding their actions to be like those of prisoners of war: and refused to hand over any of them. Some had moved on to freedom in Jamaica. In an editorial of 1 February 1842 *The Times* stated a slave had 'the right to rebel' and 'the right to rise and seize his freedom by force'.

The treatment of people of African descent in America had been symbolized by two items on page 5 of *The Times* of 16 July 1840. It quoted the *New York Courier*'s report that the president of the Republic of Texas (it was to join the U.S.A. in 1845) had proclaimed that 'all persons of colour to remove therefrom before the 1st day of January, 1842'. And the *New York Express* had noted 'a dreadful outrage' when a mob raped and set fire to the 'mulatto' wife of a 'coloured man' in Delaware, burning her to death. She had been thought to have been white. 'In a Christian land, and among a civilised people, it is indeed disgraceful.' The newspaper-reading

British could learn of the continuing movement of African slaves from the pages of *The Times* in January 1842. News came from the Atlantic island of St Helena that HMS *Acorn* had rescued 500 slaves bound for Brazil, and reported the appalling conditions found on the slave ship.

The London contacts of slave-servant Walker are unknown, and we have few details of those made by Harriet Ann Jacobs who was to acquire fame as Linda Brent following her 1861 memoir *Incidents in the Life of a Slave Girl*. This was reviewed in Britain's abolitionist press. Her sexual exploitation and being forced to live in a secret hideaway in a relative's North Carolina home made powerful testimony. In *Incidents* she mentions working for Nathaniel Willis, as a children's nurse, in England in 1845. She had spent ten years as a fugitive, hidden for seven, before reaching New York. Her freedom was purchased in 1852, so she was a slave in England.

Much of 1845 was spent in Steventon in Berkshire (now in Oxfordshire), which she described as 'a small town, said to be the poorest in the county' where the largely farming community 'lived in the most primitive manner; it could not be otherwise, where a woman's wages for an entire day were not sufficient to buy a pound of meat. They paid very low rents, and their clothes were made of the cheapest fabrics'. Jacobs 'visited them in their little thatched cottages'. She and her charge resided with a clergyman's family. 'I never saw the slightest symptom of prejudice against color'.[22]

She was in England for ten months, and would have been known to most of the villagers – Steventon had fewer than 1,000 inhabitants. Ten miles from Oxford, it had a train station and the road carried carts and wagons. Escaping would have been easy. Her presence in England in 1845 raises several questions.

The British public were not unused to seeing dark servants – it was quite normal for employers to bring servants with them from China, India, Africa, and the Caribbean, and at one time Americans were thought to be black due to the numbers of slave-servants attending to their masters. There was the 23-year-old 'African servant' of the Revd William Hepworth reported in the *Bury and Norwich Post* of 3 January 1844. Bristo Hepworth had died at the rectory, Finningham on 26 December 1843. This isolated village is in northern Suffolk (its train station opened in 1849). The *Bentinck* sailed from Calcutta for Suez (the canal did not open until 1869) with 184 passengers for England. Fourteen were listed as 'native servant' in the *Standard* (London), 20 April 1846. London Missionary Society worker Henry Russell and his wife Elizabeth went to Jamaica in 1835, and had three children: the youngest after his father died in 1839. The widow and children were in London in July 1840. With them was Ann Elizabeth Styles, an illiterate black servant. Every London census from 1841 to 1901 lists her. Ann Styles died in January 1903, aged 80, at 8 Eldon Road, Hampstead, where she lived with Elizabeth Russell Hough's children.[23]

Females seem rarer than males. One early example is Mary Ann McCam or Macham of North Shields.[24] McCam arrived in North Shields on Christmas Day, 1831. She had escaped from Virginia where she was born in 1802 to an enslaved woman and a slave-owner. She is said to have crossed the Atlantic on the *Atlas*, arriving in Grimsby. The master of the ship took her to North Shields where she was taken in by the Quaker Spence family and worked as a domestic servant in the homes of various members of the family. In 1841 she married a local man, James Blyth. The Tynemouth registration of the marriage has her surname as McHam.[25] Her surname has also been written as Macham, suggesting a different pronunciation, but McCam is an American name. Blyth was a rope maker and later a banker's porter, possibly at the Spence family bank. James and Mary Ann lived in various houses on Howard Street in North Shields. After he died, around 1877, Mary Ann continued to live in North Shields and for a while stayed with relatives of her husband in South Benwell. She died in 1893 and was buried in Preston Village cemetery in North Shields. No children have been identified.

William Jeffers from New York had been active in black self-help groups there, leaving in 1840 and obtaining a clerical role in a London bank (several banks were Quaker-owned and -influenced). Jeffers died, in his thirties, in Southwark in the early summer of 1841. Philadelphia-born Robert Douglass studied art in London in 1840–41. He returned to America, and migrated to Jamaica in the mid-1840s where he stayed for some months. He died in 1887.

Another aspect of the African American presence in Victorian Britain was fund-raising for projects in British North America (Canada). The numbers of ex-slaves, usually having origins in the United States, in Upper Canada (from 1841 called Canada West, later Ontario) is uncertain. Between 15,000 and 30,000, perhaps.

Black refugee groups in Canada sought support in Britain, sending representatives across the Atlantic. Nathaniel Paul came from a free black family in New Hampshire. From 1832 he spent four years in Britain raising money for the ex-slave settlement in Wilberforce, Ontario. In Britain he married an English woman, and died in 1839. It had been unwise to pick Paul for this project for although he collected over $8,000 he had expenses of $7,000 plus his monthly wage of $50. The settlement had reduced to four families by 1878. Funds gathered around Britain reflected the goodwill of local people towards American slaves.

The income from the sales of narratives, collections made at meetings and donations from supporters enabled these Americans to survive in Britain. Practical help, from schooling to arranging tours, involved local abolitionists. Richard Webb of Dublin, who had been involved in founding the Hibernian Anti-Slavery Society in 1837, arranged the four-month tour of Ireland made by Frederick Douglass in 1845–46. Webb published the *Narrative of the Life of Frederick Douglass, an American Slave* in Dublin in 1845 (it had been published in Boston that year), and a second edition (a third edition was published in Leeds). The income from sales in America funded Douglass when in Britain. By March 1846 sales reached 2,000.

Webb commented on Douglass in Dublin: 'We had comparatively poor audiences here. He had no excitement to stir him up – no opposition worth talking of – no thronging crowds.' Others had different opinions. His initial appearances had been in Ireland for three months, where a resident stated 'There never was a person who made a greater sensation in Cork amongst all religious bodies' … 'he is indeed a wonderful man'.

Often reported as 'Douglas', his appearances with white American anti-slavery activist William Lloyd Garrison were in 'densely crowded' public halls. Often they were supported by Quakers as in Sheffield in September 1846.[26] He was a fine speaker who told audiences he had received no formal education. Supporters centred on Anna (Mrs Henry) Richardson a Quaker in Newcastle who arranged to purchase Douglass from his owner, and £150 was paid in 1846.[27] Some saw this as a compromise for it meant recognizing the right of the slaveholder to sell him. Following his return to America he established a newspaper, and copies were distributed in the British Isles.

He sailed from Liverpool on the Cunard steamship *Cambria* in April 1847. The shipping line's officials insisted he took his meals alone and did not mix with the white passengers in first class. In a letter written in Liverpool and published in *The Times* on 6 April 1847 Douglass stated 'I have travelled in this county 19 months, and have always enjoyed equal rights and privileges' until he had been forced into second-class accommodation on the *Cambria*. The editor thundered about the U.S.A. being 'a nation talking largely of equality and liberality while practically drawing one of the meanest and most senseless distinctions that it is possible to conceive'.[28] Samuel Cunard promised nothing like this would happen again (it did) and exposed a bogus author named Burrup who said he worked for Cunard and claimed most white passengers did not want to travel with 'blackamores'.[29] Promises were made – and broken – about unequal treatment for black passengers. African Americans were aware that ships which did not fly the stars and stripes would be likely to give them better treatment.

Douglass wrote about his months in Britain and Ireland in his *My Bondage and My Freedom* (1855). He mentioned the Cunard experience. In Scotland and the north of Ireland Douglass had been deeply involved in what Presbyterians in those regions felt to be a matter of major importance. The fervour of Victorian Christian politics is largely outside modern experience. Religious and civil domination by the Church of Scotland had led to a schism in May 1843 when over 400 ministers resigned and the Free Church of Scotland was founded. The new organization needed to provide for them and their housing and families, buy or lease land for new church buildings (and to build them), and to support education and mission work. A delegation was sent to the United States where it moved among Presbyterian and Scottish groups and gathered support. They were exposed to slavery, and it was clear slave-owners had been among the donors. Their money was tainted. In early 1846 Douglass was in Scotland, and was involved in the controversy.

Douglass had earlier stated his mission was an anti-slavery one: 'I only claim to be a man of one idea.' But the 'Send Back the Money' campaign became the dominant element. From Dundee he wrote to Webb 'all this region is in a ferment'. Webb printed another 2,000 copies of Douglass's *Narrative* which brought in £150.

When Belfast was pasted with posters 'Send Back the Nigger', Webb blamed a visiting South Carolina churchman. With the numerous church appearances and public statements by various divines, the reality of slavery-founded money was understood in many places in Scotland and the north of Ireland, and Douglass's already substantial public image was enlarged. He told British audiences 'I am a slave still by the laws of the United States', where he could be auctioned and the proceeds given to the Scottish delegation that visited America 'to build their churches and pay their ministers' in Scotland. The money was not returned but as Douglass commented, 'the people [had been] thoroughly acquainted with the character of slavery'.

Douglass reported to the Massachusetts Anti-Slavery Society 'it is quite an advantage to be a nigger here. I find I am hardly black enough for British taste, but by keeping my hair as woolly as possible I make out to pass for at least half a negro at any rate'. Some thought Charles Lenox Remond 'was a white man who had assumed the Ethiop [*sic*] tinge to suit a purpose'.

Other African Americans were known to the groups in which Douglass moved. 'There is another traitor to the cause here, a Mr. Gloucester a coloured minister from Philadelphia – on a mission to raise money, to clear a debt of £1200 on his chapel' who was later described as 'an outrage on all decency, & a scandal to the name of anti-slavery'. British abolitionists and their American friends could be fiery and happy to have internecine squabbles.

The texts of narratives have been examined by James Olney. He observed in 1984 there is a sense 'of overwhelming *sameness*' to slave narratives and there was repetitiveness: 'more and more of the same', and asked 'Why should the narratives be so cumulative and so invariant, so repetitive and so much alike?' Some listed places visited and people met in Britain, a useful addition to the texts, usually in later editions as with Roper. Olney suggests conventions in the narratives were enforced by the very intention of the narrative to be a picture of slavery as it is. There were conventions in illustrations too, which have been noted by Marcus Wood.

The narratives were produced to meet the demands of the market. It was possible to earn a living in Britain through their sales and collections taken at public meetings. Roper toured both Canada and Britain. Many of the refugees had been illiterate, and the influence of abolitionist sympathizers on their texts seems overwhelming. 'In one sense the narrative lives of the ex-slaves were as much possessed and used by the abolitionists as their actual lives had been by the slaveholders.' The style of the narratives continued these conventions decades after abolition had been achieved in the United States. The slim *Life of the Late James Johnson (Coloured Evangelist) an Escaped Slave from the Southern States of America: 40 Years resident in Oldham, England* was published in Oldham in 1914, the year he died in that Lancashire town. As with Roper and many others it starts 'I was born'. Olney suggests for the ex-slave 'it was his existence and his identity not his reasons for writing, that were called into question'.

Johnson had escaped from North Carolina during the Civil War, making his way to a Union ship blockading the Confederacy. He worked on that ship and reached the North and then crossed the Atlantic.

John Brown escaped from Georgia and then worked with Cornish miners in Michigan. Following his arrival in Liverpool in August 1850, he worked as a carpenter in Bristol. Brown went on to Cornwall to renew contacts but was frustrated as his major contact had died. This was described in the local newspaper:

'LECTURE ON SLAVERY,—On Monday evening, John Brown, a man of colour, who stated that he had escaped from slavery in the United States, addressed a large audience at the Town-hall, Truro, to whom he gave a description of the treatment to which he was subjected whilst under the power of the slaveholder. The chair was occupied by Mr. Barlow, who said he had seen documents which satisfied him that John Brown was in reality what he represented himself, an American by birth but an African by blood, who had been a slave, and when in bondage, had been subjected to all the cruelties which a despotic and tyrannical taskmaster could inflict. Mr. Barlow also read a paper signed by four persons living at Redruth, Joseph Vivian, Richard Pascoe, Thomas Williams, and Thomas Champion, who stated that they had worked with John Brown in Lake Superior mine, in North America. They stated that Brown was a slave in the State of Georgia; that he had been four times sold, and came to Lake Superior in 1847, where he was employed by the mining company there for a year and a half, and was found to be a quiet, honest, and industrious man. His object in coming to England was to see Captain Joseph Teague, of Redruth, who had promised him support; but Captain Teague had unfortunately died in America, which John Brown did not know until he arrived in Redruth. He was now without support; and they, (the persons signing the paper) had helped him all in their power, and would do more for him if they could.'[30]

The names of these four Cornish miners fill out the evidence of British support for black refugees.

Brown started lecturing on slavery, and considered migrating to Canada and also Liberia. He later worked as a carpenter, earned a living as a herb doctor, married an English woman and is said to have died in London in 1876.[31]

No matter which branch of the Christian faith the refugees shared with British associates, that once-enslaved individuals moved among co-religionists and in the homes of Britons had positive results. As Moses Roper had discovered, there were Britons who would finance education. Aristocrats, members of parliament, journalists, reformers and church leaders supported the enthusiastic albeit often quirky abolitionists and gave practical support to the refugees. Few of them had met a person of African descent until they had contacts with ex-slaves in Britain. And Americans met people from the Caribbean and Africa for the first time when in Britain.

There were opportunities to meet others from distant lands if you worked on the thousands of ships that flew the British flag. Lancashire's textile mills required prodigious amounts of cotton every week, and countless ships brought the bales into Liverpool. The misunderstandings over the *Creole* were not the only marine problem between Britain and the United States.

American states passed laws with international affairs being the responsibility of senate and congress in Washington DC. Some laws of the Southern states offended foreign countries. Restraints on free black sailors in South Carolina had been initiated following a plot in 1822 led by a free black in Charleston. Black sailors were imprisoned until their ship was about to depart when the captain had to pay the costs of their detention – if that was not paid the sailor could be sold into slavery. In 1829 Georgia required free black passengers or crew to be quarantined for forty days. North Carolina copied Georgia's legislation in 1831 and a captain and two black crew members were imprisoned in Wilmington. Daniel Fraser, a British subject and cook on a ship from Liverpool had been imprisoned in Charleston in November 1830, and only released when the costs had been paid.

Years later London's *Daily News* of 13 August 1853 was to name a Charleston victim John Glasgow who was married to an English woman and had a family in Britain. His captain had sailed without him and he had been sold into slavery. He had been born in British Guiana, his wife was from Lancashire where he had settled. His enslavement was back in 1830, and had taken place in Savannah (not South Carolina). Labouring near Milledgeville, Georgia he met John Brown who was inspired by Glasgow's tales of life in Britain. After Brown met Louis Chamerovzow, secretary of the British and Foreign Anti-Slavery Society the story was published in the *Anti-Slavery Reporter* of July 1853, where the *Daily News* saw it.[32] In Brown's dictated *Slave Life in Georgia*, published in 1855, Chamerovzow printed the declaration made before a London lawyer by Brown in May 1854. It was hoped this would aid Glasgow and assist Glasgow's wife and family.

John Brown gave a talk on 4 May 1868 when he was billed as the 'American Botanist', to a background of cracking nut shells and noisy children attempting to listen outside the hall. The *Western Gazette* gave half a column to its report.[33] This must be the same individual who worked as a herbalist in Taunton where back in mid-1865 he claimed an unpaid bill, being careful to describe this as for herbs and not medicines. The *Dorset County Chronicle* compared Brown to ex-slave and entertainer Henry 'Box' Brown when both were in Taunton in March 1865. His advertisement in the *Sherborne Mercury* on 30 October 1866, and both 22 January and

29 January 1867 stressed he was a black man, the 'celebrated American herbalist' offering pills and tinctures for the stomach, liver, coughs and the eyes. He was based in Durngate Street, Dorchester: the 1865 *Kelly's Directory* states he was a medical botanist.[34]

Combining showmanship and a tale of slavery, Henry 'Box' Brown toured around Britain for over twenty years. Born in Virginia in 1815 and a slave there, then North Carolina, he escaped to Philadelphia in 1849 inside a box despatched 350 miles. He became a lecture hall sensation, fleeing to Britain by 1850. He was assisted by the free-born James Caesar Anthony Smith but their partnership was ended in July 1851. Brown's *Narrative of the Life of Henry 'Box' Brown: Written by Himself* was published in Manchester in 1851. That year he re-enacted his escape, being boxed up and sent from Bradford to Leeds, a ninety-minute trip.

In 1852 he won a libel case against the *Wolverhampton and Staffordshire Herald* which represented him as an ignorant 'darky'. Henry Brown made a successful appearance in York early 1853. With his English partner Jane Floyd he had three children. In April 1855 he was in Bristol exhibiting a panorama (large painted scenes) and in June 1856 he was in Ventnor, Isle of Wight when the 'celebrated fugitive slave' lectured, showed his box, talked about slavery and closed with 'a Negro song' at the end of each lecture.[35] In March 1865 'Mr. H. Box Brown' was billed as the 'African magician' in Taunton, when he was assisted by a female clairvoyant. Brown moved into theatrical appearances after American slavery was abolished and his children helped in those shows. In 1875 he, Jane and their youngest daughter went to America and Box Brown was reported near Boston in 1878. Brown died in Toronto (Canada) on 15 June 1897. The widow Jane lived with a daughter and son-in-law and duly appears in the United States census of 1900, 1910 and 1920.

Represented out of all proportion to their numbers in the general population, Quakers, Unitarians, and other Christian dissenters were active in the several but always small anti-slavery societies which promised guidance for newly-arrived Americans. The network was fractious: officials of the British and Foreign Anti-Slavery Society were in disagreement with American anti-slavery activists. Indeed, the Society's founder Joseph Sturge (1793–1859) has been described as being a 'leading exponent of exaggeration'.

'The whole British anti-slavery movement had become, by the mid-fifties, very much a marginal affair, with more than its share of cranks, visionaries and habitual schismatics.' Their archived letters and publications have provided historians with considerable information but the people they had set out to assist are often not mentioned. The narratives often name-drop, a style not unknown to many authors, and so we have the names of the aristocrats, members of parliament, reverends, businessmen and property-owners in whose company Americans could be found but rarely those of the people who gave their pence to support the sable strangers, although they attended their meetings, read their publications and thrilled at their testimonies – and formed the grass roots of the British abolitionist movement of the 1840s and 1850s.

The tales told at meetings and detailed in the narratives led some Britons to formalize their sympathies towards African Americans. For example the Ladies' Society to Aid Refugees from Slavery, active from 1853 to 1856 arranged to relocate some to Australia, Canada, New Zealand, the British West Indies and West Africa. The Ladies' Society for the Aid of Fugitive Slaves in England paid for Francis Anderson, who had fled Baltimore and worked as a waiter in England, to attend the Voluntary School Establishment in Walworth Road, London, and in late 1855 sent him to Canada where he worked as a teacher. John Williams, who had a 'respectable livelihood in England' was disabled in an accident and could no longer look after his wife and three children, so they too were sent to Canada. He may have been the 'J. Williams' who was in Rye in February 1854.[36] Funds were found for Cassie Stevens, who had been born in Richmond, Virginia and had taken care of the Liverpool family of a British sailor until he died, and in the case of Lewis Johnson, born free in Charleston, South Carolina but enslaved in Mississippi, they funded him after he reached London via Glasgow and found employment as a valet to a Frenchman who was going abroad.[37]

A British slave-descent family has been traced in Chelmsford in Essex where a slave who escaped from New Orleans had put down roots. The 1871 census recorded Joseph Freeman and his Lincolnshire-born wife Sarah with their six children in the town. He worked as a labourer at an iron works as did his 19-year-old Suffolk-born namesake son. His wife seems to have been Sarah Smith who married him in Boston, Lincolnshire in 1849. Their second child Susannah was a dress-maker born in Morton, Suffolk around 1854 and her brother William had been born there; Mary Ann, Eliza and Sarah had all been born in Chelmsford and were still at school in 1871. Their father died in Chelmsford in November 1875 aged 45. His gravestone states he was 'JOSEPH once a slave in New Orleans who escaped to England and became also a FREE MAN in Christ' and asks 'Reader! Have you been made free from the slavery of sin?'[38] There was the Chelmsford Ladies Anti-Slavery Society in Chelmsford but any connections to Freeman are untraced.

Chapter 2

Ellen and William Craft

William and Ellen Craft escaped slavery in Georgia in 1848. They then lived in Boston sheltered by abolitionists. After the enacting of the Fugitive Slave Law and the arrival in that city of slave catchers from Georgia they went to Canada and sailed on Cunard's *Cambria* from Halifax, Nova Scotia to Liverpool in late 1850.[1] Ellen Craft inherited her complexion from her white father, which had enabled her to impersonate a white man accompanied by a slave servant (William), when they escaped by train and boat from Macon, Georgia. William Craft was darker. They made many appearances in Britain, mixed with people of influence and the nameless throngs at meetings, and generated knowledge of American slavery amongst the British. In Scotland in early 1851 William Craft described their escape and then Ellen took the stage. The *Aberdeen Journal* (12 February 1851) carried an announcement with Ellen described as the 'white slave'. British audiences were listening to experts, who spoke well. They had not been plantation workers. That Ellen Craft was not dark was a powerful point. A crowded meeting in York heard Craft say that his father, brother and sister and Ellen's mother and grandmother continued to live a 'miserable life' in slavery.[2]

When Britain's census was conducted at the end of March 1851 the Crafts were staying in Leeds with Wilson Armistead who declared them to be 'Fugitives from America, the land of their nativity' which was widely reported.[3] At Woodhouse Mechanics' Institute in Leeds they were described as 'very interesting and intelligent persons. Ellen is a gentle, refined-looking young creature of twenty-four years, as fair as most of her British sisters, and in mental qualifications their equal too. William is very dark, but of an intelligent reflective countenance, and of manly and dignified deportment'.[4] A meeting in Bristol on 9 April noted 'Mr. Craft is a fine and intelligent young man, but his Negro character is unmistakeable; his wife, however, has a complexion very little darker than that of our country-women. She was neatly dressed and exhibited a modest demeanour; indeed, it struck us that she seemed somewhat embarrassed by the marked attentions paid to her.'[5]

Armistead was deeply involved with the Leeds Anti-Slavery Association and already had written the 560 page *A Tribute for* [sic] *the Negro: Being a Vindication of the Moral, Intellectual and Religious Capabilities of the Coloured Portion of Mankind: with Particular Reference to the African Race.* It was published in 1848. It and he were known to many British abolitionists. His *Five Hundred Thousand Strokes for Freedom* reprinted eighty-two of the Association's tracts in 1853. He and his associates, who included many women, were well-placed to assist the Crafts.

The Crafts made four public appearances in Aberdeen in February 1852, with William Craft described as 'a favourable specimen' and both being 'interesting strangers'. At one meeting 'several negro melodies were sung'.[6] Collections and donations at such meetings must have underwritten their new lives.

It was beneficial to become literate to earn a living and achieve independence, reduce patronage and charity, and settle down. The extent and speed with which these were achieved by Ellen and William Craft were remarkable. William Craft's skills as a carpenter did not require total literacy nor did ladies' maid Ellen Craft need to read and write: those skills were acquired in Surrey. They stated in their *Running a Thousand Miles for Freedom* that neither could read the passes they had obtained and she bandaged her right hand to avoid being exposed when registering in hotels on their flight from Georgia in 1848.

The 1851 census noted that William Craft was a cabinet maker. That trade became an advantage as soon as the Crafts got to know Lady Byron and Stephen Lushington and his two daughters Frances (Fanny) and Alice, all supporters of Ockham School near Ripley in Surrey: the Crafts went there. The school was managed by the two sisters. The Crafts lived with Lushington.[7] They progressed well and were offered positions as superintendent and matron.[8] William taught carpentering and cabinet making to the boys, and his wife taught domestic crafts to the girls.[9] Nothing seems to have been retrieved on what the children thought of their ex-slave teachers.

The parish church's memorial to lawyer Lushington (1782-1873) who lived in the adjoining Ockham Park for twenty-six years notes his 'especial devotion to the Abolition of the Slave Trade'. There is a smaller brass to Thomas Heath Popplestone who died in Sierra Leone, aged 37, in 1872. He had been head of Ockham School for nine years and had gone to Africa to supervise schools in Sierra Leone in the 1860s; Craft recalled his master was Thomas Wilson.[10]

John Bishop Estlin, Bristol surgeon and anti-slavery campaigner on whose arm Ellen Craft attended that 9 April meeting, wrote to the *Bristol Mercury* in October 1851 saying there were people working to obtain the release of Ellen's mother.[11] The Crafts's first child (born in Ockham on 22 October 1852 and described as her 'first free-born son'[12]) was named Charles Estlin Phillips Craft.[13] His father informed the registrar that Ellen's name had been Collins (a Collins had once owned her).

There were plans to operate a boarding house in central London at 3 Arundel Street in 1854;[14] but William Ivens Craft was born on 16 November 1855 at Beavor Cottage in Hammersmith in west London. The birth registration stated that his father was a 'gentleman' and Ellen declared her maiden name had been Atwaters. The Crafts purchased 12 Cambridge Road, Hammersmith in 1857 and their children – there were to be six (two girls) – started school. Their third son Stephen Brougham Dennoce Craft had the name Brougham in recognition of Henry Brougham (first Baron Brougham 1778-1868) an anti-slavery spokesman who knew Lushington. He and his sister Alice Isabella Ellen (known as Ellen) were baptised in Ockham in April 1863. Going to school was not compulsory in England at this time, and little has been recovered on these children. They may have boarded at Ockham, of course.

William Craft, who with Ellen and the children was now based in Hammersmith, was in Worcester in April 1856 and in Leeds in October. On 24 October he was to speak at the East Street Chapel: 'though of African blood and bred in servitude, he speaks with the facility and accuracy of an English gentleman'.[15] On 3 November Craft was at the Philosophical Hall in Huddersfield when a local magistrate introduced him: 'a tall, intelligent-looking man, with a slightly retreating forehead' he was 'received with applause'.[16] A day or so later Craft went on to Halifax where he spoke on 10 November to a very large audience and a collection was made to 'aid Mr Craft to travel from one place to another'.[17] He appeared in Oldham some weeks later, lecturing on slavery and the escape from Georgia.[18] In mid-1857 he was in Newport on the Isle of Wight speaking to a densely crowded hall in which clergymen were numerous.[19] The 1861 census for 12 Cambridge Road lists Ellen 'fugitive slave United States' and her three sons Charles, William and Brougham.

One of the refugees in 1850s Britain was William Wells Brown who had travelled via Ireland and England in 1849 to be one of 800 delegates at the Peace Congress in Paris in late August. Twenty of those delegates were Americans, three being African Americans (all travelled on to England).

Brown's *Narrative of William B. Brown, an American Slave, written by Himself* was already in print and a British edition appeared in 1849. In London, Brown met a destitute fugitive slave to whom he shared his last shilling. Brown had a collection of slave songs published in Newcastle in 1850. His *Three Years in Europe* appeared in 1852. He went on a lecture tour of Britain, sometimes meeting people who had aided Frederick Douglass.

In Pennsylvania in 1849 Brown had aided the Crafts and then for 'four months, Brown and the Crafts went on lecture tours which carried them over all of Massachusetts'. In these and other ways future fugitives had developed contacts and support in America, and American abolitionists introduced them to sympathizers in Britain. Similar links were made within the British Isles.

In Britain there were opportunities to meet people from the ends of the earth, notably at the 1851 Great Exhibition, as well as through casual contacts and formal meetings. The Great Exhibition in London's Hyde Park was where Wells Brown and the Crafts made a protest next to a statue. Garrison's *Liberator* published in Boston reported how Brown and the Crafts had stood by a statue of *The Greek Slave* by Hiram Powers in the American section of the grand international exhibition. Using a page from the London weekly *Punch*, which suggested an enslaved black woman would be a more appropriate subject, they tried to provoke American visitors in the crowd of 15,000 visitors. This seems to have escaped the attention of the general London press, and as *The Times* indicated all visitors including staff on that day totalled 12,732 we may be seeing propaganda.

The great glass building was ultra-modern, dubbed 'the crystal palace' it was removed and erected on Sydenham Hill on the edge of southern London, a district still known as Crystal Palace although the building was destroyed by fire in 1936. The items on display were the creations of industry and by artists. Foreign visitors were expected, the exhibition had interpreters available who could speak Arabic, 'Hindostanee, Bengalee', Persian, Mahratta, Chinese, Malay and 'Orissa'.[20] 'Never before was so vast a multitude collected together within the memory of man' commented *The Times*.[21] More than six million people went to the Great Exhibition in 1851. Right from the opening show-business activities took place, despite the somewhat solemn and educative nature of the exhibition, strongly influenced by Queen Victoria's husband Albert, the German-born Prince Consort.

One African American visitor was David Dorr, a mulatto (one black grandparent) from New Orleans who travelled as the slave-servant of his owner, a businessman. Dorr arrived in Liverpool on a Sunday in June 1851 and was immediately struck by the absence of people: which he put down to the English being 'a moral people' who had paid attention to 'the sweetest sacred music I had ever heard' from the church bells. This is in sharp contrast to Zilpha Elaw's criticism of the crowded Sabbath streets of London. He spent two weeks in Liverpool then took a train to London. He dismissed the American exhibits at the Crystal Palace as 'the most worthless trash' and mentioned the proposal of a South Carolinian to bring 'half a dozen haughty and sinewy negroes to the Fair' which had been abandoned because of the chances of 'escape from slavery to freedom'. Dorr moved on, reaching Turkey and the Holy Land.[22]

At a Unitarian meeting in Nottingham in mid-1851 'Considerable interest was given to the meeting by the presence, as spectators, of W.W. Brown, W. and Ellen Craft, Alexander Duvall [*sic*], and F.S. Anderson, who are all fugitive slaves.'[23] Duval and Francis Anderson had reached Liverpool from Boston at the end of March 1851. Anderson carried a letter from America's leading white anti-slavery activist William Lloyd Garrison. Anderson had escaped six years earlier and worked as a waiter until forced abroad by the Fugitive Slave Act. Duval, armed with a letter from Revd Samuel May of Boston addressed to Revd Francis Bishop of Liverpool, had escaped slavery in Maryland two years before and worked as a barrel maker. His wife and child remained in Massachusetts.[24] Duval was to have problems which could not be resolved. He had some work as a gardener, otherwise he begged in London.

On 14 October 1859 a meeting at the Countess of Huntingdon's Connexion's Spa Fields Chapel in London, heard American activist Revd Samuel May update the audience on anti-slavery activities in America. Listening were Sarah Parker Remond (sister of 1840s visitor Charles Lenox Remond), and Ellen and William Craft: Remond had been lodging with the Crafts.[25] The Crafts had now been in Britain for almost ten years. Even so when Ellen Craft handed her son Charles (born in 1852) to May who declared 'This boy would fetch in the United States 200 dollars' the printed report added '(Sensation)'. The meeting was told that the boy was 'a true-born Englishman' and Lady Byron was his god-mother and Judge Lushington his god-father. William Craft addressed the meeting.

Tweedie published William Craft's *Running a Thousand Miles for Freedom; or, the Escape of William and Ellen Craft from Slavery* in 1860. It went on sale in the summer.[26] Scholars believe Ellen made a considerable contribution to the book.

On 19 June 1861 William Craft appeared at an 'enthusiastic meeting' at the Portman Hall in London's Carlisle Street, a meeting in aid of newly-arrived fugitive John Anderson and the Revd Thomas M. Kinnaird, a minister in Hamilton (Ontario) following twenty-one years in American slavery.

William Craft continued to appear before anti-slavery gatherings such as that in Leeds on 25 March 1862 alongside British abolitionist George Thompson.[27] In April he was in Bristol at an anti-slavery bazaar in aid of fugitive slaves, held at the Victoria Rooms from 9 to 11 April 1862.[28] But his activities were not always focussed on negatives, for fired by ideas on education observed at Ockham's school, Craft was to establish a school in Dahomey (now Benin), West Africa.

As well as associating with other black Americans, the Crafts met influential Britons as seen at the British Association's annual meeting in Newcastle in August 1863. This was held over several days with outings to local natural and industrial sites. The geography and ethnology section's meeting on 28 August was crowded, the learned audience attracted by James Hunt's paper on 'Physical and Mental Character of the Negro' for 'it was known that Mr. Craft, a gentleman of colour, recently from Dahomey, and formerly, it was stated, a slave in the Southern States, would reply'.[29] *The Times* noted that despite the scientific nature of the gathering, opinions expressed were directly related to attitudes to the two sides in the American Civil War. Hunt's paper had no original views but was a compilation: as he was the president of the Anthropological Society he had influence. Hunt said that nowhere had the Negro shown signs of improvement except when 'intermixed with a higher race', that the Negro is a distinct species inferior to Europeans and there were closer analogies between Negroes and apes than between Europeans and apes. Some of the audience applauded and there were 'numerous expressions of dissent, not to say loud hisses'.

Craft told the audience that his grandfather and grandmother were pure Africans and that he had recently been in Dahomey. He had noted considerable differences between Africans in Africa, pointed out that given opportunities 'they were capable of making good use of them', mentioned Queen Victoria's England-educated African god-daughter and African churchman Samuel Crowther and reminded the hall that Caesar thought the British 'were such stupid people they were not fit to make slaves of in Rome'. He did not say so but surely because of his months in Ockham he was able to contrast agricultural workers in southern England with Africans. 'Mr. Craft spoke with great fluency, and at the same time with great modesty, and on sitting down was loudly applauded'.

Craft remained in Newcastle and again to a crowded hall, gave a presentation on the final day, 2 September 1863. He said he considered himself 'an Englishman of African parentage, unfortunately born in America'. He spoke of his recent visit to Dahomey where he had been attracted by differing tales and 'extraordinary accounts'. The British Under-Secretary of State for Foreign Affairs had told Craft he did not expect him to survive but supplied a letter asking the British governor in Lagos to aid and assist him. Craft sailed to Lagos from Liverpool 'about nine months ago' and reached Dahomey by canoe. He saw two or three thousand of the women soldiers (Dahomey's Amazon Warriors were a subject of fascination to Europeans). He met the king who asked if Craft had been sent by Queen Victoria. Craft told him he had been sent by friends who were anxious to encourage legitimate trade (not slaves).

Craft told the audience that Dahomey's human sacrifices resulted from three causes: religious, festive and as demonstrations of power. Only adult males were killed. Cotton grew in the region and could replace the trade in humans. Craft warned the African monarch that Atlantic slavery was under attack and that it would not last forever, when the market for slaves would collapse. Craft exhibited handicrafts he had acquired including cloth, a sword and bamboo baskets. Craft said that the king and his people would be unlikely to adopt cotton-growing as a Christian act but they would do so on a large scale if they found it profitable. He was 'warmly cheered'. Craft the escaped slave had held the attention of an informed audience (and no doubt in less formal meetings during the evenings). He had contributed at the time when British scientific thought was developing theories of innate racial differences. As he had said, he was black enough to argue against Hunt's paper.

It has long been believed that the 1850s saw scientific and popular racism established in Britain but the publications of Hunt and other pseudo-scientists were never as popular as slavery narratives and those hundreds of public meetings with earnest black speakers, all promoting humanitarian and egalitarian ideas around Britain. The refugees and supplicants moved in every level of society and were friends with influential people.

In December 1863 Craft again went to Dahomey, with the support of the Countess of Huntingdon's Connexion to establish a school in Whydah (Ouidah). He also had the support of Ferdinand Fitzgerald of the new Company of African Merchants, which he represented. His small school opened in mid-1864. Its regime, based on ideas gathered at Ockham, attracted students and teachers at nearby mission schools. The *Freed-Man* reported in 1865: Craft 'is at the present time in Africa, at the peril of his life endeavouring to open up commerce with the king of Dahomey, and in other ways to promote the welfare of the race to which he belongs'.[30] The article also said the Crafts, including Charles, had lived in Lushington's house in Ockham. Craft's now teenaged son Charles appealed for funds in London in 1866. Craft returned to England in 1867: the *Freed-Man* of June 1867 noting he had 'recently returned from the kingdom of Dahomey'. The slave trade across the Atlantic was ended and Dahomey's economy was now based on the export of palm-oil nuts and palm oil. But until scheduled steamship services to Europe started in 1889 trading was irregular.

Craft returned to his wife and children in Hammersmith. It was from Cambridge Road and on behalf of his mother that Charles Craft wrote to the *Freed-Man* on 23 June 1866. They were seeking help to continue the education of 'three little African boys that were given to him [William Craft] as slaves'. They had been at school for three years but the recent deaths of two British sponsors left costs to be met by Craft, who could not afford the £12 annual school bill for each lad. The lads seem to be in school in Africa.

The family in Hammersmith had been joined in late 1865 by Ellen's mother Maria. Ellen Craft was able to have American associates have Union General James Wilson locate her mother in Georgia, and she duly arrived in England. The American *Liberator* had those details many weeks before the *Freed-Man*'s report in December 1865. Maria Smith had sailed on the *Persia* from New York on 18 October, the fares and indeed the costs of the search having been paid by Lushington. The Crafts were an exceptional family but one wonders what the British-born youngsters thought of this elderly black lady who was their grandmother. When the family met up at the London rail terminal it was noted that Charles, Ellen Craft's 'little boy' had 'more of the dusky shadow on his brow than his mother'.[31]

Ellen Craft was active in raising money for America's now-freed slaves and helped form the women's auxiliary of the British and Foreign Freed-Men's Aid Society. She also pressed friends to help with a girls' school in Sierra Leone. As the 1860s aged, Ellen Craft was involved with the new Women's Suffrage Association. In the Craft descendants' papers in South Carolina are two documents linking them to Ira Aldridge, an African American actor who settled in England in the 1820s.

Aldridge was usually touring continental Europe by the 1860s. The public appearances of Americans provided opportunities for exaggeration and invention, ploys to sell tickets and make ventures financially sound. Aldridge, the New York-born dramatic actor who also played comic roles and sang, had been billed as 'The African Roscius' when he toured throughout Ireland in the late 1830s when it was claimed he had been born in Senegal. There were also errors, such as the report of his death in the *London Times* in 1845.[32] Aldridge had been in Britain since the 1820s, and as well as the limited if not to say absence of roles for black actors in the United States, the life had attractions. In January 1848 he earned over £15 for six nights at the Theatre Royal in Norwich. Biographer Bernth Lindfors has attempted to assess why Aldridge, who had 'great success in the provinces and in Ireland' failed to have any London employments from the 1840s. One reason was that theatre managers were often actors and they played the major roles in the theatres they ran. Aldridge's star status and reports of intimate relations with white women are seen as the principal causes. An illegitimate child is known through reports of a London court in early 1856 when lawyers representing William Stothard told how, when holding ambitions to be an actor he studied with Ira Aldridge in 1849. The black actor was the best man at Stothard's wedding to young Emma, who lived in Tunbridge Wells in Kent as her husband toured the country. In March 1853 she had a child which 'had strong indications of its paternity' and the judge said its father must have been a Negro – but 'Aldridge was not the only man of colour'. The court had to consider compensation for Stothard. The young mother had been left in the hospital and the judge thought her husband was unlikely to have spent 'the noon and evening of life in happiness with his wife' – the jury agreed, and awarded damages of two pounds. The male baby had died, aged three months, from dysentery.[33] The entertainment weekly *Era* ran the story on 20 January 1856 – 'Caution to Theatrical Husbands Who Neglect Their Wives'.

Aldridge married the Swedish mother of his children. Amanda Aldridge's Swedish text and her husband's brief letter (also of 19 December 1866) were kept by Ellen Craft, this evidence revealing two of her London contacts. Although Aldridge was a serious actor – not a music hall performer – the theatre was not seen as respectable at this time, especially among Nonconformist Christians. Given the latter had long been supporters of fugitive slaves, the connection between the Crafts and Ira Aldridge was unexpected.

The Crafts's Hammersmith address – it was a boarding house, it seems – was used by a younger African American actor, Samuel Morgan Smith on 13 October 1866. Smith and his wife Mary Eliza were living close by in Shaftesbury Road when Mary died on 6 October 1867.[34] They had been in England since May 1866: and had brought their namesake son with them.

Mary Smith died from epilepsy and apoplexy, aged 27. The registrar was told of this by Ellen Craft who had been 'present at the death' which took place at the Smiths' home in Angelo House, a couple of streets away from Cambridge Road.

Smith was playing Iago in *Othello* at the Theatre Royal in Rochdale in early November 1867, when the *Rochdale Pilot* noted 'the singular novelty of a naturally black Iago and an artificially copper-coloured Moor'. Othello was played by a local man; Morgan Smith's acting was not described.[35] Smith died in Sheffield in March 1882 when it was noted he was survived by his wife and a son. This wife was an English actress named Harriet who married Morgan Smith in Glasgow in 1869. They had a son who died, days old, in August 1870 when they were all in the Isle of Man. That month young Samuel Morgan Smith died too. The two boys were buried in Douglas where their father's theatrical work was drying up. Harriet went to Australia where she died in 1915.[36]

Aldridge died in Poland in 1867 and two daughters lived well into the twentieth century. They had musical training in Belgium and England. Years after their father's death, visiting African Americans called on them in London and black Britons had music lessons from one.

On 13 June 1866 Ellen Craft and her mother were on the platform of the Trinity Congregational Church in Wandsworth Road, South Lambeth (London) along with the Revd William H. Jones. She was associated with London philanthropist Clementia Taylor (and thus Sarah Remond) in gathering items for a bazaar which aimed to collect funds in part for a new school at Cape Coast (today: Ghana). In March 1867 she was with Jones in Brighton.[37]

The Revd William Henry Jones was based in Chatham, Ontario, and had come from Canada to gather funds for that community. He was a leading member of the Coloured Methodist Episcopal Church, and his credentials were accepted by the British and Foreign Freed-Men's Aid Society whose June 1866 edition of *Freed-Man* carried details. Born of free parents in Pennsylvania around 1826 he was said to represent 100,000 black Canadians – an impossibly large figure, of course. Jones seems to have made a base in Mansfield where he was joined by his niece (nameless, 'a young lady of colour') by Easter 1860 when both appeared at the town's General Baptist church. He was billed as a 'coloured missionary from America' by another poster, announcing his appearance at the United Methodist Free Church in Mansfield, and he also appeared at the town hall.[38] He had been described as a 'coloured minister from Canada' when speaking in Dorchester in May 1866 where he was successful in that town's Wesleyan chapels before moving on to Wimborne.[39] He was in Poole on 28 May and at a meeting in London's Old Kent Road on 21 June. He then went to Tunbridge Wells where he appeared with Ellen Craft. On 1 July he was with Ellen Craft and her mother.

William Craft's trading obligations in Dahomey could not be settled by selling slaves, but his employer held him responsible for debts so they sold their home in late 1867. On 26 September 1868 Ellen gave birth to her sixth child, Mary, at 124 Stockwell Park Road in Brixton. She told the registrar that her maiden name had been Smith and that her husband was a 'General Foreign Merchant'. They left Liverpool on 24 August 1869: Ellen and William, Charles, Ellen, Alfred and Mary left Brougham and William Jr to continue their education.[40] The boys were at Brixton Lodge School in Atkinson Place off the Brixton Road when the 1871 census was made – their family seem to have rented accommodation close by in 1869. Other students had been in France (one was British) and one in Haiti. Brougham Craft, at 12, was one of the younger pupils.

William Ivens Craft returned to England in 1881. Born on 16 November 1855 in Hammersmith he completed his education and had joined his parents in America by 1873. From 1876 he was active in Republican politics near Savannah, Georgia where his parents were running another school. Whites made it dangerous for blacks to vote and young Craft failed to be elected to the state's senate. Back in London he became a clerk. He lived at 16 Little Titchfield Street (north of Oxford Street) and there on 17 April 1884 his daughter Ellen Louisa was born. Her mother was Louisa Mary Le Jeune, a married woman who made waistcoats. Mrs Le Jeune married Craft in 1888. Their daughter's birth registration had been under both surnames (Craft and Le Jeune). Louisa had four sons by her first husband and she was to have four children with Craft – Ellen, Clara, William and Brougham.

Descendants of African Americans in Britain have been largely unnoticed in studies of Victorian life.

Chapter 3

Children

The four daughters of Moses and Ann Roper and the six children of the Crafts, the two sons of Morgan Smith, the children of Jane Floyd and Box Brown, the six children of Sarah and Joseph Freeman, the children of Ira Aldridge (one son died in Australia, another in Yorkshire) were not the only children born to black Americans in Victorian times.

Said to have been a slave in Florida who came to England in the 1850s Henry Parker worked as a stonemason. In 1854 he married Louisa Handy and they had at least seven children: Celia, George, Emma, Louisa, Mary, Thomas and Alice. His middle name was Codrington, which has Caribbean associations. Parker who, the family say, became a lay preacher, had many descendants and there are photographs of the patriarch, his wife, a daughter and a granddaughter. It is from them that we learn that a grandson lies among the 900 soldiers buried in the Roclincourt Military Cemetery in the Pas-de-Calais in northern France. Twenty-year-old Rifleman Edwin 'Bertie' Head of the London Regiment had been killed in March 1918.[1] He had been born in Chertsey, Surrey.

It is not clear where stories of Parker's slave origins came from. His birthplace is given as Bristol in every census in which he appears and there are no published reports of lectures or presentations, which so many ex-slaves from the Americas gave to add to the larger society's awareness and understanding. More needs to be researched on Henry Parker, and the question of his birth place resolved. Bristol had Atlantic contacts for centuries and African people were not rare there.

Other children include those born to Sarah and Alexander Crummell. Alexander Crummell was born in Brooklyn, New York in 1819 and, despite rejections because of his colour, became ordained and in 1844 was an Episcopal priest in Philadelphia. He became pastor of a New York church and in 1848 he crossed the Atlantic seeking donations for a new chapel. In August 1848 he was in Everton (Liverpool) where he informed an American patron that he had already obtained over £150 and over one hundred 'valuable books'. Supporters in Bath offered to pay for the tickets to bring his wife to England, and another agreed to pay for her education. Sarah Crummell and the children came to Bath. His namesake son died in England in 1851.[2] Daughter Frances was born in Bath in June 1849 and Dillwinna in Ipswich in 1852. They had moved to Cambridge where Alexander was an undergraduate at Queen's College when the 1851 census was recorded: four children were listed including Sophia who was only fourteen days old.

Crummell spoke in many places in England, including at the British and Foreign Anti-Slavery Society's annual meetings in 1848 and 1849. In England he met Liberia's president Joseph Jenkins Roberts and their conversations influenced Crummell's decision to migrate to Africa. He did in May 1853, with Sarah, three children and a servant. In 1861 Sydney was at the grammar school (Lord Weymouth's School) in Warminster in Wiltshire when his father was working in Africa. The school files note that at the prize-giving on 17 June 1863 he won first prizes in history and geography, and French.[3] In January 1864 he was in Liberia, where he introduced courses in Latin and algebra at his father's Liberia College. His sister Frances was at Oberlin College near Cleveland in Ohio in 1863-66. Dillwinna was studying in Ohio too. Sydney (or Sidney) Crummell returned to America in 1873. His strained relationship with his father is seen in that he failed to attend the latter's funeral in 1898.

William Wells Brown travelled via Ireland and England in 1849 to be one of 800 delegates at the Peace Congress in Paris in late August. Twenty of those delegates were Americans. The African Americans included Crummell. Brown's *Narrative of William W. Brown, an American Slave: Written by Himself* was already in print and a British edition appeared in 1849. The *Narrative* earned Brown a modest income, was translated for European sale, and launched his successful life of letters as playwright, historian, and the first black American novelist. Moving to London Brown met a destitute fugitive slave with whom he divided his last shilling. The man who had received Brown's gift was one of the refugees in Britain reduced to beggary. Many knew little other than tropical farming, lacked a network, and were illiterate (as were many Britons). Brown's letter of 27 June 1851, 'Don't Come to England' was published in *Frederick Douglass' Paper*. Brown then wrote to *The Times* that 'Many of these people have, within the past six or eight months, come to this country, seeking employment and that liberty and protection which is denied them in their native land' and proposed unemployed fugitives could be found work in the West Indies.

This was wishful thinking for agriculture in the Caribbean did not need more hands.[4]

Brown had left his two daughters in America. They were escorted across the Atlantic by George Thompson in July 1851, studied in France and then attended the college of the Home and Colonial School Society in London which qualified them to work as teachers in England.[5] Josephine Brown, born 1839, described their experiences in a letter of 27 April 1854.[6] It was headed East Plumstead School, Plumstead, Woolwich; which was in south east London.

> On our arrival in this country, we spent the first year in France, in a boarding-school, where there were some forty other young ladies, and never once heard our color [sic] alluded to in disrespectful terms. We afterwards returned to London, and entered a school where more than two hundred young ladies were being educated; and here, too, we were always treated with the greatest kindness and respect. As we were trained in the last mentioned school for teachers, we were somewhat afraid that our color [sic] would be a barrier against our getting employment as teachers; but in this were happily disappointed. My sister is mistress of a school in Berden, in Essex, about forty miles from London. I have a school here with more than one hundred pupils, and an assistant two years older than myself. My pupils are some of them sixteen years of age, while I am not yet fifteen. I need not say to you, that both my assistant and pupils are all white. Should I return to America, it is scarcely probable that I could get a school of white pupils, and this makes me wish to remain here, for I am fond of teaching.

Plumstead was dominated by the Woolwich dockyards, and few of the area's children would have attended school after the age of ten. Berden, Essex was a farming village near Saffron Walden, with a population of around 400. Clarissa Brown has been traced there, as has her marriage in St Anne's, Soho, London, on 8 October 1855 to Fritz Alcide Humbert. Humbert was a Swiss watch engraver. She never returned to America. The 1861 census listed her as a governess lodging at 3 Greengate in Salford the manufacturing town close by Manchester – her husband had died. By 1871 she was working as an entertainer and had married George Wainwright Sylvester in Bradford. They are listed in the 1871 census in Manchester Road, Huddersfield. She died in Leeds in the spring of 1874. The grave is unmarked.

Her father wrote for anti-slavery publications and London newspapers, and a pioneering novel *Clotel* published in London in 1853. In 1854 British supporters subscribed $300 to purchase his freedom – largely organized by Henry and Anna Richardson of Newcastle who had done the same for Douglass. In September 1854 his ship reached Philadelphia.

Josephine Brown returned to the United States in 1855 and completed the biography of her father which she had started in France. The *Biography of an American Bondman by his Daughter* was published in 1856. She remained in America, married and died from tuberculosis in Massachusetts in January 1874.

The Home and Colonial School Society trained two young sisters from Dominica in the British West Indies. Mary Anne Titré and Sarah Titré had gone to Canada in 1854 and then trained in England and returned to Ontario to face the extremely cold winter of 1855-56. An August 1856 report stated 'The two young colored females, natives of Dominica, who conducted the Infants' School, had been for a short time students at the Home and Colonial Training Institute, England' and the Canadian winter 'very seriously undermined their health, and to have sown the fatal seeds of consumption' and so they had returned to 'their native island'.[7] Tuberculosis (consumption) was not understood at that time.

Henry Highland Garnet from Maryland arrived in Britain in 1850.[8] His invitation was from the Richardsons of Newcastle. As well as lecturing on the free (not produced by slaves) produce idea Garnet spoke about the Fugitive Slave Act. He wrote from Hitchin, Hertfordshire in December 1850, days after the train station had opened, that 'The Fugitive Slave Law still fills the minds of the British people with wonder and amazement. Until America wipes that foul blot from her Statute book, she will have but little or no political influence upon Europe.' Garnet believed that it had led Britons to think about slavery and the extent they supported slavery 'by consuming its productions'.

Slaves who had escaped to the Northern states found, as Roper had, that they were at risk of being recaptured. Individual states in the North had enacted legislation regarding black fugitives, but a right to a trial by jury or to seek a writ of habeas corpus had been declared unconstitutional by the Supreme Court in 1842. The Fugitive Slave Act made it clear that slave catchers could operate in every part of the United States. Indeed this law ordered both state and federal authorities to cooperate in the capture of fugitives. Anyone who aided a runaway was liable to a fine of $1,000 or six months in prison. Black testimony was not allowed in courts. Thus the Northern states no longer provided a safe haven and fugitives who had settled across the border in Canada were also at risk from slave catchers. Crossing the Atlantic eastward became more attractive.

In Dublin in February 1851 at an anti-slavery meeting Garnet was 'received with loud cheers' and confirmed the previous speaker was right to consider the Irish 'ought to be interested in the welfare of the United States of America' and Irish people who had information about slavery would 'use their influence with their friends in America'. 'Mr. Garnett [*sic*] resumed his seat amidst loud cheers from all parts of the room.' In Belfast on 21 October he spoke at a 'densely crowded' meeting, remarking that he had never seen such an attentive audience. 'The common people heard him gladly.' On 28 October he was a guest of the ladies of the Belfast Anti-Slavery Society at the Wesleyan Methodist chapel in Donegall Square East. One month later in Dundee, Scotland this 'Presbyterian coloured Minister from the United States' was to lecture on the religious condition of America's three million slaves and to give a public lecture on American slavery the next Monday. He was to go to Jamaica in 1852.

In the months before Garnet sailed to Jamaica he worked to assist John Weims a free black in Washington DC whose wife and seven children were slaves; one daughter Stella had come to Britain with the Garnets and was living with them. He raised £300 in three weeks. Julia Garnet, daughter Mary and a son, along with Stella Weims, all went to Jamaica in late 1852 when Garnet was a missionary for the United Presbyterian Church of Scotland. Stella Weims died there in 1856.[9] Britons who welcomed Julia Garnet and Stella Weims into their homes heard their stories of life in 1840s America: an impact that can only be guessed at. Mary Garnet and her brother have not been documented after 1852.

At a Dublin gathering in February 1851 free-born William Powell was described as 'a coloured gentleman, who had come to this country to procure for his children that education and means of supporting themselves by the acquirement of trades or professions denied them in Boston on account of their colour'. Powell's father and grandfather were slaves; his 17-year-old son worked as an apothecary but US employers usually rejected him.[10] In 1832 Powell married Mercy O. Haskins who was of Native American descent, and they ran the Colored Seamen's Home in New York City from 1839. It closed when the Powells went to Britain, reopening in 1861 on their return. The 1850 US census shows their seven children: William P. (Jr) born 1834, Edward B. (1836), Sylvester (1838), Mercy (1840), Isaiah (1842), Sarah (1845) and Samuel (1849). William Jr studied medicine in

Dublin and London and qualified with a MRCS (Membership of the Royal College of Surgeons) in 1858, then worked as a surgeon in two Liverpool hospitals.[11] We know nothing about the British education of his six siblings.

Mercy Haskins Powell was surely fully occupied with running the family home in Lancashire, so we focus on her husband. His early years are uncertain, but a New York City birth and five years spent at sea, probably on whalers out of New Bedford, Massachusetts, are likely. Days after the Fugitive Slave Law came into force in September 1850 Powell and associates tried to see New York's mayor over the city's policy on 'free person of color' seized by slave catchers. Other activities followed before he and the family relocated to England 'where character and not color – capacity and not complexion, are the tests of merit'.

The Powells reached Liverpool on 12 December 1850. His campaigning now included confronting those in America who believed slaves in America had better lives than the Britons who laboured in factories and coal mines in England. He pointed out to the New York *Sunday Times* in March 1851 that the British were subject to parliamentary laws, and not 'to corporeal punishment, whips and chains, and separated, parents from their children, and husbands from their wives'. As early as March 1851 Powell was aiding new arrivals in Liverpool, informing Mary Ann Duval of the safe arrival of her husband Alexander. Powell obtained employment with ship's broker Christopher Bushell in Liverpool.[12]

Powell was present at a lecture in early 1856 on 'the African race' at the Tuckerman Institute hosted by Revd Francis Bishop. (Joseph Tuckerman, an American clergyman and social worker who died in 1840, had inspired this institute.) Also present was 'Josephine, the slave who has lately arrived here from New Orleans ... accompanied by several coloured friends, and the audience loudly cheered her as an expression of their sympathy and good wishes'. Hidden for the twenty-five days of the voyage by the boatswain of the *Asterion* she reached Liverpool on 16 February 1856. There had been a $500 award offered in New Orleans. She was 'a mulatto' aged 20 or 23. 'At the close of the lecture, Mr. Powell, a coloured gentleman addressed the meeting with some humour and considerable ability.' Bishop presided over a later talk there, by American anti-slavery campaigner Parker Pillsbury whose claim Josephine the slave bribed a customs officer was investigated by the Collector of Customs at Liverpool. His refutation supported by a letter from Powell was published in the *Liverpool Mercury*. Powell was 'a coloured gentleman of much intelligence' employed by C. Bushell and Co. He had attended the investigation. His letter dated 18 March 1856 was from

113 Field Street, in Everton. He was living there three years later. Powell may have aided escaped slave Tom Wilson whose story in the Liverpool press was copied by the London *Times* on 25 February 1858. Four of Powell's sons served in the Union forces in the Civil War – William was one of thirteen black doctors in that army.

Mercy and William Powell assisted newly-arrived Americans. William Allen informed America's leading white abolitionist William Lloyd Garrison in 1853 that on arrival in England he had spent two weeks in Liverpool 'rendered more agreeable by the kindness of our mutual friend, Wm. P. Powell, Esq., formerly of New York'.[13]

Like the Powells, William G. Allen had fled across the Atlantic. Born free in Virginia he taught at McGrawville College in upstate New York where he married Mary King, a white student – they fled and settled in Dublin where his 34-page *A Personal Narrative* was published in 1860, and 'sold by the author'. They moved to London where from 1864 he ran a school. They seem to have remained in Britain. The Cash brothers of London published his *The American Prejudice against Colour: An Authentic Narrative* in 1853. Allen was described as 'a refugee from despotism'. In November 1854 Allen gave a number of lectures in Manchester, invited by four clergymen of different denominations.[14] One about Sunday schools in America was 'listened to with great interest'. He had one black and three white grandparents, it was noted. A future talk was to be on the origin, history and literature of the African race, which had already interested audiences in Leeds and Edinburgh. There were children but the activities of Mary and William Allen are also not easy to trace.

In September 1851 'a young African prince in Liverpool' had been interviewed by a reporter of the *Liverpool Standard*, reprinted in London's *Daily News*, *Morning Post* and provincial newspapers.[15] 'A pleasing interview with a remarkably intelligent boy' aged 5½, Thomas Canray Caulker the son of the 'King of Bompey' (Bumpe) in Sierra Leone had come to Britain with Captain Swinton of the Newcastle ship *Adeline*, Swinton acting as his guardian. The reporter thought the habits and culture the lad was to receive in Britain would benefit his country. He was at school in Liverpool for two years but some thought Swinton was unsuitable and custody should be with a church or another individual, and a writ of habeas corpus was served on Swinton in April 1853 and the African was produced in court.[16]

The sympathizers (or busy-bodies) who so publicly expressed concern for this dark stranger – and resorted to law to have their views enforced – were part of a pattern of British behaviour which affected Americans in Britain. It was so different to affairs in the United States.

The *Cheltenham Examiner* noted Caulker's new guardian was the Countess of Huntingdon's Missionary Society (active in Sierra Leone). He had lived in Cheltenham, Gloucestershire for six years where many residents had seen 'a coloured boy walking with his friend and instructor, the Rev. J. K. Forster'. His parents died, his uncle became the heir and he became blind. He had given 'clear proof that the African mind, under proper cultivation, is capable of intellectual and religious attainments' and had learned to read 'with his fingers' (Braille).[17] Caulker died in Islington, London on 1 June 1859. Classmates from the Blind Asylum sung a favourite hymn at the interment at Abney Park cemetery, London's main Nonconformist cemetery. His headstone stated he was 'A native of Western Africa'.

The British could feel smug when it came to reuniting families torn apart when one member (usually the male) fled across the Atlantic. That was true of James Watkins of Maryland. Watkins reached Liverpool, his fares paid by friends, and there in April 1851 he bumped into fellow fugitive James Pennington. The latter wrote a note to confirm that he had known Watkins in Hartford, Connecticut for years, to help the new arrival avoid accusations of cheating.[18]

In October 1851 Watkins gave two lectures in Wigan, both 'numerously attended'. In April 1852 in Lancaster, Watkins 'a fugitive slave' spoke at two meetings, telling of the horrors of slavery. A collection was made to help redeem his parents from slavery. The second lecture was extremely well attended.[19] Watkins was well-known in Britain's provinces throughout the 1850s. His *Narrative of the Life of James Watkins* was published in Bolton in 1852 (a third edition was printed in Birmingham in 1853). He noted that 'audiences [were] easily obtainable, when it has been understood that a "black man was going to address them about slavery."'[20] He spoke in Sheffield in March 1854 telling audiences that he had purchased the liberty of three siblings, and his wife and three children on their way to Britain were delayed because an American ship refused his wife as she 'was tinged with African blood'.[21] Her surname was Wells, and she gave the forename Mary when writing to her husband in January 1852.[22] The nineteenth edition of his memoirs notes British support had enabled him to purchase the liberty of a brother and two sisters, and it had been a Cunard ship which refused his family. His children (again, no names) attended the grammar school in Birmingham where he lived for several years. This is not unusual for this era; women's names are also difficult to uncover.

The Birmingham newspaper *Aris's Gazette* published his letter dated 18 May 1854, which also advised 'I intend to commence some little business in this town.' His wife was with him in Barnsley in June 1854. Watkins was 'quite popular' and 'a great attraction'.[23] They lived in Birmingham for six years then his free-born wife returned to America as she was unwell, and he moved to Liverpool then Manchester. In 1856 he was at the Wesleyan chapel in Stoney Middleton (north of Bakewell, Derbyshire) addressing 200 people. The 1860 edition of his autobiography says that this was at the invitation of Lord Denman (son of the Lord Chief Justice of England). Watkins had 'the manners of a gentleman' and 'a satisfactory collection was made'.[24] He spoke at the Corn Exchange in Belfast in mid-November 1856 to a crowded audience and received 'loud and continual applause', ending the meeting by singing a hymn. He was to speak elsewhere in Belfast.[25] On 12 May 1859 at the Methodist chapel in Pepper Street, Chester, Watkins, now in his tenth year touring the British Isles, addressed 1,000 people; the lecture to be repeated in another Chester hall the following week. The nineteenth edition of his book was printed in Manchester in 1860. He was in Yorkshire in mid-1861 having been registered in Manchester in the census earlier that year.[26] He was boarding in Piccadilly, and listed as a 'lecturer on slavery' aged about 30, born in America. Page 56 of the 1860 edition of his book stresses Watkins's appreciation of 'the thousands and tens of thousands of the poorer classes … who have received me with unexampled kindness'. Over a dozen pages list places where he had spoken, from Altrincham to Beeston, Bridlington to Crewe, Matlock, Nottingham, Pickering, Shrewsbury, Warrington, to Wigan.

Watkins was a skilled lecturer, that in Settle on 17 July 1861 being described as 'very interesting'. He told the audience that a proportion of the funds he had collected had purchased the freedom of a brother and two sisters. He gave a third lecture in Settle on 4 August, and one at nearby Ingleton on 22 August. There was a 'very large attendance' when he spoke in Clitheroe on 24 January 1862, his three lectures were 'crowded every night to excess' in Stockton-on-Tees in September 1863.[27] He had not been traced in Britain after that. A professional lecturer perhaps with a small business that paid enough for his children's school fees, Watkins surely had a reliable income from all those editions of his autobiographical narrative. He had been seen by many thousands in Britain and Ireland, at public meetings and out and about in those towns and villages.

Early photographs showing school and church groups with some of these black children may have survived. Some of the narratives had portraits of the authors. Other images are of black people who worked as entertainers.

The 'African Twins' were on display in a room opposite the Midland Hotel in Bradford in June 1856. 'They appear to be united together in the fashion of the Siamese twins.'[28] Born into slavery in North Carolina in 1851, Millie and Christine McKoy were linked at the lower spine sharing a pelvis. The family referred to them as 'sister'. They had arrived in Liverpool in July 1855, moved via Scotland to London, toured provincial towns and were subject to legal disputes. In these fights Millie-Christine was kidnapped in Dundee, appeared at Bow Street court in London, and was said to be subject to a legal document issued by the state of Pennsylvania – but 'the law of this country does not recognise the power of Pennsylvania, or of all the States in the Union, to confer a right of property in human beings'. The tour criss-crossed Britain throughout 1856: with announcements that the girls were from Africa and Cuba. They were re-united with their mother in Birmingham in 1857, Monemia then shared the billing. They were advertised in the *Caledonian Mercury* of 24 January 1857, appearing at the Waterloo Rooms in Edinburgh. The girls and their mother fled to America.

The American exploiters of Millie-Christine were challenged: the laws of Britain did not recognise slavery in the United Kingdom, and a Pennsylvanian legal document had no strength there. Monemia had given birth to a daughter in Scotland, which raised the question, how could a slave who had a child in a land without slavery have produced a slave child? Had she enslaved her own child and if so, was this a breach of the American ban on foreign slave trading? Millie-Christine was to return to Europe in 1871 and sing for Queen Victoria.

We know less about George Lewis Ruffin and his wife Josephine who left Boston for England in 1858 and settled in Liverpool where some say three children were born, Hubert and Florida surviving. With their parents they went to America almost as soon as the Civil War started. He was to be the first black graduate of Harvard Law School (in 1869).

Then there was ex-slave John Sella Martin. He spoke in Sheffield on 13 July 1863 claiming to be an Englishman not by birth 'but by the far more emphatic title of deliberate choice'. He believed that the Union forces would prevail over the Confederates. Born in North Carolina in 1832, Martin escaped from New Orleans and reached Chicago in early 1856. He became a clergyman, and moved to England in 1861 on a lecture tour. Aided by Harper Twelvetrees and others, he gathered $2,500 (much from workers at the Twelvetrees' huge factory in Bromley-by-Bow in east London) to purchase his sister Caroline and her two children, and returned to the U.S.A. in early 1862. Martin was appointed minister at Twelvetrees' lecture hall-cum-chapel in Three Mills Lane, Bromley in May 1863. On 16 June some 850 people sat down to a celebration tea there, including Liberia's consul (the white American Gerard Ralston) and William G. Allen. Martin was very active amongst groups opposing the Confederacy. In that work he met many high-placed sympathizers and helped influence British opinion. He spoke to a gathering in Northampton in February 1864.[29] He left Bromley to replace Henry Highland Garnet in New York in mid-1864.

Martin returned to Britain in 1865 representing the American Missionary Association, tasked with obtaining financial support for the education of the freed slaves hence his association with the Freed-Men's Aid Society. He was with his wife Sarah J. Martin and their daughter. He stayed there for three years. He was noted in the *Freed-Man* attending the national committee's quarterly meeting in London on 14 September 1865 and passing over a collection of £890. The *Freed-Man* published his Sheffield talk on the cotton question in the issues of November and December 1865. He had moved on to Scotland, appearing in Glasgow on 22 September 1865 and then in Dundee. Martin seemed to be more successful in Scotland than in England. Two-thirds of the £600 he collected in Scotland was from the long-established thread manufacturers J. and P. Coats of Paisley, handed on to the society in 1868.[30]

Martin spent almost three years on this post-abolition work, including visiting the continent. Conflict with different groups around Britain, bouts of ill-health, fatiguing travel, his wife's illnesses, had all been a strain but it had been relatively successful. He died in New Orleans in 1876, aged 44: half of his life had been spent in slavery.[31] His daughter is a cipher.

Kentucky-born Robert James Harlan, wealthy through his success in the California gold fields, seems to have left England after nine years, returning to the U.S.A. in 1868, where he became active in politics. This American ex-slave was known in Britain as an importer of racehorses. His horses had won two races at Doncaster in 1859 for example. His horse Des Chiles was not a winner at Epsom but in 1860 his Maid of the Mist won by two lengths at Doncaster.[32] The *Morning Post* of London, 1 March 1861 page 8 had reported the death at 14 Canonbury Villas, London, from tuberculosis, of Lara Frances Harlan, 'daughter of Robert Harlan, Esq., formerly of Cincinnati, Ohio, America'. The death registration has her as Laura. Her widowed father, and sister Mary (aged 23 born in Kentucky) and brother Robert (aged 7 born in Ohio) were living in Baron Street, Clerkenwell on 7 April 1861 when the census recorded their father was a 'gentleman'. He died in 1897. The education of his son and daughter in Britain is untraced.

Thomas Wiggins sometimes known as Thomas Bethune and called Blind Tom, was born into slavery in Columbus, Georgia in May 1849, and was blind from birth. He and his parents were purchased by James Neil Bethune whose daughters played several musical instruments and sang. Blind Tom was attracted to the piano. He could reproduce new tunes and pieces within minutes of hearing them for the very first time. He became an attraction in theatres and gave recitals, had his compositions noted, published, and performed them in concert halls. Tom toured Britain in 1866-1867.[33]

Now we know about autism, and more about what makes a child prodigy, we can be scornful of those who just observed Tom stumbling, talking gibberish, and behaving in idiotic ways. The *Brighton Gazette* advised that Tom was 'not only sightless but also completely idiotic'. But after he played in Brighton the *Gazette* commented 'It is stated that Blind Tom is an idiot, but his performance would denote him to be anything but that.'

His first British appearance was at the Queen's Concert Rooms in Hanover Square, London in July 1866. He then was based at the Egyptian Hall in London. The *Evening Standard* referred to him as 'this poor, half-demented lad'. The provincial press reported events in the metropolis and the *Hereford Journal*'s 'London Letter' had: 'The last new thing here is a musical idiot. He is black, blind, a fool, and a musician; and his name is "Blind Tom". He possesses – or rather his friends profess for him – that he is able to imitate on the piano any tune after a first hearing.' The cynical journalist asked 'how are we to know he had never heard them before?' That was resolved by local performers and composers presenting their works – including discords and weird harmonies – to the blind teenager. In mid-August 1866 the *Morning Post*, reporting on his scheduled London appearances at St James's Hall before embarking on a tour of the provinces, noted 'he possesses to a marvellous extent the facility of playing "by ear"'. He had 'an elastic touch, and plays with much expression. He has not only a good memory, he has something of the imagination which no executive or test of true merit can be without'. That he applauded himself at the end of each piece 'smacks quite as much of contempt for his audience as of personal vanity'.

For the *Dundee Courier* Tom was 'of almost imbecile mind' but was 'without a parallel' as a musical curiosity, and it advised 'those going expecting to see an astonishing musical prodigy will be in no way disappointed'. Indeed, the *Dundee Advertiser* warned that audiences should not suppose 'his notoriety is another species of Barnumism' (showman Barnum was famed for hoaxing audiences). It was clear that 'his ability would be marvellous even if he had his eyesight'. The show-business weekly *Era* noted that when he was at St James's Hall in London he was 'really and truly a wonder', and 'superhuman'.

Tom toured Scotland, Manchester, Birmingham – and went to Paris in April 1867 – then Newcastle, Bradford, Leeds, Dover, Derby, Accrington, Huddersfield and Sheffield, leaving for America in June 1867. In Montrose (Scotland) he was described as the 'inexplicable phenomenon' (November 1866); in Manchester 'the entertainment was most interesting as well as unique' (September 1866); in Birmingham where he performed six evenings at the Exchange Assembly Rooms in September 1866 he was 'the musical prodigy'. He was advertised in Edinburgh as 'Blind Tom's Concerts and Entertainment Scientific and Humorous'. Charles Halle, the well-respected concert director in Manchester, wrote that Tom was 'quite marvellous', 'most remarkable', and was a 'most singular and inexplicable phenomenon'.

He copied new music and tunes, he played with his back to the keyboard, he played two different tunes at once and sang a third, he impersonated people. Showman, oddity, entertainer, pianist, and a black person tied by contract and American tradition to white bosses who benefited from the substantial receipts. The *Birmingham Daily Press* noted that Tom was 'professedly of defective intellect and sight, and obviously of uncouth manners ...he is obviously no fool' and as a pianist 'Tom is distinguished rather for vigour than delicacy'. The reviewer thought that musical people would be outnumbered by 'sight-seers and marvel-hunters'. Tom's activities were reported in Ireland where the *Dublin Evening Mail* stated: 'Any one to look at Blind Tom would never imagine he possessed such wonderful powers.'

Thomas Wiggins played the piano for hours on end. His sightless world was made of sounds, and his compositions seem attempts to reproduce, at the piano, the sound of rain, wind, and bird song. British reports seem to be based on publicity hand-outs, but there was that distinction between the facility to play 'by ear' (and the question of how the audience could be sure that the 'new' music had never been heard before), and his physical skills as a pianist. Most British commentators lacked time to assess him and so we seem to have no knowledge of what contemporaries thought of his musicianship. In other words, was his playing good because he was blind? How did his renditions compare to those of sighted instrumentalists? Tom's act fell out of fashion in America where his activities were curtailed by law suits against those who were his managers/exploiters; but in the 1900s he performed on the variety stage, in shows and theatres that otherwise avoided black acts. He died in New Jersey in 1908.

CHILDREN

The Countee family deserves attention. Nelson Countee from Virginia gave a talk on Africa in Leamington Spa in October 1867. He re-appeared in Leicester in 1870. A temperance group in Leicester had their picnic attended by 1,000 'of the working classes' in July 1870 when Nelson Countee a man of colour and fugitive slave from Virginia addressed the gathering. Countee had lectured in Leicester in February that year, when the hall had been 'crammed'.[34] He was in Leicester in 1872. Countee was still talking about his life as a slave in 1877 when the 'popular coloured preacher' spoke in the granite quarrying village of Trevor (Trefor), North Wales and in 1878, when he preached in Belbroughton near Stourbridge: the collection was for the chapel not him.[35] The Baptist chapel (English speaking) at Mountain Ash in South Wales heard a 'Mr. County [*sic*], a man of colour' talk about slavery in October 1878: he had taken two services the Sunday before.[36] Countee re-emerged in Derby in August 1879 when he was billed as an escaped slave. He was accompanied by his children and also preached and sung. They were in Mountain Ash in November 1879. There are four registrations of the births of children with the very unusual name Countee between 1865 and 1880.

Countee is in the 1871 census with his wife Maria and two children: 4-year-old Charles born in Leamington and baby Louisa born in Banbury. He worked as a cooper and was a local Methodist preacher. The 1881 census found him staying with a gardener in Westbury-upon-Trym in Gloucestershire, the enumerator noting the 'evangelist' had been born in the U.S.A. and had been naturalized. Maria was with the children in Aston, Birmingham. The oldest, Charles, was listed as an office boy. In September 1881 his father gave two sermons, followed by lectures on the two days, at the Wesleyan Reform Chapel in Sheepshed (today Shepshed) near Loughborough.[37]

Francis Nelson Countee died in Leicester in 1886 aged 53. The 1891 census lists Charles and a 21-year old Eliza Countee boarding in the coal mining area of south Wales. Maria and her daughters were living in the Aylestone suburb of Leicester. She was described as a 'bible woman', a widow aged 46. Three daughters worked in the hosiery business and Florence the youngest was a 'fitter shoe'. Maria Countee is recorded as dying in Leicester in 1922, aged 77. Louisa Maria Countee was born in 1869 and married in London in 1918 to James Forrest; Mary Ann was born in 1872, Lucy in Aston, Birmingham in 1875 and Florence a year later. Mary Ann Amelia Countee's daughter told her granddaughter that Maria and her sisters were 'beautiful quadroons'. That granddaughter was raised in Leicestershire but migrated to America and was living in California in 2016. Lucy married Ambrose Day in Leicester in 1901. A photograph of that wedding clearly shows her African descent.

The American's grandchildren were Frances Mabel Countee born in Leicester in 1888 and married in Cheltenham in 1911, and William Nelson Countee who appears just as Nelson Countee, born in Blaby in Leicester in 1889 and married to Amy Page in 1911. That Countee is sometimes 'County' is additional to the usual family history research problems when forenames are dropped and familiar names substituted for official ones. It is a rare name in America too, where this settler originated in Loudoun County, Virginia.

House slave Isaac William Cisco, born in July 1848, had connections to Weldon, in northern North Carolina. He was a member of the Wilmington Jubilee Singers who were in Britain from 1876. The extremely unusual surname enabled the following British details to be located from the census and civic registrations.

Isaac William Cisco married Mary Jane Turner in Ormskirk in the early summer of 1878. They are known to have had seven children: Ann Maud Cisco was born in West Derby (Liverpool) in the summer of 1879 and her brother William Henry in Liverpool in 1880. He died in Bolton the following year. The Bolton-born children were Gertrude (born 1883), Edith (born in 1884 and died when a baby), George Washington Cisco born in 1887, Herbert born in 1890 died when a baby as did his brother Henry, born in 1892. Their mother Mary Jane Cisco died in Bolton, aged 52 in 1904 and her American husband died a year later, aged 52. The three children who reached adulthood lived together in Manchester Road, Bolton for the 1911 census has the head of the household as Ann Maud, listing her 'confectioner' sister Gertrude, their brother George working as a cotton spinner. Two were to be married: Gertrude in 1919 and George in 1920. George Cisco, who served in the Loyal North Lancashire Regiment 1917-1919, died in Bolton in 1935.

Thousands of people worked entertaining the British, including children. Children who showed an African ancestry had opportunities in theatrical productions of *Uncle Tom's Cabin*. 'Cabin' shows appeared all over Britain and Ireland, as will be seen. We know George Walmer who played Tom in 'Cabin' shows was black because of newspaper reports after his 3-year-old London-born daughter Cassy attracted the attention of the police when they were performing in Leicester's Theatre Royal in late 1891. Walmer said he had been educating her. She seemed bright and intelligent, and no further action was taken.[38]

In 1892 when a 'Cabin' show reached Birmingham's Theatre Royal a locally-born woman, 21-year-old Esther Ann 'Hettie' Johnson joined. She was the daughter of an African American vocalist named John Alexander Johnson who had settled in Birmingham where he was listed in the 1871 census, living with Hannah Greaves. Weeks later on 16 August their daughter Esther Johnson was born. She had an older brother (John Albert Johnson) and Charles Albert Johnson who was seven years younger according to the 1881 census. Their father died in Birmingham in 1879, aged 43. Hannah died in 1889 and in 1891 Hettie was listed as a machine-press operator. She was working as a factory hand when she took advantage of her skin colour. She had a career as an actress.

In January 1887 the antics of the 'African Blondin' were noted in Bristol. A rope fifty feet (12 metres) above the floor was where this entertainer walked, in shackles, pushing a wheelbarrow, whilst blindfolded.[39] He was an African American named Carlos Trower who, aged 19, married Myra Clay in Stoke-on-Trent in October 1864. He married Annie Emmett in Barnstaple in October 1875. He was to perform with their daughter Celia (known as the Black Star) in later years. Conditions which had surely driven him from America had changed and he re-crossed the Atlantic in 1878, coming back to England in 1879. He worked in Germany, and in the popular English resort of Blackpool as well as the Crystal Palace. His last known public performance was in Swansea in May 1888. He became ill and was placed in an asylum in Bow, London where he died in April 1889, destitute. Annie Trower sought assistance from readers of the *Era*; a benefit was held. There were three children including a grandparent of Ron Howard who, with relatives, is researching the 'man of colour', the African Blondin, 'high rope walker'.

The Salvation Army's activities involved Agnes Foster and her family. Websites note that she had been instrumental in establishing the Salvation Army in Jamaica in the 1880s after forty years in England, and suggest that she had been taken to England as a slave. The British census of 1851, 1861, 1871 and 1881 recorded her as born in Jamaica, the wife of an English farmer named John Foster, with four Yorkshire-born children. The black wife of a Yorkshire farmer is outside stereotypes.

The London archives of the Salvation Army located Agnes Foster and her daughter Jane (aged 25, a 'teacher of music') at 8 Vernon Avenue in Barton, Eccles (Manchester). She was a widow. She joined the new Salvation Army in Eccles and became an officer, based in South Shields into 1883. She went to Jamaica soon after and although unauthorized, she founded the Army's work in Kingston in 1887. Officially adopted by 1888, the first edition of

Kingston's *War Cry* in 1888 noted that one of her daughters was an officer of the Salvation Army in England.

The 1891 census lists her as an 'evangelist' visiting a house in Gate Street, Swinton (Eccles). The 1901 census located her in Bristol, a widow aged 74 living at 56 North Hill, Bedminster. The Jamaica *Gleaner* of 25 October 1902 noted that she was living with a daughter in Eccles. She died in Eccles, aged 87, on 18 March 1910. Agnes Bizzett Foster spent most of her adult life in England. Acknowledged as 'Mother Foster' by Salvationists in Jamaica, her activities in Britain deserve investigation. This is a black British family and the lives of her children may reveal more about Victorian times and could detail American Salvationists. The Salvation Army was in favour of temperance and still is, one of the survivors of the era of Victorian anti-drinking organizations.

At the beginning of September 1895 the *City of Paris* docked in Southampton and among those taking the train to London were the Revd Daniel Jenkins, his assistant and fourteen youngsters. They took lodgings in Catherine Street, the Strand but Jenkins found that his plans were going to be thwarted. The boys played band instruments but English law did not permit children aged below eleven years to be taken about to sing or play, or gather alms. Jenkins and his party went to Bow Street police court to seek advice and were mentioned in *Lloyd's Weekly Newspaper* (Sunday, 8 September): 'A Troupe of Niggers at Bow Street'. Jenkins was a 'tall, well-spoken man, of evidently pure negro descent', his assistant was 'a young man of similar appearance, in a blue serge suit' and the fourteen boys 'all in uniform dress' were sitting on the bench facing the magistrate. They were aged from five to ten. Magistrate Sir John Bridge said he could not give advice but if the group played on the streets they would cause an obstruction. Jenkins ran an orphanage in Charleston, South Carolina which needed money hence their venture to London. He asked 'what will we do? We are here without money, and must starve'. Sir John gave Jenkins a sovereign (£1) from his own pocket. The assistant (Paul Daniels) told the reporter that the American consul was unable to help them.

On Monday the *Pall Mall Gazette* picked up the story.[40] 'Sad Plight of Thirteen Little Nigger Boys', the report said their ages were from five to fourteen and Jenkins 'a coloured Baptist minister' and the band had been stopped whilst playing in the street on the Saturday morning. On another page the *Gazette* said there were fourteen boys and with a laboured humour noted that the court had taken on the appearance of a juvenile St James's Hall (a hall often used for minstrel shows). The young men 'might break into a breakdown [dance] at any moment'; also there was nothing said or sung about the Old Folks at Home because they were orphans. The newspaper hoped they would be able to return to America. When the *Standard* reported it had 'John Jenkins'. The daily cost for all of them was one pound. The wrong name and the statement they had not played in the streets were repeated in the *Yorkshire Herald*.

The *Daily Telegraph* commented 'to let loose a brass band of thirteen [*sic*] Negro children upon an urban population suffering from nerves is likely to create almost as many orphans as it would relieve'. The court assisted by putting Jenkins in contact with the Society for the Prevention of Cruelty to Children. Jenkins had made contacts with British Baptists, possibly through visiting the Metropolitan Tabernacle or the orphanage in Stockwell, London, both founded by Charles Spurgeon, for the orphanage's Vernon J. Charlesworth wrote to the *Baptist* on Sunday, 10 September asking for support for Jenkins had found 'it impossible to appeal for help in our thoroughfares'. He added Jenkins was to visit the orphanage of George Muller in Bristol and would be attending a gathering of the Young People's Society of Christian Endeavour in Stockwell. Jenkins was assisted by Sir George Williams (founder of the YMCA), a wealthy and charitable evangelical in London whose son Howard helped run the orphanages of Thomas Barnardo. Sir George's letter of support was dated 30 September 1895. One reader of the *Baptist* declared that Americans were rich enough and American Baptists were numerous enough to support their own appeals and added that no more charity should be 'bestowed upon the impecunious representatives of wealthy America'.[41]

There is evidence that the children did perform in the streets, from Jenkins's later comments in orphanage publications and the memories of holiday-making members of a patrician white Charleston family, that of Augustine Smythe who heard 'the unmistakeable nostalgic strains [of the band] coming round the London corner', and soon assisted them. Jenkins and Daniels seem to have remained in Britain for months. Twelve boys including three of Jenkins's sons, plus Frank Wallace aged in his early twenties left on the *Teutonic* from Liverpool on 16 October. Daniels studied in Colwyn Bay, Wales until 1899; Jenkins negotiated to be sole US agent for the instruments made by Abraham Collins of London, a reflection of his sagacity revealed through a rare copy of the orphanage weekly newspaper, the *Charleston Messenger* in 1898.[42]

Jenkins and the orphanage secretary Eloise Harleston came to England in 1906 and their daughter Olive was born in Wigan, Lancashire. She went to school in that coal mining and cotton mill town until 1920. Her half-brother Edmund Jenkins came to London, aged 20, with another band in 1914, and remained to study at the Royal Academy of Music for seven years.

Other Americans found Britain to be better than the U.S.A. The children had opportunities for education, not restricted to under-financed and inferior blacks-only schools and colleges in America. In America as young adults they faced discrimination in every walk of life. No wonder William Ivens Craft returned to London and Clarissa Brown Sylvester never left. Isaiah Powell returned to England and was listed at a boarding house in 53 Saxony Road, West Derby in the 1901 census which recorded that he was a cooper and unmarried. He was living in Prescot Street, West Derby in Liverpool and his brother Dr William Powell Jr was with him when he died on 7 June 1902. The death registration states he was a journeyman cooper (self-employed barrel maker). William remained in Liverpool, moving to a nursing home in Kirkdale where he died in April 1916, aged 81.

Chapter 4

Minstrels and *Uncle Tom's Cabin*

Nineteenth-century Britons experienced African people in various ways. Slavery narratives and lectures were widespread; from the 1840s there were stage performances by minstrel troupes, and from the early 1850s stage acts based on the best-selling novel *Uncle Tom's Cabin*. All involved whites using burnt cork to impersonate people of African descent and many included men, women and children who were genuinely black. This (mis)use of black imagery had a long history in Britain, with the Jack-in-the-Green celebrations which marked the end of winter and the seasonal reduction in work for chimney sweeps. The first of May was often called Sweeps Day, and as they and friends performed in the streets in the hope of donations, a black face seems to have been de rigueur.

Customs of the common people, that is, 'folk' or 'vernacular' activities, are difficult to document. An activity which continued over decades if not centuries might be noted by visiting strangers. If and when it ceased, it would be mourned by few who were literate. Folk songs were hardly noted in England until the late nineteenth century, and it was not until photography became widespread that costumed dancers were documented. The magazine *Folk-Lore* founded in 1889 published (Volume 4, 1893) a photograph of May Day celebrations in Cheltenham, some participants appear to have blacked up. That is, white men blackened their faces. Explaining this phenomenon has led to various suggestions and beliefs.

Were such dancers enlisted from chimney sweeps with sooty faces? Were the dances and costumes due to northern African (Moorish) elements, an opinion encouraged by the name 'Morris dancers'? Was there a desire to disguise the performers so that the powerful had problems in controlling the often-ribald and usually drunken activities? The revival of morris dancing, with local traditions in costume, dance styles, and melodies added a romantic 'historic England' image to what is known to have been far from rare back in the seventeenth century. And to the chagrin of deeply Christian late Victorians, how could their modern society accept the fertility symbols, the pagan images, and the bacchanalian celebrations? In these complexities there remains the matter of what black-faced dancers were suggesting. Sweeps were welcome as guests at weddings in England and elsewhere in Europe, but why darken faces to present 'Moors'?

An unexpected source is the 1957 memoir of Ernest Shepard, born in London in 1879. His *Drawn from Memory* was later published by Penguin Books (1975). Probably best known for his *Winnie-the-Pooh* illustrations of the 1920s, Shepard's small book tells of life in London in the late 1880s. On 1st May 'a motley group of men rigged up for "Jack-in-the-Green"' appeared near his house. One was 'completely covered with greenery ... only his legs were showing'; another was dressed as a clown; and 'a third, in striped cloth coat and trousers, with a huge collar and a blackened face, was beating a tambourine'. Another was dressed as a woman. They cried out to Shepard 'what have you got for Jack-in-th'-Green, little gentleman?' His sketch of the four shows these outlandish individuals. Perhaps the black-face performer had copied theatrical minstrels? The Jack-in-the-Green fertility image seems to have been centuries old. But Shepard's clear memory of late Victorian St John's Wood, London with these apparently rustic 'folk' celebrants of spring both reminds us that black-face entertainers were not restricted to the theatre and that these four men were performing in the street in the hope of coins (the 'woman' had an umbrella to catch donations thrown from windows). A quick scan of Victorian newspapers, and later editions carrying letters and articles describing events of the recent past, shows that the May Day celebrations with a performer clad in branches and leaves were widespread.

The *Illustrated London News* in May 1843 shows a Jack-in-the-Green group with some darkened faces. The *Gloucester Echo* in 1938 reported that Cheltenham chimney sweeps had been active in the May Day celebrations 'years ago'.[1] May Day was also called Sweeps Day it seems. A Somerset newspaper in 1937 commented years before 'you could come across half-a-dozen "Jack-in-the-Green" parties in any suburban area' and that the leading dancers were always known as Black Sal and Dusty Bob. Those names are very suggestive. Recollections of May Day in rural Kent were published in the *Sunderland Daily Echo* in 1939 when 'the central figure, Jack in the Green, [was] surrounded by boys with blackened faces – why blackened, I wonder?'[2] From Shepard's illustrations it seems that black-face minstrels had impacted on the older British street frolics.

Presentations by black performers made much of Southern plantation life, a genre developed in America in the 1840s although black-face white performers dated back into the eighteenth century. Sheet-music covers reveal posing, strange clothing, and often banjo players. A pioneer American show in Liverpool in 1842 had Joel Sweeney, a black-face performer, sing and play the banjo. He met with success and toured to London. He was one of the first white Americans known to have taken up the banjo, an instrument so little known that a review of the Virginia Minstrels (which Sweeney joined) in Manchester explained it was 'a rude guitar'. Soon American songs with lines such as 'I'm off to Alabama with a banjo on my knee' were performed to Britons.[3] Four men, the 'Ethiopian Entertainers' singing and playing violin, banjo, tambourine and castanets appeared in London in May 1844.[4] Blacked-up minstrels had a banjo player to offer the British public.[5] Taking American names added to the illusion: the Tenessee (*sic*) Vocalists had a banjo according to the advertisement for their appearance at the Casino de Venise in London's Holborn in February 1848.[6] 'Black minstrelsy matured in the 1870s and black-led troupes toured America and Europe.

Dancer William Henry Lane, known as Master Juba, worked in Britain from 1848 and had considerable fame, encouraged by a report from America by Dickens in 1842. He vanished from the theatrical press in 1852, and died in Liverpool in early 1854; researcher James Cook has recently unravelled the misspelling of his death registration as Bois Juba. He had a dominating place in British entertainment for two or three years, and might be considered an originator in tap dancing. He certainly was often mentioned in British newspapers in 1848. His fame was drowned by minstrelsy.

Minstrelsy was a musical and humorous entertainment style popular in Britain from about 1850 to 1970. Minstrel shows were seen by millions. The entertainers blacked up, a grotesque parody of black Americans of the Southern slave states. When African-descent entertainers participated, they too wore burnt-cork make-up. Minstrel shows were musical, vibrant, amusing, and capable of swiftly adapting to new circumstances. Most societies have entertainers who use masks and gaudy clothes, speak with false accents, dance in exaggerated ways, and play musical instruments with visible enthusiasm. The minstrel show did all of these. A minstrel show was a self-contained entertainment.

Minstrelsy showed both the evils of slavery and the allegedly happy plantation slaves. Stage versions of the best-selling novel *Uncle Tom's Cabin* added dramatic elements; then spirituals contributed songs including 'Go Down, Moses' and 'Steal Away to Jesus'. Costumes ranged from ragged hand-me-downs to primary-coloured broad-striped fashions, tuxedo jackets, and the eighteenth-century styles favoured by 'court minstrels'. There were shows which lasted well over an hour, and acts which appeared in other entertainments. Minstrelsy encouraged audience interaction. Opening with the entire company in a semi-circle, with individual acts including dialect songs and dances, the cast would join in the chorus. In the centre was the pompous interlocutor, or master of ceremonies, personifying dignity. The endmen had comic roles, making jokes often about the interlocutor. The audiences joined in their mockery. With malapropisms and vulgar dialect the endmen – Brudder Tambo and Brudder Bones – were in turn mocked by the interlocutor. He directed the action on stage, swiftly responding to the audience: another reason why minstrel shows were very successful. The show could include handsome tenors singing emotional songs. This sharply contrasted to Tambo and Bones, who made puns, contorted their bodies, and wore the most flamboyant costumes. The second act could include a range of entertainers, using the time for the closing act's set to be put up behind the curtains. Almost any style of act might be seen, but a major attraction was a stump speech. An ill-educated, verbose, over-serious speaker would include the latest political and local news in this act, which usually ended when he fell off his soap-box. Local dignitaries and leaders of society were parodied. This was the heritage of the jester.

Victorian music publishing, the manufacture of inexpensive musical instruments, and easy movement afforded by railways all led to composers and performers of popular melodies achieving fame and fortune. Minstrel shows led to so-called dialect songs reaching most parts of Britain. Audiences enjoyed minstrels singing of 'Away Down in de Kentuck [Kentucky] Brake', 'Dixie', and 'Dar Is a Place Call'd Loozyann [Louisiana]'. The sentimental sighed when they heard 'Old Mass Was de Best ob [sic] Men'. Men and women purchased banjos – and mandolins and guitars – and played the songs at home. Groups played together; singers performed to the piano in domestic music-making. Amateur groups were widespread: the squire's in rural Oxfordshire in the 1880s is recalled in Flora Thompson's *Lark Rise to Candleford* memoirs.

Professional groups reached every town in Britain. Several groups named the Christy Minstrels notably that run by George 'Pony' Moore had continuing success. St James's Hall in Piccadilly, London, a 550-seat basement beneath a grand hall, became a centre for minstrel shows until it was demolished in 1904. The Moore Minstrels set the standard for four decades. Moore and Burgess claimed to have been minstrels since 1865 and in 1876 had forty-five performers.[7] Christy Minstrels included a 'Happy Uncle Tom Dance' in their London show in 1857.[8] Although Tambo and Bones and the interlocutor retained vital roles, the scope widened to include plantation and Southern themed songs, Irish songs, comic songs and dramatic ballads sometimes presented by operatic singers. Presentations could include all-female troupes, black performers, and varied costumes. The show-business weekly *Era* on 22 February 1876 listed thirteen minstrel troupes including Sam Hague's, originally the Georgia Minstrel Troupe of twenty-six freed slaves which had opened in Liverpool in July 1866. In time white performers replaced many of them. Aaron Banks was the longest-surviving original member working in Britain. Other African American minstrels in Britain included composer James Bland and the comedian Billy Kersands.

Minstrelsy's success was due to it being a family show, with choral and solo singing, instrumental selections, humour, topicality, sentimentality and joy. African-descent performers were often first-class, as with the Bohee Brothers, Canada-born banjoists – as we will see. Burnt cork was just one of minstrelsy's negative images of blacks. The entry of a watermelon cart would lead to the entire cast breaking away to munch the sweet fruit; scenes set in a bar would involve card players cheating and threatening each other with razors. The cast would stop to dance at the slightest opportunity.

The legacy was almost toxic, for audiences associated African Americans with music, dance and humour. Given the so-limited opportunities elsewhere, the late nineteenth-century entertainment world attracted black men and women who would have met with success in other walks of life had American discrimination been less severe.

The number of performers working in British burnt-cork minstrelsy was substantial. Veteran-turned-historian of the genre Harry Reynolds recalled that 'at one time no variety programme was complete without the inclusion of two or three black face acts; turns famous for their versatility and laughter-producing propensities'. He thought 'burnt cork was a quaint and inoffensive disguise'. One effect of black-face performers was the permanent confusion over identities: Ethiopian Troubadours were not Africans, the Musical Kaffir had no link to South Africa and 'negro comedians' usually meant black-face. The lyrics of the often-tuneful songs they presented libelled life in the Caribbean, Africa and the U.S.A. Generally termed 'plantation songs', samples provided by Reynolds include the lines 'Her face was so black dat you couldn't see it well', 'Feet so large and comely, too, Might make a cradle ob each shoe' and 'He's a knock-kneed, double-jointed, humpy-plumky moke, But he's happy when he whistles this tune'.

The sheet music of these and countless other songs spread the warped images around Britain, the covers having illustrations usually by artists who had never seen a person of African descent. Indeed, like the American popular songs published round the world from the 1920s, the lyrics were by writers who had not seen cotton growing, sat by any of the rivers mentioned, or been present at a church service or in a bar in Afro America. The impact was enormous – even young British Guiana-born James Risien Russell, bound for Edinburgh University and an MD, a medical scholarship to Paris and Berlin, and a professorship at University College London, played Bones in a school presentation in 1880s Scotland.

Entertaining the crowds at the Cowes Regatta in August 1861 were a military band, strolling musicians, a solo violinist and 'a sable Sambo with his melodious banjo, [who] was sailing about among the boats ... and reaping a golden harvest' with his songs.[9] He may have been a burnt-cork performer. A group of amateurs had put on a minstrel show, in aid of charity, in Market Harborough in February 1861, collecting £21.[10] Professionals who can be seen in newspaper reports include the thirteen performers of Rumsey and Newcombs' Minstrels, reported in Sheffield at the beginning of 1862.[11] The Matthews brothers claimed to have established their troupe in 1863. They played the Christmas season at the Colston Hall in Bristol in 1875-1876.[12] A minstrel company was formed by members of the Dublin police.[13]

Then there was a man named Height who, with a scene painter from a Bradford theatre, was accused of consorting with a married woman named Liepke, they were named in a divorce case in late 1876. She had left him to be with Height, who worked with Hayes Minstrels, from February 1876.[14] One minstrel was Jacob Baltimore who had been employed as a valet in London in 1889. He was 'a negro servant' witness in Viscount Dunlo's divorce case in mid-1890: Lady Dunlo having been a music hall singer.[15] The 1891 census finds him in Hackney, a 'professional singer' aged 17, born in Maryland. The twenty-five Kentucky Minstrels who appeared in Huddersfield in October 1893 included one genuine performer of African descent, Frank Broom. A humorous version of *Il Trovatore* was well received, as were the singing and the stump speech.[16]

Minstrel performances can be traced in local newspapers and on theatre bills. We cannot be certain if the performers were of African descent or using burnt cork, and it is likely contemporaries were also baffled. What they saw and heard added to the British general idea of African Americans. For those of African descent, like Esther 'Hettie' Johnson, minstrel shows were an opportunity for employment, along with presentations based on *Uncle Tom's Cabin*, dramatic works, and recitals of African American songs. The men, women and children who worked in these presentations in the second half of the nineteenth century left a remarkable legacy in Britain which, whilst uncomfortable to the modern mind, strongly influenced the larger society. News of their reception reached America, which encouraged others to cross the Atlantic: without the desperation of Roper, Douglass, the Crafts, Watkins and the other refugees.

The initial impact of *Uncle Tom's Cabin* has been easier to date. A work of fiction, *Uncle Tom's Cabin* had a considerable and lasting impact on British perceptions of black people, for this American novel sold many thousands of copies and led to countless songs, plays, anti-slavery lectures, books, illustrations and newspaper reports for decades. These affected Americans and others of African descent in Britain, and influenced the highest in the land.

In 1852 *Uncle Tom's Cabin* was reported to be selling 1,000 copies daily in the U.S.A.[17] A London reviewer commented that the book was 'so good that even the most refined among English readers of fiction will pursue the story with interest'.[18] The elderly slave Tom manages the estate for his owner who sells him to pay off a debt, and Tom leaves his wife and family behind. His new master promises him his freedom, but dies. Tom is purchased by a brutal cotton planter. Two slaves and their child escape. The very nature of American slavery was exposed. *The Times* thought the book would prolong slavery in America but the liberal *Leeds Mercury* thought that *Uncle Tom's Cabin* would develop a sense of 'the sinfulness and inhumanity of Slavery'.[19] The book was available in several editions, was published in magazines and reviewed in many newspapers. By late 1852 it had been three times translated into German.[20] Passmore Edwards wrote *Uncle Tom's Companions* to refute criticisms from *The Times*, using evidence gathered from 'men who have walked, or who now are walking, the streets of London', these witnesses being Garnet, Douglass, Wells Brown and Pennington.[21]

Uncle Tom's Cabin was on stage at the Standard Theatre and the Royal Olympic Theatre in London in September 1852. In October 1852 there were London productions at the Marylebone, Queen's and the Victoria theatres. One production reached its hundredth performance in mid-January 1853.[22] Performances at the Pavilion in east London included auxiliaries playing slaves, probably black people.[23] A *Cabin* show in Manchester was into its third month in February.[24] Another was in Hull in early February.[25] A version on horseback was in London from late November 1852 and was playing in Bradford in mid-February.[26] In Edinburgh Pablo Fanque (the son of a black Briton) dropped *Rob Roy* and put on an equestrian version of *Cabin* from mid-February 1853.[27]

Ex-slave lecturers brought aspects of the novel into their talks as with Wells Brown in Newport, Isle of Wight on 10 February 1853.[28] *Cabin's* authoress Harriet Beecher Stowe arrived in England in May 1853 and received much publicity. The decision by the Pope to ban her book led to further publicity.[29]

The Duchess of Sutherland, one of the Queen's ladies in waiting, was a wealthy hostess whose support of the anti-slavery movement led Thomas Carlyle to call her home (Stafford House) 'Aunt Harriet's Cabin', Queen Victoria called it a palace. The Duchess was to see Samuel Ringgold Ward's *Autobiography of a Fugitive Negro: His Anti Slavery Labours in the United States, Canada, and England* dedicated to her.[30] She hosted Stowe. Stowe then wrote *Key to Uncle Tom's Cabin* and extracts duly appeared in the British press. Beer houses were named *Uncle Tom's Cabin* in Huddersfield, Sheffield, London, Preston and Bradford. The Royal Porcelain Works, Worcester issued an image of Uncle Tom and Eva. The Staffordshire potteries issued two, each 26cm high. Dickens mentioned such an ornament in *Household Words*. By December 1853 Stowe's book had sold 600,000 copies in Britain. It was translated into Welsh. In June 1854 the play was at Newport, south Wales and another version was at Bolton. By 1855 music publishers used *Uncle Tom* in the titles of a march, a lament, a waltz and a quadrille. Teachers in Sunday schools told children about slavery in America, using *Cabin*.[31]

Realising that some thought its story was exaggerated, William Craft told an audience in Sheffield in December 1855 that nothing in print exaggerated the horrors of slavery. Box Brown enlarged his panoramas and took them to Ryde on the Isle of Wight from 12 May 1856: fifty-thousand square feet of canvas showed views of *Uncle Tom's Cabin*. The two-hour show had music, and tickets cost two shillings for reserved seats, one shilling for seats and 'working people' were allowed access for sixpence.[32] An illustrated edition of *Cabin* was published and Stowe dramatized her novel as *The Christian Slave*. The book's continuing sales led to the joke that some wondered where all the copies had been stowed.

Theatrical versions included a scene on ice, the Ohio River was crossed when it was frozen, the slaves heading from Kentucky north to freedom. Eventually bloodhounds were on stage for a chase scene, as in Portsmouth in 1860.[33] Stowe abridged the novel and readings were given including by her associate the 'mulatto' Mary Webb around England in 1856.[34] Song-and-dance minstrel shows included Uncle Tom as early as 1853.[35] The leading troupe the Christy Minstrels included a 'Happy Uncle Tom Dance' in their London show in 1857. London's Victoria Theatre revived *Cabin* in October 1858, as did the Theatre Royal in Bristol. The City of London Theatre produced a version in late May 1859. Belfast was to see *Cabin* performed again in 1860 (the *Era* also noted Ira Aldridge was in Cork). In Bradford a new venue, Uncle Tom's Music Hall, was almost ready in December 1860.[36] The wide acceptance of *Uncle Tom's Cabin* in its many guises did not extend to Catholics, and a priest denounced the book when visiting the workhouse in Cardiff, telling a woman reading a copy that it and she should be burned. That led the workhouse guardians to rule that Catholic priests would only be permitted to enter the workhouse when requested by an inmate. Birmingham's New Theatre Royal claimed in June 1861 that *The Horrors of Slavery, or Uncle Tom's Cabin* was 'an original version'. It had music too.

With Eva and Uncle Tom ornaments on the mantelpiece, *Uncle Tom's Cabin* on the bookshelf, versions in theatres, as sheet music, and melodrama, the images created by and from Stowe's novel had a wide-ranging circulation in Victorian Britain. *Uncle Tom's Cabin* companies and singing groups strongly influenced the minstrel shows – generally whites in black face – which amused the British from the 1840s well into the twentieth century. The slavery experiences of Richard Sayer, reported in the *Chelmsford Chronicle* on 12 May 1871, after he spoke at Coggeshall, read like a summary from *Cabin*. In all these ways *Uncle Tom's Cabin* influenced British views and had an impact on black people in the British Isles.

When contemporaries referred to a person's role in the *Uncle Tom's Cabin* story we should assume the individual may not have claimed such an association. A pious semi-fraudster Revd William Mitchell from Toronto obtained alms by begging. In Falmouth in 1861 a free lecture at the Polytechnic Hall on slavery was given by 'Mr. W. Michell, [*sic*] a coloured gentleman, one of the characters in the pathetic tale of "Uncle Tom's Cabin"'.[37] The census in April 1861 recorded the 45-year-old 'preacher' lodging with the Perry family in South Street, Yeovil.

The novel's impact on Josiah Henson was substantial, for he *became* Uncle Tom. The warping of the story of Henson who became regarded as the inspiration for Stowe's Uncle Tom has lasted for more than a century and remains alive to this day. How this came about is important. The Stowe-Henson-Uncle Tom story shows how even, with the best of intentions, there was duplicity.

Henson was born into slavery in Maryland in 1789 and ill-treatment led to him being maimed. He walked to Canada in 1830. His autobiography

The Life of Josiah Henson, formerly a Slave, Now an Inhabitant of Canada, ghost-written by Samuel Eliot of Boston appeared in 1849. By 1851 it had gone into a third edition in Britain.[38] The *Liverpool Mercury* reporting the arrival of the Crafts on 13 December 1850 listed the passengers from Boston and Halifax on the *Cambria*. From Boston there were twenty-four including 'J. Henson' who surely was the future Uncle Tom. Henson brought some black walnut boards, produced by his ex-slave community in Dawn, Ontario to be exhibited at the Great Exhibition.

Stowe had started her novel in February 1851, and had not met Henson at all. The books attributed to Henson were written by white ghost-writers. *Uncle Tom's Cabin*, Stowe's writings and comments, and the much-amended editions of Henson's autobiographies plus the stage melodramas, made the link and brought the larger society's focus on Canada as a haven for fugitives and the destination of the Underground Rail Road. Donations to Dawn were numerous, but as recent visitor Wells Brown wrote in 1861, 'no place has proved itself less deserving'. Problems had been created by John Scoble, who had settled in Canada and misused his reputation as an ex-official of the British and Foreign Anti-Slavery Society of London.

It was to Henson's advantage, and to the benefit of the causes he espoused, to accept the association with Stowe's saintly creation. In December 1876 he gave two addresses at the Congregational church in Herne Bay, Kent where six guineas was collected for him.[39] In March 1877 Josiah Henson went to Windsor Castle where he was greeted with enthusiasm by Queen Victoria. He died in Dawn in 1883, aged 93. Many of the settlers there had returned to slavery-free America. Historic markers, books and websites continue to tell the false story of Henson's impact on Stowe. *Uncle Tom's Cabin* continued to attract Britons.

Chapter 5

Frauds and Impostors

The activities of black men and women whose claims were false, who lied and cheated, obtaining financial and other support from the inhabitants of the British Isles, and misrepresenting fugitive slaves were reported, sometimes at length, in Victorian newspapers. The details reveal something of the extent of support for black Americans, and how these antics created problems for genuine refugees.

We have noted the 1840s free-born Charles Lenox Remond was sometimes considered to be 'a white man who had assumed the Ethiop [*sic*] tinge to suit a purpose'. George Borrow in *Wild Wales* (1862), his account from travels in the mid-1850s, noted in Chester that an ex-slave blacksmith from Antigua told him 'Any black might live in England without working; that all he had to do was attend religious meetings, and speak against slavery and the Americans' and that he was going to marry 'a religious lady'.[1]

Chancers and opportunists, liars and beggars, are to be found in most societies. The parvenu produced 'anew by each generation with incomparable monotony' is to be found among 'defamed peoples', but the black impostor in the African Diaspora has been little studied or understood. Their successes were often due to white sympathies. The widespread sympathy towards people of African descent was seen in 1849 when a beggar in Cornwall 'lately blackened his face and hands, and successfully appealed to the sympathies of several householders of St. Austell as a distressed and deserving negro; but he forgot he had a hole in his trowsers [*sic*]'. He was sent to Bodmin prison for three months.[2]

Alfred Wood had been charged with false pretences in Manchester in February 1852, for he was said to have obtained £15 by presenting a letter signed by President Roberts of Liberia. The case was dismissed. Wood told the police that he was a Baptist minister and had preached in London. His manner 'closely resembled that of the coloured preachers who are frequently to be met with on our missionary platforms'.[3] Seven weeks later the *Liverpool Mercury* of 23 March warned that this man had 'obtained certificates from several clergymen under false representations' as did the *Blackburn Standard* on 31 March. In Newcastle in September, Wood gave a lecture on American slavery and claimed to be a minister and doctor from Liberia. The meeting was crowded.

Wood's downfall was reported in the *Newcastle Courant* eight days later. He had been charged in Hull with obtaining money on false pretences, namely collecting for a chapel to be erected in Monrovia, the capital of Liberia. 'Alfred Thomas Wood, alias Dr Wood' had claimed he knew Josiah Henson (regarded as the stimulus for Tom in *Uncle Tom's Cabin* the best-selling slavery novel of 1852). Two receipts signed by Wood were placed before the court. One for £12 10s deposited in Dublin on 26 September and the second for the same amount but in 'Malton' (a Yorkshire town) on the same day suggested fraud. Contact was to be made with Malton. The *Hull Packet* said that Wood was aged 35 when reporting the charge of fraud in the court which dealt with complicated legal matters into the evening. London's *Morning Post* declared that it was 'extraordinary'.[4]

A Hull vicar had given Wood one pound on 9 November having seen a book listing subscribers and a document saying Wood was authorized to collect for the new chapel. Both were now alleged to be false. Wood told another minister in Hull that his congregation in Monrovia numbered 2,000 but the whole town had only 1,500 inhabitants as the British consul would testify. The two Hull clergymen made their statements, then a Manchester police inspector told the court he had arrested Wood in Liverpool in February 1852 on a charge of false pretences but the case was discharged as there was no evidence that Wood was not – as he had claimed – associated with the Commercial Banking Company of Monrovia. A Liverpool merchant who knew President Roberts said the signature on one of Wood's documents was a forgery as was the seal attached to it. The Revd Augustus William Hansen who had been acting British consul in Monrovia for sixteen months said he knew Wood whose congregation was 200. The jury found Wood guilty on three charges. He was sentenced to eighteen months in Hull's prison, with solitary confinement for the first and last months.

Wood returned to court two days later, a formality as his plea of not guilty on two more charges was accepted. The judge remarked that fresh information had reached him since the sentencing which, had he known, would have led him to sentence Wood to be transported to Australia. The *Liverpool Standard*'s report of the Hull trial also reminded its readers of its warning about Wood back in March 1852, which had led Wood to threaten libel. Summaries of the Hull trial appeared in several newspapers in January 1853.[5]

William Wells Brown's *The American Fugitive in Europe* of 1855 devotes a chapter to Joseph Jenkins who had several roles in 1850s London: distributing advertising bills, sweeping a crossing in Chelsea, playing Othello when he was billed as 'Selim, an African prince', a Christian preacher and temperance lecturer, and a band leader. Jenkins told Wells Brown that he was born in Ethiopia-Sudan, and had a son and daughter. Jenkins was a fictional character, based on a real African Selim Aga. Wells Brown wrote a pioneering novel, *Clotel*. Fact and fiction merged elsewhere.

Reports in the British press indicate that pious fraudsters and begging clergymen were not rare in the 1850s: and who were 'the coloured preachers who are frequently to be met with on our missionary platforms'?[6] Frederick Douglass had commented in Belfast in 1845 that he had been challenged by those who said he 'was not what he pretended to be, and [he] could not exhibit any credentials from persons of respectability'. He had never been asked for credentials before although he had given about fifty lectures. By 1852 the *Temperance Chronicle* recommended 'persons representing themselves as fugitive slaves' should 'be required to produce introductory certificates from well-known friends of the anti-slavery cause, and all collections made on their behalf should be forwarded to some person in Great Britain or Ireland who is willing to act as trustee, and whose name will guarantee that no more than the sum required shall be solicited, and that it shall be fairly appropriated to the object specified. These precautions would protect the public against fraud, and the coloured race and the anti-slavery cause against the odium to which both are subjected when benevolent persons are swindled in their name'.[7]

The subject was raised in the *Anti-Slavery Advocate* in August 1853, which warned of 'a coloured man named Charles Hill' who claimed to be collecting funds to redeem his wife from slavery. It recommended would-be donors to exercise great caution. Hill was Reuben Nixon who posed as a fugitive slave and is known to have done so under the names Henry Smith, Charles Hill, William Love, David Clarry, Andrew Baker and Hiram Swift. He was sent to prison on two occasions. Before reaching England he seems to have been known as John Allen, William Johnson and Charles W. Swift. In 1854 the *Cambridge Independent* pleaded readers should 'place the public on their guard' against this 'incorrigible' impostor and the *Brighton Gazette* noted his lies.[8] The *Brighton Herald*'s long report of 23 March 1854 was reprinted in the *Anti-Slavery Advocate* on 1 May, noting 'it shows that a man, though black and no better than he should be, may still be a very clever fellow'. His statement to Secretary Louis Chamerovzow that he had arrived in England on the *Summers* did not match port records. He was sentenced to three months with hard labour for obtaining money under false pretences. The *British Friend* of 4 April 1854 also noted that he had been in Belfast and recently convicted in Brighton. On release from Lewes prison he returned to trickery.[9]

He was an escaped slave named David Clarry when he appeared in Portsmouth in 1856 with letters of introduction and a 'plausible tale from the man himself', which led to a successful public lecture. He said he wanted to open a hairdresser's shop, having been a valet in America and anxious to settle down with his white wife. He opened his shop in Cross Street, Southsea and put up the hairdresser's pole and also stocked toys. In mid-1856 he disappeared along with items loaned to him (books and clothing) and the shop's goods. 'The kind-hearted people who assisted him have now to regret their misplaced generosity, whilst their guest is doubtless carrying out the same system in another part of the country'. The *Portsmouth Times* ended its report 'Rather tall and thin, [he] has quite a gentlemanly appearance, and walks very erect'. The cape he usually wore in Portsmouth had been loaned to him by a lady, and he 'took it away on leaving the town'.[10]

A description was published in the *Waterford Mail* of 2 September 1856 when a resident of Lismore warned the charitable against giving money to the 'man of colour' who was wandering around Ireland. 'Very tall, with large bushy whiskers' he said he was Reuben Nixon and sometimes David Clarry, and other names. He travelled with his wife and baby, the wife being from County Cavan but was said to have met her husband in Baltimore, U.S.A. His owner had sent him to Alabama and he escaped. In fact the pair had married in Dublin where they were servants and took to begging as 'more pleasant and profitable than an honest way of living'. They had been in Plymouth and elsewhere in England and in Ireland had appeared in Cork and were thought to have planned to visit Fermoy and Waterford.

The *Perthshire Advertiser* was noted by the *Anti-Slavery Reporter* in March 1857 having issued a 'warning: Reuben Nixon again'. He had been working as Smith in Dundee and Dunfermline in 1855, and in January 1857 as William Love in Darlington. The *Montrose, Arbroath and Brechin Review* of 6 February 1857 noted (as Love) he had spoken at a crowded meeting for two hours. One week later it noted he was an impostor who was solely a fugitive from 'those whom he had duped and fleeced. He has a new story for almost every place in which he appears' and a 'different name for each character he assumes'. It then described him. The *Montrose Standard* of 13 February 1857 noted 'he had ample testimonials in his possession'. At the northern end of Ireland far from Waterford, as William Love, Nixon toured and lectured, and pawned a watch he had borrowed. The Dublin marriage detail was repeated but there was now the suggestion that he had been involved with the police in Sunderland.[11] Another prison term was in the winter of 1857-1858.

In Cambridge in April 1856 a man named Watson was sentenced to one month with hard labour for fraud. A William Quant had a letter in the 28 May edition of the *Bury and Norwich Post* advising that he had known the Revd Dr Watson for ten years and had helped him go to London's Borough Road School as part of his training to assist 'his sable brethren' in the British colonies. He was responding to the *Post*'s report of 24 April – which noted that Watson's abilities picking oakum and walking on the treadmill showed he had been in prison before. Watson was to repeat his trickery. A lecture on 'the coloured subjects of the Queen' in Bradford on 14 October 1856 was given by William Watson, 'a person of colour, and a late student of King's College, London'. The chairman had known Watson for about ten years. 'The lecture was marked by talent and intelligence, and spoke volumes in favour of educating the escaped slaves in the British Colonies'. Watson had established societies for that purpose in Jersey and Guernsey (Channel Islands) and Devonport (Plymouth). There were 80,000 (*sic*) escaped blacks in Canada where he planned to establish schools.[12] Earlier that month a man reported as Henry (*sic*) Watson, claiming King's College and Channel Island associations had been in Huddersfield, saying he intended to give a lecture to raise funds for the education of African children. He visited the retired chief constable and was referred to the current chief constable, and then 'decamped, under the pretence of going to Lindley, leaving an unpaid score at Dearnally's beerhouse, Castlegate; and he has not yet thought it necessary to return and pay'. William Watson was to present a lecture on the general education of the coloured people of the British Empire at the Guildhall in Worcester in November 1858, with Sir Charles Hastings in the chair. Sir Charles was a well-regarded doctor and social reformer in Worcester. The meeting was not well attended. William Watson was a rogue. When he was scheduled to speak on his usual topic at the town hall in Cheltenham in late 1858 he was both late and intoxicated.[13]

An unnamed 'black man, of rather genteel dress, and speaking good English, who described himself as an escaped slave' received 'pecuniary assistance' from chapels, schools and Quakers in Saffron Walden at the beginning of 1856. Just as a collection was to be made at his lecture the local police chief said that he was a 'discharged and disgraced gentleman's servant' and a mob chased him from the small Essex town. 'He ran as fast as his legs could carry him' towards Cambridge. His foolishness, 'singing immoral songs and quaffing gin and water to excess' in local pubs must have alerted the police.[14]

In Leicester at the beginning of 1853 an anti-slavery meeting was addressed by the Revd Kelley, a fugitive born in 1818. The Fugitive Slave Act had driven him from Massachusetts to England where he collected donations to purchase his freedom, which the mayor said was an extraordinary state of affairs. He needed £166 13*s* and already had about £50 from collections in large towns in Britain. The collection on this occasion was the largest so far, almost £18.[15] He was probably Edmund Kelley, born in Tennessee, who had arrived in England in 1852, seeking funds to redeem his family and himself, first in Britain where his arrangements were questioned, and then – successfully – in Ireland. He went back to New Bedford, Massachusetts in mid-1853. His *A Family Redeemed from Bondage* had been published in New Bedford in 1851. It named his wife and four children, and that their purchase price was $2,800 plus $365 expenses, and named him Edmund Kelley. Perhaps he had borrowed the capital to free his family, and crossed the Atlantic to recover the money? Because he lacked a trustee his credibility had been questioned. In Ireland he met with considerable success. In Dublin the *Freeman's Journal* described him as having 'a highly intellectual and gentlemanly appearance'.[16]

H.E. Lewis, 'a gentleman of colour…the Negro Mesmerist…a native of Africa' was an American. He hypnotized strangers: he made them fall asleep and then act on his suggestions. Appearing in Sheffield then Roscommon (Ireland) in May 1850, Lewis had considerable success in 1850s Scotland, advertising his lectures in Dumfries in September and October 1850. The *Aberdeen Journal* of 23 July 1851 advertised thirteen locations where he was to lecture between 24 July and 7 August 1851. Lectures in the town hall were to attract 'all the families of distinction' within 8 miles as well as 'gaping rustics'. Probably suspecting trickery or a sophisticated fairground act, his performance was studied and the February 1852 *Edinburgh Monthly Journal of Medical Science* reported on an 'Examination of Mr. Lewis's Pretensions at Aberdeen'. There was another challenge.[17] The *Journal*'s report was to be reprinted in William B. Carpenter's, *Mesmerism, Spiritualism, &c.* (New York: Appleton, 1895).

Lewis moved on to Liverpool where an advertisement appeared on the front page of the *Liverpool Mercury* of 27 April 1852. He was to lecture on mesmerism for four evenings from 4 May. His reputation in Scotland was such that his colour was seldom mentioned there. He modified his programme, lecturing on American slavery when back in Aberdeen in February 1853 (*Aberdeen Journal*, 2 February and 9 February 1853). A year later, 'well known in Scotland' this 'native of Africa' was mentioned in the *Newcastle Courant* of 10 February 1854. He was at the town hall in Alnwick, a meeting chaired by a minister.[18] Later that year when appearing in Leeds he was a 'man of colour' (*Leeds Mercury*, 2 December 1854). He has been traced elsewhere in Yorkshire (Huddersfield, Holmfirth and York) in February-March 1855.[19] In 1855 Lewis 'the Negro Mesmerist' was to appear at the Marylebone Literary Institution in London on 16 and 17 May, according to advertisements in the *Morning Post* (12 May 1855) and *The Times* (14 May 1855). He was said to be an American who had travelled globally. He now included phrenology in his presentation (the study of the shape of the cranium as an indication of character).

The *Croydon Chronicle and East Surrey Advertiser* of 15 March 1856 reported Lewis the 'African Mesmerist' gave a lecture in the Lower Hall on Crown Lane. 'The audience was not very numerous, and but few persons came forward to be acted upon, and over those Mr. Lewis had but little power, sending a few to sleep, but operating successfully on a little boy. In justice to Mr. Lewis it should be mentioned, that he conducted his experiments in a fair and straight forward manner, clearly showing that to the science alone he was willing to trust.' There was singing by Mr and Mrs Brady.

Lewis was employed to make a phrenological study of the children of the Martin family in Durham city, and the family papers survive.[20] He signed the ten pages on 15 February 1857 in the St Leonards district of the city of Durham. Probably of Virginian descent he was a British citizen born in St John, New Brunswick. A legal announcement in 1855 gave his name as Henry Edward Lewis. He died in July 1857, aged 39, after he was thrown from his horse in Blackheath, London.[21]

Press reports of late 1857 told of 'two remarkably good-looking young coloured girls' who had been arrested in London for begging. Holding a sign stating they were fugitive slaves they had collected from people in the street. They told the magistrate at Southwark that they had been slaves in Kentucky and had escaped to Philadelphia where they had their fares paid to Greenock (Glasgow's port). Unable to obtain work they came to London but failed to find employment as servants. They said that they thought they could earn a living through knitting, so the magistrate gave them money from the court's poor box. Charitable people made donations, and the pair returned to show what they had made with the wool purchased with the gifts. The magistrate had received offers of help from distinguished people: and one letter suggesting they were low characters. Told they were living in Wentworth Street, Whitechapel the court's clerk said this was 'full of low lodging-houses'. The girls said that a coloured man and his large family lived in the same court. Responding to questions the magistrate was told that their fares had been paid by free blacks and their ship to Scotland was the *Jane*. Investigation had not been completed but the tale seemed sound, another five shillings was provided from the poor box and the pair were to reappear a week later. Named Rose and Minnie Avery when the *Standard* (2 December) reported a donation of five shillings for their support, *The Times* (9 December) named them Rose and Minnie Avon.

Falsehoods were revealed when Mendacity Society officials reported days later. The elder girl was living with a black man at 1 Crown Court, Wentworth Street and the younger with her mother 'an Irish woman' and visiting her father in St Luke's workhouse in Chelsea on the other side of London. Greenock port authorities said that no ship named *Jane* had called there in the last eighteen months. An elderly black man from the workhouse said the girls were not his although he had two daughters. The woman who claimed to be his wife said neither was her child. The workhouse porter said the younger one visited the old man, which she denied but the assistant porter was emphatic that she had been there often, leaving coins. The wife of the black man said she had a daughter named Besse Richards or as *The Times* had it, Becca Richards (the name on a letter seen by workhouse staff) who was married to a man named Sylvester who lived in the same court but she was not one of the Avery girls. The magistrate thought there was deception. The younger Avery said she had not written that letter as she could not write. Fabrications were mixed with truths: the older girl seeming to have solid knowledge of America for example. The younger girl was an impostor, the older one probably so and the woman lived on their collections. Those who had donated funds to help the pair should tell the court how they wanted the money disbursed if it was not to be placed in the poor box. 'The girls then left the court very much dejected' having been warned against begging.

Selling religious tracts involved Asian beggars, mentioned and pictured by Henry Mayhew in his *London Labour and the London Poor.* He noted this selling of tracts was a 'line peculiar to the Hindoos'. Charles Williams, accused of begging in the public streets on Sunday, 10 January 1858, appeared in Southwark's court two days later where a policeman stated he had seen Williams, with a placard round his neck describing himself as a fugitive slave, in Newington Causeway (in the Elephant and Castle area of south London). He displayed a heavy iron ring which he said had been fixed to his leg. Having seen two or three people give him money the constable arrested Williams, who pretended not to 'understand the English language, but he was perfectly acquainted with it, having been a professional beggar for more than two years'.[22] His wife, who was Irish, told the court that his claim was false for he had been a sailor, and had turned to begging, sometimes bringing home two pounds a day. That was not through the 'dodge' of claiming to be a fugitive slave but by selling tracts and almanacs. He had been imprisoned for two weeks a year or so before. The magistrate said that Williams was a gross impostor and sent him to prison with hard labour for two weeks.

There were other temptations which led to court appearances. In Wolverhampton in 1858 Henry Smith 'a man of colour, from South America' (this often meant the southern U.S.A.) was sentenced to two months with hard labour for stealing sheet metal from his employer, iron brazier John Evans.[23]

Pious fraudsters included the Revd William Mitchell from Toronto who obtained alms by begging but used 'old and fraudulent credentials' and kept no records. In Falmouth in 1861 a free lecture at the Polytechnic Hall on slavery was given by 'Mr. W. Michell, [sic] a coloured gentleman, one of the characters in the pathetic tale of "Uncle Tom's Cabin"'. William Mitchell's *The Under-Ground Railroad* had been published in Manchester in 1860. In February 1861 he was in Chipping Norton and returned in March when he again had a popular meeting. He thanks the local people for the donation of a large box of clothes for blacks in Toronto. Truro in June 1861 had two lectures given by the Revd W.M. Mitchell who was reported as a minister to ex-slaves in Canada. He had been born in a wigwam, being the son of a 'mulatto' and a Native America. He warned against believing those whose visits to the slave states avoided seeing the harshness of the system.[24] There was no mention of his book which has his image, says he was born in North Carolina, quotes letters of support and reviews of his talks from the *St Albans Times* of March 1860 and the *Bolton Guardian* of 12 April 1860. Mitchell said that he was gathering funds to build a chapel and a school house in Canada. In January 1863 the *Taunton Courier* noted his earlier presence and that he had been highly recommended by the secretary of the Hampshire Congregational Union, but was a fraud.[25] A second visit in 1863-1864 led the *Anti-Slavery Reporter* to describe him as an impostor.

When based in Ohio, Mitchell is said to have provided accommodation for over 1,200 fugitives in twelve years, ending in 1855 when the American Baptist Free Mission Society employed him to assist fugitives in Toronto.

Some Britons were alert to false claims, and as the *Newry Herald and Down, Armagh and Louth Journal* was to remark in 1862 'coloured men have not behaved themselves better than they ought to have done in this quarter, and there is a suspicion [which] hangs over them and their antecedents'.[26]

Isaac Newton's statement that he had escaped from Virginia to Canada when in Nottinghamshire in 1862 was questioned: 'The auditors of this "escaped slave" had better have asked for his credentials' so someone was suspicious.[27] He should not be confused with the Revd J. Newton who was active in Nottinghamshire church circles in May 1873.[28]

Henry Allen alias Jacobs 'a swindler for many years' appeared for the third time before the Thames police court in March 1870. Charged with obtaining money, food and lodgings through false pretences, he was a 'most audacious and heartless person'. The Middlesex sessions in April heard that over 100 people in London had been swindled by him, and there were victims elsewhere. *Reynold's Newspaper* reported him as Henry Allen alias Jacobs alias Hunter 'with a great number of other fictitious names', said 200 people had attended the Thames police court to bring charges against him and there were 100 others this 'mulatto' had defrauded, in 'all parts of London' and Brighton, Hull, Portsmouth, Plymouth, and Liverpool. Most were poor people. He was sent to prison for five years. Allen, a sailor aged 25 had several routines including saying that he had just arrived in England and had numerous gifts, sometimes pretending luggage was entrusted to his care. Both methods led him to be well-treated, fed and loaned money. He had also stolen a coat. There had been 200 charges against the Virginian.[29] If he was a Virginian, that is.

There were black immigrants in the U.S.A. One was Gustavus Adolphus Nero Rodman Fraser who was mentioned in the British press in 1885-1886. He was a multi-named impersonator who found people in Glasgow to be receptive to his tales.

His claims were summarized by *The Times* towards the end of 1886. Fraser was aged 29. When he addressed a Manchester court 'at length' he said that he had been born in West Africa and sold with his mother to Spaniards, and spent ten years in slavery in Cuba. He escaped to South America (probably meaning the Southern U.S.A.) where he met an English missionary, worked his way to Canada, took over a school for black children in 1876 and was then a Baptist minister in Canada. In 1880 he joined the black-run African Methodist Church and 'went to his own country as a missionary'. It was suggested that he sought funding in England and so he had travelled to Britain.

At the beginning of 1886 newspapers reported on his trial in Glasgow where he was charged with fraudulently obtaining money 'from prominent citizens, and from congregations to which he preached in Glasgow' receiving some £400.[30] Named as David Nero, described as over 6ft high (2 metres: very tall for the era), he claimed to be the principal of Sumner College, Kansas and preached in 'nearly every Glasgow Free and United Presbyterian Church'. His luggage contained numerous love letters from ladies in Glasgow, Liverpool and elsewhere. The 'negro preacher in custody at Glasgow' had first been noticed in Glasgow in June 1885. Sumner College aimed to train black men to evangelize Africa. He had impressed Protestant leaders and congregations in Glasgow and in Edinburgh.

He was thought to be leading an immoral life in Scotland as he had a wife and family in Kansas. The woman called Mrs Nero lived with him in hotels but was never seen by his 'evangelistic friends'. This came to light when a dress delivered to their hotel was not paid for, and the hitherto invisible Mrs Nero became known to the churchmen. Documents indicated that he had obtained money in Ireland, England and France and his wife in America had issued receipts. His luggage contained photographs of and letters from 'daughters of local merchants and others'. The *North British Daily Mail* said that he was a 'lion among the ladies', a modern Othello who came, saw and conquered among ladies who attended special religious meetings. Three letters indicated the writers would marry Nero as soon as he had enough money to go to Africa. The families of the women whose letters had been found in Nero's possessions were 'living in terror lest the astounding folly of their daughters may be divulged'.

Having stayed in a central Glasgow hotel paying the discounted rate for missionaries, he went to less expensive accommodation in a private hotel in Bath Street where for three weeks he lived with a woman from Liverpool claiming her to be his wife. One hundred pounds (more than a working man received in a year) was found on him when the Glasgow police arrested him, and there were indications £103 had been sent to America. Those letters had been sealed up by the police. The Glasgow police had yet to hear from America although Mrs Nero had cabled her husband from Kansas. Besides, the police were busy with the 'numerous clergymen' who were closeted with them, discussing his preaching and the collections.[31]

The 'negro preacher' was mentioned in several newspapers. The *Dundee Courier* said more information was coming to light and Nero had been active in his 'pious frauds' in England too: Carlisle, Liverpool, Manchester and Eastbourne. As he waited in prison the wife of brewer and merchant W.A. Arrol initiated an action in Glasgow's Small Debt Court seeking a refund of ten pounds she had given him on 1 January, as his claims were fraudulent. The charges of falsehood, fraud and wilful impositions allowed bail to be granted and £300 was said to be the amount of the bail-bond which was raised. The news reached America where the *New York Times* published a report received by telegram from St Louis, Missouri on 3 February. Nero was known in that city on the banks of the Mississippi, as a teacher in the public schools. He was a native of Demerara, British Guiana (Guyana, South America) and had been dismissed due to bad behaviour. In St Louis he had married a woman from Chicago, having previously married in Ohio. He had gone to Britain in 1885 to lecture on 'the American Negro' and was widely welcomed, staying with the respected Baptist minister Charles Spurgeon in London. He returned to America with an English woman who, on discovering letters from other women he had promised to marry, told the school board and he was dismissed.[32]

Nero heard the two charges made against him in Glasgow on 20 February 1886. Over £55 obtained through falsehood, fraud and wilful impositions, and a further £52 through a fabricated letter. He was sent to nearby Kilmarnock to hear a charge relating to £20. The bail-bond for the first two charges was £150. His name was recorded as David Victor Adolphus Nero. He was released on bail. In Kilmarnock there were crowds anxious to see the tall 'black preacher'. Bail was granted and paid, and Nero planned to speak at a Kilmarnock hall but on returning to Glasgow he was arrested and charged with fraud in Dumfries between 30 June and 7 July 1885 when he had obtained £15 and spoke at the parish church. He was taken by train to Dumfries.[33] Interviewed he claimed to be a Foulah from the (vast) lands between Sierra Leone and Old Calabar (eastern Nigeria). No mention of slavery in Cuba – he said he had been in Martinique in the West Indies for ten years before going to Canada where he obtained a degree from the University of Toronto. He worked in a church in Windsor, Ontario and then went to 'Kansas, Missouri' (possibly the journalist's error for Kansas City, Missouri) as a head teacher until he moved to Summer (*sic*) College. His first visit to Europe was in June 1885, preaching just once in that church, returning to America. Having resigned in November he had returned to Glasgow to collect for a training institution for blacks. His elocution was excellent; he spoke and wrote French and German, and planned to hold a public meeting in central Glasgow. He did, making fun of his reputation as 'a swindler and a liar amongst the fair sex'.[34]

Gossip, interviews with journalists and allegations do not make for evidence however. The *Glasgow Herald*'s editor wrote that calls of foreign missions always had tremendous appeal in the city, and spiritual uplift for the denizens of its slums appealed less than requests to supply 'the natives of Africa with flannel waistcoats and nasal pocket-handkerchiefs' so Nero had shown much wisdom or had been lucky to work the city. His toying with the city's 'fair-sisters' led to them untying the purse strings of brothers and parents. One thousand pounds had been garnered in the city by Nero. The prosecutions had been abandoned and money found in his possession had been returned for who could prove that Nero had not collected for educational purposes in Africa? The editor warned 'a mouth full of texts does not necessarily imply a heart full of grace' advising 'stricken doves' to find consolation with admirers of 'a paler hue'.[35]

Nero surfaced next in Rochdale, Lancashire. Sixteen kilometres from central Manchester, it produced miles of textiles in numerous mills. On 15 November 1886 Nero (now the Revd Gustavus A.N.R. Fraser) was remanded on a charge of obtaining money by false pretences. His reputation was so widespread that when a pedlar named Hassan was charged with a breach of the peace in Banff on the coast of north-eastern Scotland the judge asked if he was Nero, he 'indignantly repudiated the insinuation'. In Rochdale a number of witnesses from Scotland appeared at the court. The *Rochdale Times* carried details. In late October 1886 Fraser/Nero had called on a local minister seeking the loan of a room where he could give a religious lecture. He would request donations to enable him to study at Nottingham Institute, aiming to translate the gospels into Mandingo, his native tongue. The minister agreed, the lecture took place and the 'Rev. Gustavus Adolphus' then contacted local persons of status.

A wine merchant and a clerk of the town's council both gave him five shillings. Ladies 'overeager to advance a good cause' opened their purses for him. He contacted a second clergyman and obtained permission to use his hall in the High Street. Well-attended, donations flowed. But the first minister discovered that Christian scriptures had been translated into Mandingo and there were five colleges in America where black men could train for the ministry (Nero had said it was impossible for a black man to qualify as a Christian minister in America). The two Rochdale ministers approached the police. A telegram was sent to Glasgow and the Scottish police supplied a photograph and details of Nero's career there. One of the ministers invited Nero to call: he left town immediately.[36]

Scottish interest in events in Rochdale led to more reports with the trial of 8 November detailed in the *Glasgow Herald* the next day. The charge was obtaining five shillings from one of those ministers on false pretences. The court heard that he had been active in other Lancashire towns including Bolton, Oldham, Preston, Wigan and Bury. Followed to Liverpool and arrested in Chester, Nero was said to have sought funds in order to learn Greek to do those translations into Mandingo. A book in his possession indicated over £89 had been collected between 24 September and 28 October. Claims to be from the Mandingo country and recently arrived in Britain were countered by his time in Scotland and his visit to America, which ended when he returned to Britain in September. There was also the matter of his use of different names. One duped minister testified that Nero told him he had just arrived from Africa. Having found out where the Mandingo country was, the minister discovered Nero had no idea of its location. During his lecture Nero stated that he had been there recently. Bail was opposed and he was sent on remand to Strangeways prison, Manchester to await further developments. During his short spell in Chester he had worn clerical garb, obtaining two donations by saying he had been a slave in Cuba.

During his visit to Oldham he met a fellow who had known him in Kansas City when he was a school teacher. This witness had left America two years earlier when Nero was still there. He informed the minister where Nero was to give a lecture in Oldham: Nero failed to turn up. A woman who kept a lodging house in Liverpool told the court that Nero had stayed there with a woman eighteen months earlier and left without the woman. When he returned 'eight months ago' she refused to accommodate him as his female partner was different. Letters had come from Kansas for the prisoner. Nero told one Manchester man that he was a member of the benevolent society the Foresters, belonging to a lodge in Guinea (French West Africa). He sought assistance, needing to get to Glasgow where he wanted to sue his brother who was a doctor there. Lodge members threatened to tell the police that he was an impostor. The case was again delayed.

When the trial was resumed the court heard allegations that Nero had cheated two ministers in Rochdale. The defence argued against statements relating to both Kansas and Glasgow but the superintendent of the Glasgow police testified that Nero had been bailed but flaws in the summons prevented the police seeking him when bail expired. The Oldham man who had worked in the post office in Kansas City told the court that he had met Nero in Oldham, and that his reputation in Kansas City was far from good. The case drifted on into December, the travels and impersonations of Nero meant the police had to make widespread enquiries. On 8 December 1886 he was sentenced at the Salford court to six months with hard labour. A Nottingham newspaper noted that he had been intending to study in that city. A Dublin newspaper said the crime was Nero's presenting a false letter of recommendation, which was how *The Times* reported the trial's conclusion.[37]

The problem faced by the Scottish police was how to prove a missionary was not going on missionary work. This had been avoided in Lancashire despite other problems. There was evidence that Nero had started receiving lessons, which meant that collections for an education were – on the face of it – genuine. The old acquaintance met in Oldham, who addressed the bogus minister by his earlier name, had alerted the clergyman who announced that the preacher would be speaking. Had he waited until that meeting was over, and that witness had heard information that clashed with his own knowledge, a different charge might have been made: but Nero did not appear. Those two donations of five shillings (one quarter of £1) were hardly worthy of a lengthy court hearing, and a sentence would have been days, not months. Nero said that he had written the testimonial, and thus gave the court the opportunity to consider fraud or forgery, hence the lengthy prison sentence.

The numerous swindles in Scotland were due to the credulous not realising that 'a mouth full of texts does not necessarily imply a heart full of grace' as the *Glasgow Herald*'s editor had warned. Duping lawyers, churchmen and the families of stalwart citizens had been successful. The Rochdale clergymen who discovered there was no need for a Mandingo translation and that training colleges for black clergymen did exist in the U.S.A., revealed skills Nero had not anticipated. Nero had obtained much more money than many Britons earned in a year. The willingness to support his plans to improve the lot of fellow blacks reflects well on the many men and women he deceived. When reporting the death of the Cockermouth woman who believed she was his wife, the *Workington Star* said of the former Miss Hunter that she had married a 'black sinner'.[38] Whatever else is said of the man, he left a legacy of distrust towards black preachers in western Scotland and the mill towns of Lancashire.

He was listed in the 1891 census boarding at 27 Hillary Street in Leeds. A 'theological student' aged 32, he was with his new wife, Lincolnshire-born Jennie, aged 22.

When the African American Peter Thomas Stanford was attempting to establish himself in Baptist circles in England, he 'met with an amount of ill feeling and mistrust which seemed incredible, but which, I believe, was in a great measure due to the past misconduct of a number of coloured men, and the bad impression they had left behind them'. Spurgeon told Stanford 'I have decided not to have anything to do with you.' Impostors had created this ill-will. Nero's name was mentioned in an Irish court case in 1893 when a woman claimed that her late husband's will was made when he was suffering from delusions (he was not deluded enough to fail to understand the nature of Nero, though).[39]

Chapter 6

Canada

Canada or British North America had a substantial black presence in its Atlantic provinces from the eighteenth century. The area to be known as Ontario was called Upper Canada then Canada West, and was the usual destination for the thousands who fled American slavery. Between 15,000 and 30,000 perhaps. Those black settlers were poor and seldom literate, and appealed for assistance in Britain as we have seen with Nathaniel Paul who from 1832 spent four years in Britain raising money for the ex-slave settlement in Wilberforce, Ontario. He died in 1839.

Funding black activities in Canada not only gave succour to the fugitives but allowed comparisons between British Canada and 'free' America to be made. British sympathizers financed the training of several individuals who went to work in Canada, teacher Francis Anderson was sent in 1855, and John Williams and his family have also been noted. Others who went to Canada included Moses Roper who raised his daughters there. Josiah Henson born into slavery in Maryland in 1789 with his wife and five children walked to Canada in 1830. His autobiography *The Life of Josiah Henson, formerly a Slave, Now an Inhabitant of Canada*, appeared in 1849. By 1851 it had gone into a third edition in Britain.[1] The *Liverpool Mercury* reporting the arrival of the Crafts on 13 December 1850 listed the passengers from Boston and Halifax on the *Cambria*. From Boston there were twenty-four including 'J. Henson'. The ship had reached Liverpool on 11 December 1850 'after a very tempestuous passage'. Henson brought some black walnut boards, produced by his ex-slave community in Dawn, Ontario to be exhibited at the Great Exhibition. Henson was announced in the *Daily News* of 14 May 1851 as due to attend a London gathering of the British and Foreign Anti-Slavery Society with Garnet. At this time he was a Christian minister of Canada, an escaped slave, and an author, like several individuals we have noted. Henson and 'T. Garnett' both described as 'Ministers of colour, from the United States' attended the 17 July 1851 public meeting of the Camden Town Ragged and Industrial School in London, the school being £66 in debt.[2]

The *Bristol Mercury* on 6 February 1858 reported that the Revd T.A. Pinckney, who was destined to work among the freed slaves in Canada, had preached at Clifton's parish church on 29 January. The *Nottinghamshire Guardian* of 14 January referred to him as 'a coloured clergyman from Africa' who worked for the Colonial Church and School Society and had worked in Africa for four years. South Carolina-born Thomas Pinckney had been ordained in 1853 and worked in Liberia with Crummell until mid-1857.[3] The Colonial Church and School Society's annual meeting in Birmingham's town hall on 13 April led the *Birmingham Daily Post* (14 April) to refer to Pinckney as 'a clergyman of colour'. At a London gathering some days later presided over by Lord Shaftesbury, when Pinckney was 'about to go out to Canada' the Earl described him as 'the representative of the much-wronged coloured race' according to the *Essex Standard*. Despite the Carolina – Canada – Liberia associations often claimed by cheats, Pinckney's bona fides were not publicly challenged.

In Chatham, Ontario he ran a school for black refugees. Married to Elizabeth King, an English Canadian in 1860, the couple soon left and settled in Southampton, England.[4] They made a home at 14 Avenue Road. The 1871 census indicates he was not employed as a minister and they had a 12-year-old general servant. This census says he was born in Pennsylvania and was a naturalized British subject. The 1881 census states that he had been born in Charleston. Both indicate that his wife had been born in Ashford, Kent. He died aged 70 in December 1887 and his widow in March 1889, aged 72.

Andrew Jackson was described as a fugitive slave when he spoke at Preston's Temperance Hall in 1856, hoping to collect funds to purchase the freedom of members of his family.[5] His 'spirited, eloquent, and very humorous discourse' was to be followed by one on slavery the next night. In June 1857 Jackson gave a speech in Glasgow: 'his command of the English language is far from perfect'.[6] In January 1860 the audience at his talk in Sheffield was 'moderate'.[7] The hall in Glasgow where he spoke on 26 March 1860 was more than half-filled. He explained the US legal aspects of slavery and declared he was for reform not revolution.[8] He got to know one Briton with considerable influence in both America and Britain, the Baptist preacher Charles Spurgeon of London. Spurgeon confirmed on 12 April 1860 that John Andrew Jackson was a member of his church, and that endorsement along with several from Scottish figures in 1857 appeared in Jackson's *The Experience of a Slave in South Carolina* published in 1862.

This account tells of escaping to Canada and his marriage there to a woman from North Carolina. She was Julia A. Watson, and the marriage was in St John, New Brunswick on 20 November 1852. She was with him in Britain. They were listed in the 1861 census lodging at 15 Baker Street, London. She worked as a lady's maid at that time. The Jacksons returned to America in the late 1860s after a disagreement between Jackson and Spurgeon, which left the American outside the network which had long supported him.[9]

The Revd W. Troy who spoke at the King Street Baptist chapel in Bristol in September 1860 was said to come from Windsor, Ontario.[10] William Troy was the 'coloured gentleman' who headed an escaped slave community in Canada who appealed for funds in Gloucestershire in the summer of 1861. Earlier that year he was in Hull where the census states he was 32, born in Virginia, a British citizen and a 'minister of the Gospel'.[11] His *Hair-breadth Escapes from Slavery to Freedom* was published in Manchester in 1861. The 116-page booklet details several stories. Troy seems to have been based in Manchester.

There were concerns over legal aspects of the case of John Anderson. In 1853 on his way to freedom in Canada he stabbed a slave catcher in Missouri. He then lived quietly in Canada; Americans sought his return. The status of Canadian legal practices and those of Britain interested lawyers, for the case also exposed Britain's ability to over-ride Canadian law.[12] Abolitionists and those who were anti-American welcomed the fact that the Webster-Ashburton Treaty of 1842 which set rules to apply to Canadian and American relations would permit extradition when an individual seemed to have committed murder – but not for manslaughter – and Anderson had been defending himself. *The Times* commented that there had been no offence 'cognizable by the law of England'.[13] Anderson left Canada and reached England, sponsored by abolitionists. His reputation reached Britain earlier, with a summary and a portrait in the *Illustrated London News* of 9 March 1861, for example.

On 19 June 1861 William Craft appeared at an 'enthusiastic meeting' at the Portman Hall in London in aid of Anderson, with the Revd Thomas M. Kinnaird, a minister in Hamilton (Ontario) following twenty-one years in American slavery.[14] There then was a crowded meeting (6,000 people attended) at Exeter Hall, London at the beginning of July 1861, chaired by industrialist Harper Twelvetrees. One speaker expressed pleasure that the United States was now split over slavery. Twelvetrees presented Anderson with a small bottle of earth ('England's free soil') to certify his freedom. Also present was Kinnaird. A collection was taken for Anderson who was 'surrounded by several other men of colour who had effected their escape from slavery'. The hall was full one hour before the meeting commenced – it was 'a vigorous expression of English sympathy, not only for Anderson, but also for the race to which he belongs'.[15] Anderson was soon to be 'the renowned fugitive slave'.[16] He toured, and lectured in London and the south-east.[17] At Luton town hall he was well received and a collection was made in September 1861.[18] Missing from that account was his preaching in both the Calvinistic and Baptist chapels in Holyhead, the ferry port in North Wales (strongly suggesting Anderson went to Dublin).[19] Anderson was active in temperance (anti-alcohol) circles, addressing the Band of Hope Union in London's Bloomsbury in October 1861, saying shoeless Britons were the result of boozing. He spoke in east London's Stratford at the Temperance Hall on 4 December 1861.[20] Anderson went to Northamptonshire where in the village of Corby he began the schooling denied during his years in slavery.[21]

Had Anderson been sent back from Canada, if not immediately lynched, he would have been tried in a Southern slave state.[22] In 1863 the committee's chairman Harper Twelvetrees wrote *The Story of the Life of John Anderson, the Fugitive Slave* which William Tweedie of London published. Twelvetrees, a London soap maker, was an abolitionist and the story is more about slavery than Anderson's life. Nothing has been found on Anderson's time at Corby's village school where as an ex-slave and 'murderer' (he admitted the stabbing) he would have been memorable to the children who shared the classroom. He was accommodated with the head teacher John Pool from October 1861, was known (according to Twelvetrees) to church and chapel leaders in the area, and his farewell soiree in London, 22 December 1862 included them, William Allen and George Thompson. Anderson went to Liberia: 'John Anderson, the fugitive slave. This man of colour, whose case excited so much interest in England and America a year or two ago, is about to settle in Liberia.'[23] Anderson then vanishes from history.

Others reached the British Isles including William Howard Day, free-born in New York in 1825, a graduate who founded a newspaper and mixed with what might be called America's black establishment. He went to live in Dresden, Canada in the mid-1850s. In 1859 Day went to Ireland, aiming to collect funds for his schools. With the Scottish-Canadian Revd William King he reached Scotland in November 1859. Day was still in Britain in 1861 (the census places him boarding in Manchester) promoting settlement in Africa, speaking alongside Garnet. There were insufficient funds for an independent life and he took temporary work, including teaching in Lincoln. Chamerovzow expressed the view that Day was misappropriating funds, the so-easy accusation which was seen time and again. In late 1863, his natal land afire with war, Day left England for New York.

The Revd William Henry Jones was based in Chatham, Ontario, and came to Britain to gather funds for that community. He was a leading member of the Coloured Methodist Episcopal Church, and his credentials were accepted by the British and Foreign Freed-Men's Aid Society whose June 1866 edition of *Freed-Man* carried details. Born of free parents in Pennsylvania around 1826 he was said to represent 100,000 black Canadians, an impossibly large figure, of course. Jones seems to have made a base in Mansfield, Nottinghamshire where he was joined by his niece (nameless, 'a young lady of colour') by Easter 1860 when both appeared at the town's General Baptist church. He was billed as a 'coloured missionary from America' by another poster, announcing his appearance at the United Methodist Free Church in Mansfield, and he also appeared at the town hall.[24]

He had been described as a 'coloured minister from Canada' when speaking in Dorchester in May 1866 where he was successful in that town's Wesleyan chapels before moving on to Wimborne.[25] He was in Poole on 28 May and at a meeting in London's Old Kent Road on 21 June. He then went to Tunbridge Wells where he appeared with Ellen Craft.

Jones avoided pitfalls which entrapped other touring speakers. He kept the *Freed-Man* informed of his work. He not only had those Canadian references but was accepted by the experienced Ellen Craft who must have cringed at public reports of black impostors. The monthly noted he had been in Kent and Sussex, and in the December 1866 issue which reported he was back in London, it was said that the mayor of Winchelsea, near the coast in Sussex, had chaired his meeting in that town. He said he was interested in recruiting blacks in Canada to teach in Jamaica, the recent insurrection in Jamaica now occupied many pages of the *Freed-Man*. The standard question – what was being done with donations – was dealt with by Jones stating that £20 was to be sent to Canada. Someone was concerned and the society was to define its informal relationship with Jones in the issue of November 1867. It noted 'there are peculiar difficulties arising from the long continued visit and operations of a negro agent in this country arising from the different habits of the people and the unintentional occasion of offence or annoyance that may be given'. In December 1867 he reported that he had been in Guernsey and Jersey in the Channel Islands, and listed all the donations he had received.[26] Jones returned to Canada and died there in 1874.

The once-enslaved John (*sic*) Hawkins, born in Maryland in 1811 told a journalist in Leeds in 1891 that he had escaped to Canada, and was now a Methodist Bishop in Canada where the black population numbered 23,000. He said that in Chatham, Ontario, black and white children went to different schools, and detailed some of the achievers including a doctor. He added that black Canadians feared they would become part of the U.S.A.[27] Bishop Hawkins's forename was Walter, as we will see.

The black settlers in Canada whose representatives pleaded their case in Britain may have created two quite different images: that black people needed white support, and that when away from the United States's slave society they were able to create communities from almost nothing. There were contradictions in this, as in the publicity given to New World black settlers in Liberia.

Liberia was settled by American blacks from 1822 and its independence was recognized by Britain in 1847. America's came in 1862. Black-led churches and migration supporters such as Crummell kept a strong African American influence there, also seen in the republic's flag and constitution. There had also been an attempt to find an African future for black Americans around Abeokuta in what was to be named Nigeria. Two men investigated, Robert Campbell (born in Jamaica in 1829) and Martin Delany from Virginia, now based in Canada. Delany had worked with Douglass for some years and Campbell had migrated to America in the 1850s. Campbell was in England in 1859 where he made contact with the Church Missionary Society and cotton manufacturers. The former disliked the concept, for Abeokuta was a Christian settlement founded by African recaptives from Sierra Leone. Campbell and Delany met up in Africa. Blacks in Canada rejected migration and in 1862 Britain annexed Lagos, the beginning of official British colonialism in that region which, as the British believed, it was 'unwise to attempt to procure for the American emigrants territorial rights or privileges' thwarted the project.

In May 1860 both men were back in Britain. The concept of British capital joining with African labour and African Americans with skills with cotton appealed. Garnet was supportive and he and Campbell shared a public platform in Birmingham in October 1861. African American settlement in Africa lost a major raison d'être when US slavery was abolished in 1863. Campbell was active in Lagos until his death in 1884. Delany died in Ohio the following year. Their activities in Britain had drawn British business and government attention to the Niger River region and cotton-growing. Campbell's *A Pilgrimage to My Motherland* was published in both London and New York in 1861. Delany's *Official Report of the Niger Valley Exploring Party* was also published in 1861, in both Leeds and New York.

Canada-born blacks in Britain were often regarded as Americans. George Dixon was regarded as an American because he was based in Boston, Massachusetts. He was born in Halifax, Nova Scotia in 1870. He fought in London in 1890: often billed as 'Little Chocolate', Dixon is regarded as the first black to win a world boxing championship. He wrote or allowed his name to appear as the author of *A Treatise on Boxing* of 1893. He died in New York in 1909.

The 'tall black man' on the *Shannon* which arrived in Portsmouth in January 1859 was described in the *West Sussex Gazette* as having been voted 'the bravest man we ever did see' by the officers and men of that ship. He had brought his gun into a commanding position during fighting at Lucknow, in November 1857 and had killed several Indians with his cutlass.[28] The brave man was William Edward (or Nelson) Hall born of American ex-slaves in Nova Scotia, Canada in 1821 or 1827. He left the merchant navy and joined the Royal Navy in Liverpool in 1852, served in the Crimean War at Sebastopol and had been a volunteer in the Naval Brigade sent inland from Calcutta in August 1857 to quell the uprising. The 410 seamen and marines took four field pieces and six 8-inch guns and helped relieve the siege at Lucknow (and in March 1858, captured the town). The Brigade won five Victoria Crosses in the campaigns of 1857-1858, and Hall's was for his bravery on 16 November 1857. Hall and a badly-wounded lieutenant were the only surviving crew members. Their gun made the breach in the town's walls which enabled the Highlanders to enter. The medal was presented to him in Ireland in 1859. Hall retired in 1876, returned to Canada, lived with his sisters and died in 1904. The memorial to the men of the *Shannon* at Southsea erected in 1860 noted that ten had been killed in action in India, ten died of wounds, eighty-three from disease and forty-four were wounded.[29]

There were black Canadians in both the Royal Navy and the merchant navy. In December 1871 ten sailors were charged at Ryde on the Isle of Wight with mutiny after the *Iron Duke* went aground soon after leaving London for Australia. The names included three black sailors: Daniel Watson 'of Carolina', John Henry 'of Jamaica' and Hilton Davies of St John's, Newfoundland.* All were acquitted.[30]

---

* Newfoundland became a Canadian province in 1949.

A man seen on many British streets and who experienced imprisonment in three continents was John Sayers Orr, an itinerant anti-Catholic preacher. Known as the Angel Gabriel he was in Britain, Canada and America before returning to his birthplace British Guiana in late 1855. In Liverpool at the end of July 1855 he was described as 'an undersized, strange-looking man' with a sun-burnt face and black eyes, preaching in the Exchange area.[31] His preaching led to riots in British Guiana in February 1856 and to his arrest. *The Times* suggested that he would be known to its readers.[32] The *Daily News* noted Orr had earlier caused riots in Greenock and Glasgow as well as New York and Montreal, and the *Morning Chronicle* recalled his 'ranting' in Scotland.[33] A demagogue who summoned crowds by blowing a trumpet (hence the nickname), Orr had been a member of the American Party or Know Nothings, an anti-migrant group that flourished in the 1850s, his actions in Massachusetts had led to riots in 1854, and he was imprisoned in Washington DC. The anti-black, anti-immigrant political party had this half-Scottish and half-African as a leading member. The *Glasgow Herald* noted Orr's departure for Guiana on the *Adam Carr* in its issue of 19 November, recalled he had been 'the constant cause of rioting and the breeder of ill will and religious hatred wherever he showed his face in the West of Scotland' so must have been content when it reported he had been sentenced to three years with hard labour in Guiana.[34] Edinburgh's *Caledonian Mercury* noted in 1857 that he had died in prison.[35] Orr's mother was 'a respectable coloured woman'.[36]

As we will see, Orr's status was very different to another Canadian of American parentage, the Revd John H. Hector.

Chapter 7

Jubilee Singers

Choral groups – known as jubilee singers – were to be seen throughout the British Isles from the 1870s. Following abolition, some in the U.S.A. became alert to the educational poverty of the 'freedmen' and charitable individuals and organizations established schools and colleges for African Americans. Some institutions prospered, others barely survived. The pupils lacked money so fees were uncertain, and the legacy of slavery meant few blacks were qualified to teach. Indeed, illiteracy was almost universal among the ex-slaves. The economy of the defeated Confederacy was close to bankruptcy, railways and bridges had been destroyed, harbours were blocked, towns and plantations had been burned, white leaders killed, and farms lacked equipment and workers. Banks, credit and trust were rare.

Finances for black endeavours came from sympathizers and black-led churches. Initially teachers were often Northern women, who went to the Southern states to assist and sometimes stayed there for the rest of their lives. Black teachers had to be trained, and access to white institutions was impossible in the old slave states. Buildings, libraries, pupil accommodation, and salaries for teachers had to be financed. Appealing for financial support in Britain brought Americans across the Atlantic. Decaying barracks in Nashville, Tennessee became Fisk University: it lacked books and equipment. So the pupils went out seeking funds by forming a choir which presented black songs. Historian Eileen Southern wrote thus 'A large part of the Western world was introduced to the folksongs of black America.'

Following the successful tours of the Fisk Jubilee Singers in the 1870s, black choirs found aspects of their performances were taken up by others: just as *Cabin* shows could involve drama, singing, performing animals, and music hall acts. Jubilee choirs usually numbered ten to twelve males and females. Smartly dressed and with sober if not sombre manners they generally performed before audiences unlikely to attend *Cabin*-based shows.

The initial plan was to collect funds for Fisk University in Nashville by performances in Christian surroundings. British audiences had to be made aware of the wholesome character of the entertainment – as a letter in the *Belfast News-Letter* of 2 September 1873 tried to clarify. It quoted from the *Sword and the Trowel*, the monthly publication of Spurgeon's Baptist organization in London, following the choir's performance at his Tabernacle. Their noble object, sincere Christian faith and the wonder of their singing were all recommended by Spurgeon, and it was noted that they collected £20 by that one appearance. On 9 September the choir made an appearance at Belfast's Ulster Hall, and it was a sell out. The newspaper named Jennie Jackson, Minnie Tate, Mabel Lewis and fifteen of the songs.[1]

That first Fisk choir to reach Britain, in April 1873, numbered eleven. As well as Jackson, Tate and Lewis there were Ella Sheppard, Georgia Gordon, Julia Jackson, Maggie Porter and four men: Isaac Dickerson, Benjamin Holmes, Thomas Rutling and Edmund Watkins. The British were used to African Americans fugitives, but the Fisks – except Watkins who had been lashed when picking cotton – had been house servants not field hands and Jennie Jackson, Tate and Gordon were free-born. They were neatly dressed and spoke politely having observed the manners and style of whites. Manager Gustavus Pike booked accommodation in St Aubin's Road (*sic*) in Upper Norwood where they were 'often stared at and followed by idle boys and girls on the streets'. St Aubyn's Road was a side street close to London's Crystal Palace entertainment centre, a neighbourhood used to entertainers and musicians. Ten minutes away was Hamlet Road where the family of the late Ira Aldridge resided into the 1880s.

George White rehearsed the Fisks and their initial public appearance was on 6 May 1873 before an elitist audience including the Duke and Duchess of Argyll. The duke was married to Louise, daughter of Queen Victoria and it was at their London home that the Fisks sang on 7 May. Queen Victoria visited and that encounter opened almost every door in her kingdom, although the Nonconformist community had already been supportive for that initial Willis's Rooms concert had been sponsored by descendants of the groups so recently aiding fugitive slaves. Lord Shaftesbury spoke at the concert, and pointed out that the songs were not the 'negro melodies' spread by entertainers. The review in the *Daily News* mentioned Pike's book *The Jubilee Singers* which had been published by Nonconformist publisher Matthew Hodder.[2]

In Scotland the Fisks were hosted by John Burns, whose wealth came from the Cunard shipping line: it supplied their passage over after

American-flagged ships refused. Patronage was widespread, with Greenock council not charging them for using the town hall. As we have seen, they went to Ireland, singing in Belfast and Londonderry. Audiences wanted to hear secular sings including 'John Brown's Body'. Their tour of Scotland resumed, the *Dundee Courier* noting that the simple words were very expressive.[3] They were in north-east England's Newcastle in November 1873 and when in Darlington on 17 November the event was chaired by a member of parliament.[4] They started a useful and popular association with white American evangelist Dwight Moody.

Rutling, Dickerson and Maggie Porter considered careers as solo artists in Europe. Holmes asked for income from some concerts to be set aside to pay them and not for Fisk which White rejected as it might backfire on the entire project. Dickerson's friendship with Arthur Stanley the Dean of Westminster Abbey led to suggestions that Dickerson studied at Edinburgh University. Britons offered to be patrons to Porter, Dickerson was greatly admired by English women and Jennie Jackson received at least one proposal of marriage.

The touring, rehearsals and performances brought stress and fatigue. The singers were no longer in top form and the death of White's wife affected them all. Jennie Jackson was unable to sing in Leicester and Mabel Lewis in Bristol, Holmes had a persistent cough (it was tuberculosis, and it was to kill him) and White was coughing up blood. The musical direction became the responsibility of Ella Sheppard. By the time the Fisks left England in May 1874 they had collected £10,000 for Jubilee Hall, £400 for furnishings, £250 towards a library and gifts of books from Gladstone, Spurgeon and others. Lord Shaftesbury, a Negrophile and Fisk supporter, remained staunch and able. The British press also noted the Fisks had remained modest.[5] Dickerson took up Dean Stanley's offer and Wilkins and others decided to remain in Britain for the summer of 1874.[6]

A second Fisk Jubilee Choir was in Britain in May 1875. America W. Robinson replaced Mabel Lewis, and Frederick Loudin, Benjamin Thomas and Hinton Alexander were new. Old hands were the two Jacksons, Sheppard, Gordon, Porter and Rutling. Gabriel Ousley who had been a slave of Jefferson Davis's family had completed their US tour but did not cross the Atlantic, so there were ten singers. They went to their previous lodgings in St Aubyn's Road and again toured and performed widely. Friends warned them that they had returned too soon, but they knew the Nashville building was scarcely started and funds were short. They linked with Moody's revival tour for a month which was excellent publicity, making their reputation as Christian evangelists firm.

It is easy to miss associations outside the world of music, such as the patronage of Britons who had recently aided fugitive slaves or the religious faith of so many of their British supporters. The first tour had inspired others, and there were thirty pupils of the Hackney Juvenile Mission School who, as the East London Jubilee Singers, were to appear in Colchester, Essex on 17 June 1875.[7] Among requests to perform came one from imperialist Sir Bartle Frere who wanted them to sing for the visiting sultan of Zanzibar (they did not). America Robinson was impressed by the enthusiasm which greeted the choir and Loudin the oldest singer noted 'an entire absence of race prejudice'. It was another punishing schedule with twenty-three concerts in just over one month, but there were holiday breaks.

The singers saw poverty when their concerts attracted the poor (as at Spurgeon's Tabernacle – £214 came from more than 6,000 people in the audience). They met Dickerson in Edinburgh and a daughter of the late David Livingstone. In November 1875 in Dublin they made the error of singing 'Rule, Britannia'. They performed for the inmates of the Royal Asylum for the Idiotic in Kendal and continued into 1876 with a punishing and often cold and damp tour. Ella Sheppard was so ill that Maggie Carnes joined the troupe in late January in time to appear in Manchester's Free Hall, where Loudin addressed the large audience. They then had two evening concerts in Liverpool's splendid St George's Hall. They also gave a recital for Sunday school pupils at the Victoria Hall, sharing the platform with the Hall's choir before an audience of over 10,000. Rutling spoke of his slavery experiences and 'Lowden' gave a closing address.[8] Chapels were open to them to give concerts and to charge entry. Poet and literary patron Lord Houghton was the main supporter of their concert at the Wesleyan chapel in Pontefract on 10 March 1876, which was crowded despite high prices.[9] They gave one concert in Oxford's town hall on 28 April 1876, supported by the mayor. This two-hour recital had tickets on the night at one shilling. To reserve seats in advance cost three times that price.[10]

Jubilee Hall at Nashville was being finished. Back in London the Fisks again sang for the Argylls, Shaftesbury and others in high society. America Robinson considered giving up her US citizenship; and they all bickered. Julia Jackson had a stroke, and stayed in England with Georgia Gordon when in June 1876 the Fisks took a holiday in Switzerland. In Geneva the troupe turned in on itself. Maggie Porter threatened to resign, her bluff was called and she was replaced by Ella Hildridge. Loudin's wife Harriet joined

American SLAVERY.

On TUESDAY, OCTOBER 8, 1839,

To commence at Half-past Six o'Clock in the Evening,

Moses Roper,

Who made his escape from Slavery,

WILL DELIVER

AN ADDRESS

IN THE PUBLIC ROOMS,

Jarratt-Street, Hull,

When he will give an account of his Personal experience of Slavery
as it now exists in the

UNITED STATES OF AMERICA,

And will in the course of his Lecture, exhibit several Instruments of Torture—facsimiles of those
which are mentioned in his " Narrative."

After the Address, " A Narrative of the Adventures and Escape of MOSES ROPER, from
American Slavery," the Third Edition, with a Portrait of the Author, engraved on Steel, may be had,
Price Two Shillings and Sixpence ; and also at Mr. J. PURDON'S, Bookseller, Market-Place.

M R. is pursuing his studies at " University College, London," and he is now, during the vacation,
travelling to expose the system of American Slavery ; and, at the same time, by the sale of his Book, to
provide himself with the means of obtaining further education, or continuing his studies Two Years
longer, with the view of making himself useful among the African race. He had no education before
he escaped from Slavery.

J. PURDON, PRINTER, MARKET-PLACE, HULL.

Moses Roper toured Britain in the late 1830s, married a Welsh woman, and they migrated to Canada. Roper revisited Britain, as did his wife and daughters.

William Peter Powell born in 1834 left New York with his parents and siblings in 1850. He studied in Dublin and Manchester and qualified as a doctor in 1858. He worked in two Liverpool hospitals and when the U.S. Civil War broke out, the entire family returned to New York where Dr Powell served in a Washington army hospital. He died in Liverpool in 1916. Courtesy National Archives and Records Administration Washington DC from records of the Department of Veterans Affairs, RG 15. Thanks to Jill L. Newmark of the History of Medicine Division at the National Library of Medicine in Bethesda, Maryland.

Ira Aldridge migrated to England and performed as an actor in London from 1825. By the 1860s he was often touring the continent - he died in Poland in 1867 – with his Swedish wife and young family living in Upper Norwood near London's Crystal Palace. He knew **Ellen Craft** who had escaped to England in 1850, evidenced by this note dated 1866, from the Craft family papers in South Carolina. Courtesy Avery Research Center for African American History and Culture, Charleston SC.

Ellen Craft and her husband William fled slavery in Georgia in 1848. She dressed as a white man and William pretended to be her servant. They lived in semi-freedom in the northern states but slave catchers threatened in 1850 so they sailed to England, settling in 1869 and having six children in Britain. *Illustrated London News*, 19 April 1851, courtesy Bernth Lindfors.

The novel *Uncle Tom's Cabin* of 1852 was a best-seller in Britain and America, and there were theatrical and musical spin-offs. China ornaments were produced, and became mute testimony to American slavery in thousands of British homes.

Elizabeth Taylor Greenfield was raised in Philadelphia. She was blessed with a superb singing voice, which led her to Europe after a New York City concert in 1853. In 1854 she sang for Queen Victoria at Buckingham Palace.

Samuel Ringgold Ward was born in Maryland in 1817 and escaped north, moving to Canada for two years and then to Britain in 1853 where he spoke at public meetings and collected donations for fugitives in Canada. His *Autobiography of a Fugitive Slave* was published in 1855, and it helped finance his migration to Jamaica where he died in 1866.

Jesse Ewing Glasgow from Pennsylvania studied medicine at Edinburgh University where he wrote *The Harpers Ferry Insurrection* in 1859. He died in December 1860, a few weeks before graduation.

John Brown had his *Slave Life in Georgia* published in London in 1855. He had escaped to Canada and reached Britain in 1850. He lived in Britain into 1876. He was a herbalist in south-west England, and based in Dorchester in 1866-1867 when his advertisements in the *Yeovil Flying Post* stated he was a black man.

John Anderson killed a slave catcher when escaping to Canada in 1853. He was imprisoned eight years later, which became a cause celebre in Britain in 1861 where he found refuge, some education in Northamptonshire, and went to Africa in 1862. An English associate wrote a book about Anderson in 1863.

Yours truly
John Anderson

Thomas Bethune/Wiggins known as Blind Tom toured Britain in 1866-1867, aged seventeen. His performances at the piano attracted the curious – he was often presented as a freak.

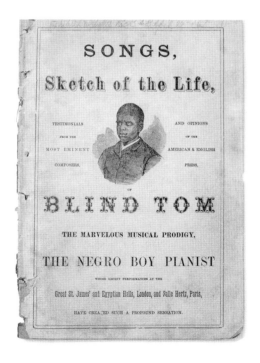

SONGS,

Sketch of the Life,

TESTIMONIALS   AND OPINIONS

FROM THE   OF THE

MOST EMINENT   AMERICAN & ENGLISH

COMPOSERS,   PRESS,

OF

BLIND TOM

THE MARVELOUS MUSICAL PRODIGY,

THE NEGRO BOY PIANIST

WHOSE RECENT PERFORMANCES AT THE

Great St. James' and Egyptian Halls, London, and Salle Hertz, Paris,

HAVE CREATED SUCH A PROFOUND SENSATION.

Horace Weston was born in Connecticut in 1825 and died in New York in May 1890. He was closely associated with banjo makers S. S. Stewart & Co of Philadelphia. This image is from his obituary in *S. S. Stewart's Banjo and Guitar Journal* June 1890, which indicates Weston played in London in 1878 and Germany until 1880. It quoted from the obituary in the New York *Morning Journal* of 26 May 1890 that around 1884 he had appeared before Queen Victoria and had been presented with a gold medal. No evidence of that has been located.

Calvin Harris Richardson and Thomas Lewis Johnson studied in Stockwell, London in the late 1870s. With their wives, sisters Issadorah and Henrietta, they went to Cameroon in 1878 as Baptist missionaries. Henrietta Johnson died there and her husband returned to England in January 1880, very ill. After mission work in the U.S.A., Johnson settled in London then Bournemouth where he died in 1921. His *Twenty-eight Years a Slave* was published in Bournemouth in 1909 – a much smaller edition had been published in London in 1882. The Richardsons remained in Cameroon then retired to the U.S.A. Courtesy Michael Graham-Stewart.

Frederick Loudin (fifth from left, back row) led the Fisk Jubilee Singers touring from May 1875, visiting the continent 1877-1878, and returning to England in 1884. That group sailed for Australia in 1886 and there toured widely, including New Zealand, India and Japan. Assisting Loudin was **Marian 'Mattie' Lawrence** (second left) who returned to London and married Englishman Henry Thrift in October 1890: they lived in Croydon where she died in 1907.

This 1884 group are (standing, left to right): C. W. Payne, Mattie Lawrence, Benjamin Thomas, Georgia Gordon, Loudin, George Barrett, Maggie Wilson, Patti Malone and (seated) Willey Benchley, Minnie Tate and Jennie Jackson.

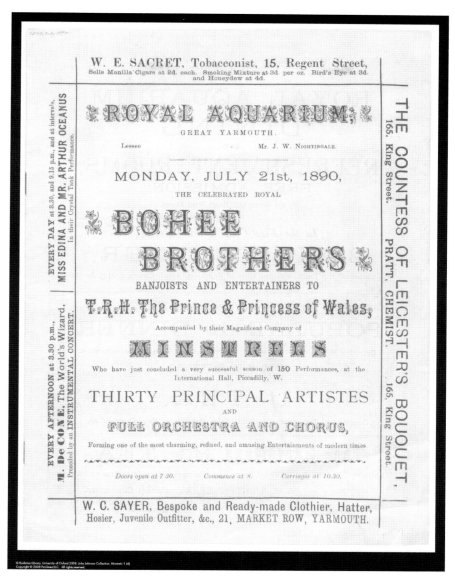

James and **George Bohee** were musicians born in New Brunswick, Canada and based in Boston, Massachusetts. Their skilled banjo playing led them to Britain in 1881. For many years they ran their own show which employed several other black performers. They correctly claimed they had entertained Queen Victoria's heir (the Prince of Wales, later King Edward VII). Courtesy John Johnson Collection, Bodleian Library, Oxford.

Peter Thomas Stanford from Virginia migrated to Canada and in 1883 to England, where he became the minister of the Hope Street Baptist church in Birmingham in 1889. He left for the U.S.A. in 1895 and published *The Tragedy of the Negro in America* in 1898.

Martha Ricks. Born a slave in Tennessee she was sent to Liberia in 1830. In 1892 she sailed from Africa to Liverpool and fulfilled a long ambition to meet Queen Victoria. She presented the monarch with a quilt showing Liberian coffee plants. British newspapers reported her venture with surprise and respect. Copyright National Portrait Gallery, London, ref 38887.

Mrs. RICKS, The Queen's Liberian Visitor.

ELLIOTT & FRY   Copyright   55, BAKER STREET W. AND AT 7, GLOUCESTER TERRACE, S.W.

Amanda Smith was born a slave in Maryland in 1837. Her Christian preaching led her to work in India from 1879. She spent two spells in Britain, speaking on her missionary work and slavery, as well as anti-drinking meetings often associated with Lady Henry Somerset. This picture is from her autobiography, published in London in 1893.

Isaac Perry Dickerson was a member of the original Fisk Jubilee Singers which toured America from 1871 and went to Britain in 1873. He left the choir to study in Edinburgh, travelled to Palestine, and spent the rest of his life as a Christian preacher in Britain, based in London in the 1890s. He was also a temperance lecturer. Courtesy David Conroy.

George Dixon was the world bantamweight boxing champion in 1888 and fought in London in 1890. He was a featherweight champion from 1891. Born in Halifax, Nova Scotia, in 1870 he lived in Boston, Massachusetts.

Paul Dunbar's poems were well received in America and in 1897 he visited England for some months. *The Times* reviewed his cooperation with Afro-British composer Samuel Coleridge-Taylor, noting he possessed an 'undeniable poetical gift'.

Eph Thompson was a skilled elephant trainer who worked in Britain from the 1890s. He was buried in Brookwood Cemetery, Surrey on 17 May 1909. (My thanks to Rainer Lotz).

NO. 1 TROUPE.   WEST END MORECAMBE.   SEASON 1910.

James Cooney (back, left) seen with colleagues in Alex Day's beach entertainers of Morecambe, Lancashire in 1910 is said to have settled in that town around 1902 but he married a local girl in 1898, having worked as a circus performer and with the Bohee brothers, and served in the Argentine navy. He died in Morecambe in 1932.

him, and in September they returned to England via Paris. Julia Jackson was able to hobble but improvement was slow. Rutling became ill and stayed in St Aubyn's Road. Hildridge was frail and unable to tour, so went home. Georgia Gordon became infatuated with Loudin, Porter returned and the group again went to Dublin to sing before thousands, and were invited to form a Freemason lodge (they did).

A Dutchman in London arranged a tour of The Netherlands, and after time in Ireland (Belfast, Ballymena, Coleraine and Londonderry from 5 to 12 December[11]) they set off in January 1877. The success of the Fisks had been noticed in America, and the Wilmington Jubilee Singers of North Carolina followed them to Holland. Like the Fisks, the Wilmingtons had toured the U.S.A., in 1875 when they numbered twelve (five males). The first British appearance by the Wilmingtons in Liverpool in November 1876 had Lord Shaftesbury's support.[12] The Wilmingtons were in Worcester on 23 January 1877, Bridgnorth on 25 and 26 January, and Liskeard (Cornwall) in April.[13] The success of the Fisks encouraged other black choral groups and there was 'no end to jubilee singers' almost an 'epidemic' in New York including the Hampton Colored Students.

The Fisks still had problems. Julia Jackson was taken back to America, Maggie Carnes fell ill, Jennie Jackson remained in Amsterdam, unwell, and the survivors limped back to Arundel in Sussex in May 1877. Attempts were made to lure a Wilmington singer into the Fisks, Georgia Gordon and Mabel Lewis went back in July and the choir had two new members: Lucinda Vance and Minnie Butler who arrived from America in September, joining the stalwarts who had been on holiday in Scarborough, Yorkshire. All were scheduled to tour Germany.

There were still large audiences at public meetings with ex-slave speakers, such as that in Aberdeen on 27 August 1877 when a full hall listened to E.T. Anderson.[14] Loudin spoke of slavery, too.

The public confused the two groups and the *Northern Echo* (Darlington) on 10 August 1877 carried advertisements, placed by both groups, next to each other. The Fisks were to sing in Stockton on 14 September and advised 'friends and the public not to be deceived by other companies calling themselves Jubilee Singers', whilst the Wilmingtons, scheduled to perform in Redcar on 10 August claimed 'no connection with the Fisk party'. The Wilmingtons when in Middlesbrough sang at a service involving William Wells Brown. This was Brown's first visit since 1854, and involved the temperance movement's Order of Good Templars.[15] They were in Guernsey in the Channel Islands in September, a sell-out concert for the ten members.

Charles and Ida Washington were named, and a Mr Davis spoke of his experience of slavery.[16] They were in Williton, between Bridgwater and Minehead, in early May 1878 when both Washingtons were named.[17]

In the Fisks Patti Malone replaced Jackson and Minnie Butler went home as well. The German tour through forty-one towns had them perform in sixty-eight concerts in ninety-eight days as well as events in homes and churches. Although their finances would have gained by returning to Britain for a short tour after Germany, the Fisks sailed direct in July 1878, leaving America Robinson to study singing in Strasbourg (then in Germany) and Rutling to recuperate in Switzerland. Maggie Porter stayed in Germany for some months and Watkins remained in Europe for a time.

Friendships among associates must have impacted on the larger society, what did other residents of Crystal Palace, street urchins apart, think of these other Victorians? Whilst Edinburgh University was not unused to black and Asian undergraduates, Dickerson's presence must have been noticed, and the nurses and doctors who attended the frail singers must have asked questions. Above all, the many thousands who attended their concerts had a new musical experience, as well as seeing people of African descent in positive ways.

The Wilmingtons were in Newport on the Isle of Wight in July 1878. Members had broken away for the *Isle of Man Times* reported a series of concerts by Mr Davis, a bass and 'late leader of the Wilmington Jubilee Singers' and his wife in which he was to describe his twenty-three years as a slave.[18] One problem seems to have been the limited audiences attracted in the Channel Islands that summer, even though the group had reduced to seven members, including both Washingtons.[19] Money was short and Ida Washington led a protest against the management of the Revd H. Parsons of Brighton who had not paid them for two weeks. The unpleasantness at a concert in Littlehampton on the south coast was made public, Parsons paid some of the arrears, and quit.[20] In November 1878 Charles Washington, living at 14 Addington Street near the Thames in London, announced in the *Era* that the Wilmingtons were now in their third year in Europe and were open for engagements. They had twice performed for the royal family. Mr and Mrs Davis were – as the Wilmington Jubilee Singers – appearing in Flint, North Wales in December. In January the 'farewell tour through South Wales' continued.[21]

Alexander Davis and his wife performed (singing and lecturing) on the Isle of Man in the summer of 1879 but were dissatisfied with the financial results. Some suspected their charitable project was 'a blind' and the couple were threatened with being exposed as impostors. It was decided to close up and send the net balance to Fisk University.[22] Wilmington in North Carolina needed funds for black uplift but the troupe had not indicated what institution would receive the donations.

Davis placed an advertisement in the *Era* seeking a white or coloured manager for the singers in October 1879.[23] In Oxford in November he was claiming that the singers were collecting funds to build a mission hall in Wilmington. They were in Ipswich days later when a lecture on slavery was to be given, too.[24] Washington's troupe numbering eight was in Ealing (west London) on 25 and 26 November, Sydenham near the Crystal Palace on 28 November, in Grimsby from 1 to 5 December when they moved to Doncaster to appear at the Guildhall on 5 and 6 December. The *Doncaster, Nottingham and Lincoln Gazette* of 5 December described them as freed slaves. They had no contracts until opening in Glasgow on 1 January 1880 but within a week employment had been found in Lincoln, London, Sunderland and over Christmas in Belfast.

The Belfast newspaper named them: Matilda Giles, Mary White, Amelia Stokes, Miss Washington and Charles Washington, Peter Stokes, William Jones and pianist-soprano Miss Blechoff.[25] As with the Fisks, there had been changes in personnel since that booklet was on sale in Bridgnorth in January 1877 which named nine (three females). Ida Washington had been born in Macon, Georgia in 1856 and had been an enslaved house servant; her husband Charles L. Washington had been born in Virginia in December 1849, and had been educated at Hampton. Peter Lewis Stokes had been born in Petersburg, Virginia in September 1852. The other six originals had departed – Alexander D. Davis born in Wilmington in February 1850 had settled in New York; Miss Rebecca Samuels a 'quadroon' born in late 1848 in Norfolk, Virginia; Samuel H. Hill had been born into slavery near Wilmington in February 1855; Elijah White had also been born (1 August 1851) near Wilmington but had been sold to Arkansas; Miss Fanny Lyman a 'mulatto' had been born in Tallahassee, Florida in October 1855 and sold with her mother to Wilmington. House slave Isaac William Cisco, born in July 1848, had connections to Weldon, in northern North Carolina. We have noted that Isaac William Cisco married Mary Jane Turner in Ormskirk in 1878. They died in Bolton in 1904 and 1905. Three children reached adulthood and lived together in Manchester Road, Bolton according to the 1911 census.

In mid-January the Wilmingtons were in Hinckley and obtained £4 3*s* 2*d* for the new hall; then there were three performances in Melton Mowbray.[26]

Blechoff seems to have left for the singers were in the Lincolnshire horse-racing town of Market Rasen when they advertised in the *Era* of 4 April for a good sight-reading pianist. In November they participated in a Liverpool benefit for Sam Hague, who had fame as the director of a black-face minstrel troupe: which performed at the event.[27] Untraced thereafter, perhaps the remaining Wilmingtons took a ship to America?

The legacy of the Fisks and of the Wilmingtons was the acceptance of the spirituals as a black musical creation, and the awareness that African Americans could both move as equals among high society and perform music to the standards of the European art song traditions. The sum of $150,000 was raised for Fisk University. *The Story of the Jubilee Singers, with their Songs* was published in London in 1876 and often republished, with a new group photograph each time. The 112 songs were played and sung all over Britain, for jubilee singers were part of British entertainment and continued to be so into the 1950s.

Frederick Loudin took another choral group totalling nine to eleven, using the Fisk name and also 'Loudin Jubilee Singers' to Europe and around the world and spent over two years in Australia and New Zealand in the 1880s. He was back in England in 1897. His assistant was Mattie Lawrence, 'a really superb soprano',[28] who left the antipodes in 1889. On 21 October 1890 she married an Englishman in Croydon, near London. When and where she met Henry John Thrift remains unknown, but her husband's family had a solid position in the town's business community as well-established provision merchants. Her father-in-law was an alderman and a justice of the peace. British documents have her forename as Marion and surname as Lawrance and the marriage registration declares her father a 'medical officer U.S.'. Newspaper announcements state her father had lived in Washington DC and was dead.

In 1890 the *Dundee Courier* of 25 February noted that the *Edinburgh Evening Dispatch* had exposed 'a troupe of jubilee singers who were recently touring the north of Scotland'. Another jubilee musician was organist Charles Nicholas or Nicholson Darlington Pickett, who lived in Manchester. Pickett became infatuated with a singer named Macintyre and sent her presents and letters which were returned, but he continued for three years and in October 1891 was charged with threatening to murder her. He pleaded guilty to sending the letter. He was cautioned and £500 was paid which would be forfeited if he did not appear if summonsed in the future. The London court record has her as Mary Ann Margaret Mackintyre and his first name as Levy.[29] Widely reported but seldom stating he was black or a jubilee troupe member, his fate is untraced but there was a mention of insanity.

The Pennsylvania Jubilee Singers who were in Sheffield in March 1891 were a quartet that included aspects of *Uncle Tom's Cabin* during their several days there.[30] In 1890 they had appeared at the Congregational Schoolroom in Wombwell on 27 March and at Doncaster's Subscription Room on 31 March 1890.[31] They were billed as 'descendants of Freed Slaves' when they were to give four recitals at the Town Hall in Middlesbrough 22-24 June 1890 and two at the town's Temperance Hall. They were in the Isle of Man in August, where a collection at the door overcame the ban on commercial entertainments on Sundays.[32] Loudin's colleague, Orpheus McAdoo, took black American music to South Africa (he died in Australia in 1900).[33] One of his colleagues, Laura Carr, advertised for work in the entertainment weekly *Era* on 31 July 1897, declaring she had worked for five years with McAdoo and had just returned to London from South Africa. In 1899 a black jubilee choir appeared in Rishton and Great Harwood, Lancashire.[34]

Pioneer Fisk Isaac Dickerson went to Palestine and then worked as a temperance lecturer and Christian minister in Plumstead, London from the mid-1890s, where he died in 1900.[35] The 1891 census finds him a visitor at 7, Bruce Grove, Tottenham the London home of the octogenarian widow of pioneer meteorologist and Christian, Luke Howard. Another pioneer Fisk was Thomas Rutling. He settled in Britain and worked as a concert singer. He participated in a concert in York in November 1893. His 'very fine mellow' voice was the main attraction although other musicians included a young pianist, a violinist, a soprano and a baritone. He was billed as 'the African tenor'. His songs included items by Gounod and Schumann, and his encore was 'Home, Sweet Home'. He was one of eight performers at a concert in Leeds in January 1896, winning 'the approval of the audience'. He had been living in Leeds since 1895 when he was reported attending a talk at the Quaker meeting house on 'the negro race in America' given by a white Bostonian who pointed out that the people who had once owned Frederick Douglass (who had recently died) felt their lives were of 'utter insignificance' compared to Douglass's 'life of great usefulness'. Rutling 'of this city ("the African tenor")' seconded the vote of thanks.[36] Rutling was listed as a singing tutor, lodging in Manchester, in the 1901 census. Both Rutling and Dickerson have gravestones which declare they had been jubilee singers.

Loudin's choir in Australia included Robert Bradford Williams, born in Georgia in 1862 and a Yale graduate. He married in Tasmania and in 1890 moved to New Zealand where he worked as a lawyer and was a long-serving mayor of the Onslow suburb of Wellington. He died in 1942.[37] McAdoo's troupe included Hamilton Hodges, who settled in Auckland, New Zealand.[38] McAdoo's brother Eugene, who seems to have died in London in 1917, toured small halls in Britain into the 1910s. In his trio was veteran Laura Carr who had worked in South Africa and was in London in 1897.[39] Postcards of that trio are far from rare.

We can doubt that Wilmington's black residents benefited from the Washington-Davis choir, but Fisk University's finances were placed on a firm footing due to their choir. The organization of a lengthy tour by a dozen and more performers was complex and difficult, and the Fisks had the additional problem that theatres were not used by them. Their insistence on a formal, Christian presentation was at odds with the workplaces of other African American singers, notably those in *Uncle Tom's Cabin* shows.

The British and Irish audiences who attended the concerts and recitals had a new musical experience. The manner of the singing, the Christian nature of the songs, the integrity of the performers, all had a positive impact. How could a down-trodden people produce such wonderful music? These singers were polite and refined, distant from the capering and foolishness of minstrels.

Chapter 8

Slavery Narratives

The *Narrative of the Adventures and Escape of Moses Roper from American Slavery* was published in 1837; Moses Grandy's *Narrative of the Life of Moses Grandy: Late a Slave in the United States of America* was published in London in 1842; the *Narrative of the Life of Frederick Douglass, an American Slave* was published in Dublin in 1845 and James Pennington's *The Fugitive Blacksmith* was published in London in 1849. The *Narrative of William W. Brown, an American Slave written by Himself* had a British edition in 1849. Box Brown's *Narrative of the Life of Henry 'Box' Brown: Written by Himself* was published in Manchester in 1851. A second edition was published in Bilston near Wolverhampton in 1852.[1] *The Life of Josiah Henson, Formerly a Slave, Now an Inhabitant of Canada*, was in its third edition in England in 1851. The *Narrative of the Life of James Watkins* was published in Bolton in 1852, William G. Allen's *The American Prejudice against Colour: An Authentic Narrative* in London in 1853 and John Brown's *Slave Life in Georgia* in 1855. Douglass wrote about his twenty-one months in Britain and Ireland in his *My Bondage and My Freedom* (1855). Samuel Ringgold Ward's *Autobiography of a Fugitive Negro: His Anti-Slavery Labours in the United States, Canada, and England* was in print by 1855. William Craft's *Running a Thousand Miles for Freedom: or, the Escape of William and Ellen Craft from Slavery* appeared in 1860.

There were also publications which were less personal but presented the African American experience to the British and Irish. For example Christians of the Evangelical Alliance split over the unwillingness to exclude churches which had slaveholding members. Their summer 1846 international conference in London involved Molliston Madison Clark. Born free in Delaware he was a delegate of the African Methodist Episcopal church. He was in Britain for months, and his *Tract on American Slavery by the Rev. M. M. Clark, a Coloured Man, Now on a Visit to England from the United States of America* was published by Wardman in Bradford in 1847.

Clark noticed that the church had compromised with the slaveholders. His *Tract* and lectures, and his resignation from the Alliance, show that he became firmly in favour of emancipation. He was in Norwich in September 1846 and Brighton in October. He acquired fame in America where he died in 1872. Who purchased his *Tract*? Indeed, who purchased the other tracts? The market was substantial for William Wells Brown's now-illustrated edition of his narrative *Life and Escape* was said to have sold 14,000 copies. Brown had a collection of slave songs published in Newcastle in 1850. His *Three Years in Europe* appeared in 1852. James Pennington edited *A Narrative of Events in the Life of J. H. Banks, an Escaped Slave, From the Cotton State of Alabama, in America* which was published in Liverpool by Rourke in 1861. John Jacobs, the brother of Harriet Jacobs, had his 'A True Tale of Slavery', in four issues of *The Leisure Hour* (London) in February 1861. He wrote 'I do not think of leaving London at present. I shall wait to see what course the North intends to pursue.' He added 'let me breathe the free air of another land, and die a man not a chattel'. He left for America the following year and died in 1875.

We have noted that James Olney observed in 1984 that there is a sense 'of overwhelming *sameness*' to slave narratives and there was repetitiveness: 'more and more of the same', and asked 'Why should the narratives be so cumulative and so invariant, so repetitive and so much alike?' He suggested conventions in the narratives were enforced by the very intention of the narrative to be a picture of slavery as it is. Rather like the sale of programmes at theatres and concert halls, perhaps the slavery narratives were also souvenirs?

The economics of slavery narratives have been revealed through a court case in Bristol in 1885. Lewis Charlton of Maryland is detailed on the Maryland State Archives site (msa.maryland.gov), on Wikipedia and docsouth.unc.edu. Charlton's name appeared in a short article in *Trewman's Exeter Flying Post* newspaper of 23 May 1883. Charlton 'stated that he had been for fifty years in bondage in the State of Maryland' at a meeting at the Bible Christian Chapel in Tiverton, a lace-making town in central Devon in south-western England on 22 May 1883. He collected for a church and school planned for Westminster, in Carroll County, near Baltimore, Maryland. Born near there in 1814, Charlton's slave life had been described in a ten-page narrative by a Maine publisher. Maryland archives note he was freed in 1842, and the US census of 1870 listed him with wife and teenage son.

Charlton was a free black man who moved to Britain fifteen years after the end of the Civil War. To raise funds he published a narrative. He was connected to the evangelical Byrom Hall in Liverpool in 1881.[2] He spoke on 'The Horrors of Slavery, and the Evils of Intoxicating Drink' in Lostwithiel on 27 November 1882 at a meeting chaired by the mayor. He spoke on foreign missions at Threeburrows Primitive Methodist Chapel in February 1883 when it was indicated that he was based in Plymouth.[3] In May he was in Tiverton as noted above and in August 1884 he ('an aged negro') spoke at a temperance meeting in the brewing town of Burton of Trent.[4]

Lewis Charlton was innocently linked to a cheating employee of a printer in Bristol, as were others, and the court case reveals interesting aspects of what might be called the Slave Narrative industry of Britain. According to the *Bristol Mercury and Daily Post* of 17 October 1885 Lewis Charlton's payments had been embezzled by Frederick Perrin, a printer's manager of Bristol. Charlton 'a man of colour [who] went about the country and sold books containing an account of his life' was illiterate but his agent or secretary told the court about contracts given to Perrin's firm, and payments made. In July 1883 they were to print 2,000 posters and 10,000 handbills, and £2 5s was paid to Perrin. Two thousand copies of the book were to be printed, at a cost of £13. In March 1884 another two thousand copies were purchased. Both the printer and the typesetter confirmed that the necessary tasks had been carried out. Perrin pocketed the money and the accounts remained unpaid. Assuming Charlton had sold all the first batch of copies of his narrative, the market had been two thousand sales in eight months.

A Portland (Maine) printing is undated but suggested dates are 1860 and 1870. The Bristol printing has not survived in major British libraries but an undated *The Life of Lewis Charlton: A Poor Old Slave, who, for Twenty-Eight Years, Suffered in American Bondage* which was printed by Pitts and Crockett in Fredericton, New Brunswick (Canada) is at the British Library with a suggested publication date of 1885. It has twenty-eight pages.

Perrin's case had several witnesses who testified that they had paid him for work at the printers, and he was sent for trial at the Assizes on charges of false pretences, embezzlement, falsifying books of account, and the theft of paper and printer's materials from his employer.[5]

Lewis Charlton died in Sheffield in 1888, aged 74. A copy of the registration certificate states that Charlton had been a 'temperance lecturer'. He died in the Rock Street, Pitsmoor workhouse on 26 March 1888. His address had been 175 Pond Street, Sheffield (in the centre of the city) as was that of the informant William Hardy. Pitsmoor workhouse was generally used for children. It is probable that the 'aged negro' was buried in a pauper's grave.

What Charlton's life in Britain suggests is that, even after slavery's abolition in the United States, audiences wanted to hear about the slave experience. Before them on the platform – or within the pages of the narrative – was a person who had experienced those times. From those depths the speaker/author had risen to espouse activities which would benefit all: Christianity and rejection of alcohol. Those who sought support for settlements in Canada (and Liberia, Jamaica, and elsewhere) also appealed to the British.

With slavery's abolition in America, there was the clear need to teach the untutored ex-slaves. And the vast regions of black Africa, as described by David Livingstone in the 1850s, were also presented as needing guidance. All this led to white patronage and to European colonialism of tropical Africa, with blacks defined as in need of assistance. However, audiences in the British Isles were told of faults in their own lives: they were offered advice on the values of Christianity. Black speakers were often critical of alcohol, and formed a small but always vibrant element in the temperance movement.

Chapter 9

Education

American slaveholders feared literate blacks. They supported laws against teaching slaves to read and write because of 'a variety of fears, the simplest of which concerned the forging of passes by potential runaways'. It is estimated that five per cent of slaves could read by 1860.

Moses Roper's experiences of acquiring an education in 1830s England were greatly aided by his letters of recommendation which introduced him to three churchmen, all connected to the British anti-slavery movement. Roper moved to London where he started his formal education. He travelled through the country, selling copies of his narrative. Some of these villages and small towns had schools provided by various religious and philanthropic bodies. The established church (Anglicans) had established the National Society in 1811, and the nonconformists set up the British and Foreign School Society in 1814. These schools relied on fees from pupils, supplemented by state grants and donations from well-wishers. The nonconformists founded University College London in 1826, unlike Oxford and Cambridge open to all religions (and none). Roper's time there was curtailed by illness.

The refugees had varied experiences, with the Crafts achieving literacy and teaching at their school in rural Surrey in the 1850s. John Anderson attended the nonconformist school in the Northamptonshire village of Corby. Patronage was essential, and those narratives which detail the authors' British experiences often name those men and women; Ringgold Ward's *Autobiography of a Fugitive Negro* published in London in late 1855 named Congregationalist minister James Sherman, his host in London for several months.

Scotland's education system had few religious restrictions, and black Americans studied there, notably James McCune Smith of New York in the 1830s. A medical student rejected by American institutions, he was awarded an MD by Glasgow University in 1837. In Glasgow he was involved with the Glasgow Emancipation Society (founded in 1833), serving on the committee. It and Smith were closely linked to abolitionist George Thompson. Smith was refused passage on a ship for New York in May 1837, officers of the Glasgow Emancipation Society and fellow students honoured him and showed their contempt for the shipping company by throwing a farewell dinner party in June 1837. Smith worked at the Colored Orphan Asylum in Manhattan from 1846, contributed to medical journals, and worked with Frederick Douglass, writing the introduction to Douglass's *My Bondage and My Freedom*. No American professional association admitted Dr McCune Smith as a member. He died in 1865.

As well as meeting and being supported by well-meaning white patrons, the Americans had opportunities to meet other black people. Wells Brown noted 'three colored young men' among the students at the Infirmary, Edinburgh, and recalled that in London 'one may meet half a dozen colored men, who are inmates of the various colleges in the metropolis.' Then there were three Africans who arrived in Britain in 1855. Samuel Campbell, William Broughton Davies and James Beale Horton had attended college in Sierra Leone and had been selected by the Church Missionary Society for the British War Office following the latter's decision to recruit and train Africans to be army medical officers. The trio studied at King's College in central London. Campbell caught bronchitis and went back to Africa where he died. In April 1858 Horton and Davies passed the examination of the Royal College of Surgeons and moved to Scotland to study further, Horton to the University of Edinburgh and Davies to St Andrews. In Edinburgh Horton adopted a new second name, Africanus. He was the only student to be awarded honours in Practice of Medicine. His thesis on topography, botany and the weather of West Africa was published in London in 1859. Davies achieved his MD in late 1858 and moved to Edinburgh and wrote a prize-winning essay on botany. The pair became members of the Botanical Society of Edinburgh. Horton was awarded his MD, and he and Davies reached home in October 1859 as staff-assistant surgeons in the British Army (the rank equalled that of a lieutenant). Horton served in the Gold Coast (Ghana), retired from the army in 1880 as a Surgeon-Major (lieutenant colonel) and settled in Freetown. He wrote articles and books. His *West African Countries and People* of 1868 was a pioneering work.

There were African American students in Scotland. On 6 April 1858 Edinburgh's *Caledonian Mercury* reported a meeting on Saturday, 2 April at the Queen Street Hall, chaired by the President of the Royal College of Surgeons, when one of the university's medical students 'Mr Johnson, formerly a slave' spoke of his twenty-four years in slavery, his experiences in Canada and horrors in Ohio (which was not a slave state). The hall was filled and included many students. Johnson was surely the 'R. M. Johnston' who spoke about slavery at the Free St Paul's Church in Dundee in November 1858, for he was described as a medical student at Edinburgh with twenty-four years in slavery before his escape to Canada. There were so many people that 'hundreds were unable to obtain admission'. Nearly £15 was collected for his education and the *Dundee Courier* said it was hoped he would return to the city after his planned visit to Aberdeen. A shop in the High Street would take further donations for his training.[1] That shop was still supporting Johnson when the *Dundee Courier* of 29 December 1858 advertised his lecture at Bell Street Church that evening. Dundee Ladies Anti-Slavery Society supported the venture, and Johnson a 'medical missionary' was to talk on American slavery. He spoke in Aberdeen in July 1860 at a meeting focussed on escaped slaves now in Canada.[2]

Another American student Jesse Ewing Glasgow died in Scotland just before Christmas 1860, aged twenty-three.[3] In 1859 his *The Harpers Ferry Insurrection* had been published in Scotland. This forty-seven page booklet explained the raid by John Brown on the armaments base in Virginia.

Johnson continued with his medical studies, and continued to speak of his slave upbringing. He had been born in Lexington, Kentucky and had been a house servant to a doctor. Aged 23 he had escaped to Ohio where he worked in a hotel until 1857 when he crossed the Atlantic. He studied for four years in Edinburgh and then qualified as a surgeon in Glasgow. He became a Member of the Royal College of Surgeons, England. He was lecturing in early 1865.[4] 'It was his intention shortly to go back to Kentucky in order that he may make himself useful among his freed brethren' reported the *Rochdale Pilot* in late 1867 after his talk, introduced by the mayor, at that Lancashire town's public hall.[5] He had addressed several gatherings in Rochdale that week.[6] The *Pilot*'s report referred to Johnson as 'a gentleman of colour, formerly a slave in South [*sic*] America'.

We have to guess at the interchange of ideas between the Africans and the two Americans in Scotland.

Another American medical student in Britain was George Rice who arrived in Scotland in 1870. Born in Troy, New York of freed slaves in 1848, he qualified as a doctor at Edinburgh University in 1874. He moved to London where he became the medical supervisor at the Woolwich Union (workhouse) infirmary in Plumstead, probably in 1877. He married Florence Mary Cook and their daughter Mary Lucinda Rice was born in Plumstead in 1882.[7] He had worked at the Manchester Royal Infirmary as the house physician, and had been resident medical officer at the Charlton Union hospital.[8] He moved to the south-east edge of London, and had two sons (both died young). Dr Rice had several responsibilities, some parallel. In May 1881 he testified in an Old Bailey murder trial as the resident medical superintendent of the Woolwich Infirmary.[9] In 1887 he was the resident medical officer of the South Metropolitan District School in Sutton. He took a thoroughly professional interest in doctoring, having two research papers published by 1890. 'Glycerine Injection in the Diarrhoea of Prolapse of Children' was in the *Practitioner* in 1889, and 'Notes on an Outbreak of Influenza in a Poor-Law school' in the *Transactions of the Epidemiology Society of London* NS Vol 9, pp 104-110 in 1889-1890.[10] He moved to Sutton and worked at the large asylum in Belmont (it accommodated 1,700 patients), where most patients were mentally ill. He studied epilepsy there, into 1917. He died in 1935 not long after his wife. Their daughter Lucinda ran a private school in Sutton for several years.

Just as Queen's College prepared Crummell as a minister, and the medical schools provided professional training, other schools and colleges offered more than the bare literacy of National and British schools. We have seen that Alexander Crummell studied at Queen's College, Cambridge. After he went to Liberia his son Sydney, aged 15, was at the private grammar school in Warminster, Wiltshire in 1861.[11]

Isaac Dickerson studied theology at Edinburgh University. Thomas Lewis Johnson spent twenty-eight years in slavery, the title of a short memoir published in 1882 and of an expanded book published in Bournemouth in 1908. His fare was paid by his church in Chicago, and he arrived in Liverpool in 1876. He worked for W. Hind Smith, an officer of the YMCA in Manchester 'for some time prior to his going to Mr. Spurgeon's College and then to Africa'. His wife had a sister, Issadorah, who had married Calvin Harris Richardson, a Baptist minister and they came to England in the summer of 1877, and Richardson also attended Spurgeon's College. At that time known as the Pastor's College it trained evangelical Christian ministers. Johnson became ill in their mission field, Cameroon, and his wife Henrietta died there. (Calvin and Issadorah Richardson remained there.) Johnson returned to Britain, and worked in America before settling back in England in the 1890s where he died in 1921.

James Alfred Johnson escaped from coastal North Carolina during the civil war but remained illiterate for decades. His daughter's *The Life of the Late James Johnson (coloured evangelist), an Escaped Slave from the Southern States of America, 40 Years Resident in Oldham, England* was published in 1914, months after his death at the age of 66. There is only one known copy of this fifteen-page memoir.[12] Johnson was born near Wilmington, North Carolina in 1847. A ship took him to Philadelphia and Johnson went on to New York where he obtained employment on the *Blenheim* bound for Liverpool where he arrived in December 1862. Johnson walked across England and eventually sailed to Spain from Swansea. He had earned a living: 'I took to singing, dancing, and rattlebones, which I found was easier and pleasanter than begging.' In Sheffield he joined 'Chuckey Harris's boxing tent' and worked as a pugilist in fairs. In September 1866 he reached Oldham in Lancashire, where he obtained work in foundries. In 1869 he married Sarah Ellen Preston (she died in 1886) and 1891 he married Mary Ann Cook. Through Sarah's 'instrumentality and patience I have acquired the blessed boons of being able to read and write'. He also became a Christian evangelist.

We have seen that the Powell family came to the British Isles where the children were educated, the medical qualifications of the first-born son have been detailed. Another son was a skilled tradesman, making barrels. Awareness that the ex-slave settlements in Canada lacked schools led to the Colonial Church and School Society sending Thomas Pinckney to Ontario. And we have William Craft and his school in Benin, and Wells Brown's daughters who were qualified teachers. We lack details on the north London school established by William G. Allen, and no evidence has been uncovered to show where in Lincoln William Howard Day was teaching around 1861. Day was listed in the 1861 census (taken on 7 April 1861) as a boarder at 91 Grosvenor Street in Chorlton upon Medlock, in central Manchester. Aged 33, and married, he was listed as an 'editor and lecturer M.A'. One year later he was in central Liverpool staying at a temperance hotel near Clayton Square and soon left for America.

Students whose physical appearance or religious practices were clearly different to the majority would have experienced taunts and anti-social behaviour. Charles de Rothschild was a pupil at the expensive and exclusive Harrow School and later commented 'Jew hunts such as I experienced are a very one-sided entertainment.' The sprinkling of black teachers and life in the neighbourhood may have had different influences on other schools but the little evidence from the 1910s suggests varied experiences.[13]

Because of its location and its ambitions, we know about the school for Africans established in Colwyn Bay on the north Wales coast in the 1890s. Two African Americans went there, Paul Daniels from South Carolina in 1895-1899 and Joseph Morford from Chattanooga, Tennessee who was there from 1900 to 1904. Morford became a Christian missionary in Nigeria. Morford had worked as a coal miner in Wales, Daniels was an assistant to the founder of the Jenkins Orphanage in Charleston and had reached London with a band of orphan musicians in 1895. He studied book-keeping, scripture, and English. He helped with the printing of the Congo Institute's newspaper. He returned to South Carolina where he died in 1961 after a lifetime of working for unfortunate orphans.[14]

The African students came from several places and when Daniels was there it seems they had at least seven languages between them. The son of the president of Liberia was there in 1896. His father Joseph Cheesman's education at Liberia College would have involved Crummell. One visitor was Thomas L. Johnson; another was Sir Samuel Lewis, an England-trained lawyer from Sierra Leone. African influences on Daniels can be seen in that he added the middle name of Gabasie, a deliberate reference to West African naming traditions.

Chapter 10

The Length and Breadth
of the Country

As well as a broad range of activities among African Americans in Britain the places where they have been traced were the length and breadth of the British Isles. Roper for example when in Northamptonshire spoke in Daventry, Kilsby, Hackleton, Harpole, Kettering, Kislingbury, Middleton Cheney and the county town (Northampton). In Cornwall in the south-west he spoke in St Agnes, Bodmin, Redruth and Launceston. The expanding railway network helped this scattering of course, and certainly enabled entertainers to find work in urban theatres.

In 1866 Gustavus Allenborough 'coloured tragedian' performed in Northampton as Othello and announced his availability for 'starring engagements' and claimed his repertoire included 'Othello, Black Doctor, Slave, &c'. He played Othello in Redhill, Surrey in late July 1867.[1] In June that year Coventry saw G.P. Dunbar play the lead in *Antoine, the Savage of the Rocks*, a 'great engagement of the American Coloured Tragedian'.[2] The 1871 census listed him as George Dunbar, an actor aged 40, a British subject born in America with his Birmingham-born actress wife Julia in Walsall. In 1873 Dunbar was playing the Alhambra Music Hall in South Shields.[3] When G.A. Gross was announced to play Othello at the New Royal Adelphi Theatre in Liverpool in summer 1868 he was described as 'The only successor to the celebrated African Tragedian, Mr. Ira Aldridge' and 'the South American Coloured Tragedian'.[4]

There is confusion for the modern reader – what was the ethnicity of 'Miss Edwards (the coloured ballad lady)' and 'Yankee Henri (Negro comedian)' who were at the Hanover Music Hall in Sunderland in August 1867?[5] And for contemporaries, for even the well-known escaped slave 'Mr. H. Box Brown' was billed as the 'African magician' in Taunton, in March 1865: when he was assisted by a female clairvoyant.[6]

Some people have been noted just once or twice, and some places seem to attract dark strangers almost every year. The Powell family in Liverpool and the Crafts in Hammersmith had roles in guiding newcomers. In late 1853 Manchester, the Mechanics' Institute heard George Marshall speak of his experiences as a slave. 'A highly intelligent and interesting person' he had spent thirty years in slavery, having been born in Maryland and then lived in Tennessee.[7] He returned to America in 1855 with a recommendation from William Powell.

White liberals such as Armistead in Leeds, George Thompson in London, the Richardsons in Newcastle and Impey in Somerset had black associates. The identities of less vociferous Britons who aided refugees are obscure.

Duns, the small market town in the Scottish Borders, had an important role in securing the freedom of James Pennington. We have also noted that Harriet Jacobs lived in a village on the Berkshire–Oxfordshire border in the 1840s. John Brown's career as a herbalist in Dorchester is unexpected and so too is the presence of the Crummells in mid-century Bath. Garnet has been noted in Hitchin. It was because of Garnet that we know of James and Charity Johnson and their daughter Charlotte who relocated to Liverpool after 1850. New York-born, Johnson had been a waiter. They were sought out in September 1861 by Garnet, on his second British tour.

The lecture given by a fellow named Parnell in a school in Crowland, south Lincolnshire, attracted over 1,000 people and he obtained nearly £4 in the summer of 1858. The town was small and this event seems to have attracted a majority of the town's adults. 'G. Parnell' from Virginia lectured in Market Harborough in September 1858.[8] John Williams failed to convince contacts in Leeds that he was genuine, and in the summer of 1858 was sentenced to two months with hard labour.[9] He may have been the John 'Toby' Williams who lectured in Devon in December 1852 or the fellow who died on a prison treadmill: an 'unfortunate negro' with dissipated habits whose death was reported in a Dublin paper in 1864.[10]

Frederick Henry Williams said that he was an ex-slave from Toronto when he pleaded guilty to the theft of a watch in Stoke, an Ipswich suburb. He was sent to prison for three months. Washington Duff was said to be from Kentucky when he spoke in High Wycombe in late 1862. Ten months later he lectured at a school near Liverpool Street station in London and was in Hitchin in March 1864. Unable to read or write, he had been in England for five years by this time. His wife remained in Canada, he told an audience in the small town of Godmanchester in October. In Bedford in January 1865 he said he was born in 1829 and came from Kentucky via Canada. He had crossed the Atlantic with two other escaped slaves, Jackson and Howell. Jackson was present, and told the audience of slave life in South Carolina. Duff talked to 200 children from the Band of Hope and the workhouse.[11]

Another ex-slave J. Hughes from Baltimore attended Methodist mission society meetings in Leeds in April 1859. He remained in England for he lectured on the war in America in Trowbridge in February 1865 and in the town hall of the garrison town of Aldershot in May 1865. Hughes was in Wallingford in June and in Leicester in October where he was described as 'Rev J. Hughes, an escaped slave'. He should not be confused with Henry Hughes who was thought to be a bogus lecturer when arrested for molesting a child in Watford in July 1865.[12]

Little is known of Edward Irving who gave two lectures in Tunstall, a Staffordshire pottery town in May 1863 ('audiences were not large'). Before a 'very scanty audience' at the Temperance Hall in Bolton in early 1864 he addressed the audience; placards advised 'Think of the slaves as well as the three million bales of cotton' for the Union blockade had severely reduced shipments of cotton to the local mills. Irving was said to have 'been some years in this country'. He was still in England in April 1865: 'a man of colour, and an escaped slave' who spoke on slavery in the Primitive Methodist chapel in Coleford, in the Forest of Dean, a small town yet to be connected to the railway network. Holywell near the coal-mining town of Wrexham was where James Cheeney Thompson 'a pre-possessing young creole' presented a lecture illustrated by his own paintings in mid-1865. He claimed to have been a slave in Cuba and the South. The Scottish weaving village of Kennoway in Fife had a 'respectable attendance' at the talk given by William Johnstone in January 1865. He was seeking donations to free his children. Richard Sayers was in the school room of the small town of Wragby in Lincolnshire in late 1871, telling of his escape from slavery. He was in Denbigh, North Wales in February 1874 when he was described as 'an escaped slave from the far west'.[13]

Continuing to influence people around the British Isles were *Uncle Tom's Cabin* presentations, some retaining few traces of Stowe's creation. From the 1870s genuine African people participated in them, starting with Henry Jarrett and Harry Palmer who announced they were to take a *Cabin* show with African Americans to Britain advertising 'something that will astonish England', in August 1878. There were three companies. They were pioneer employers of black performers in *Uncle Tom's Cabin* in Britain.[14] 'Their value in imparting picturesqueness to many of the scenes' was regarded as providing completeness to the presentation. Major roles were played by whites. These shows were seen in cities and in smaller venues.

The patrons of London's Princess's Theatre were boisterous in their support. The *Morning Post* suggested that the novelty of black actors and actresses made the performance interesting. 'Several special artists are to be found in the negro ranks' and the *Post* named the Louisiana Troubadour Quartet and the dancing Slidell children, and praised the excellent banjo playing of Horace Weston. The script by George Rowe made Uncle Tom a 'tedious old nuisance' and the plot was clear only to those who knew the novel. The singers, the 'Four Jolly Coons' and Weston were the 'real attraction of the drama'. The harmonies of the singers were simple but appealing and 'wonderfully well in tune'.[15]

A *Cabin* show was presented in Dublin's Queen's Royal Theatre in September 1878 but lacked the novelty of Jarrett and Palmer's black-and-white troupe. The London show was supposed to have 100 freed slaves. The Royal Aquarium in London had a *Cabin* show in September 1878: the afternoon performance was by the Jarrett troupe which played the Princess's Theatre in the evening. These performances continued as the Victoria Theatre across the Thames in Lambeth presented another *Cabin* show which had taken note of the appeal of the Jarrett and Palmer troupe, and employed Petrie and Fish, two 'long-legged dusky gentlemen'. A preview of a *Cabin* show in Bristol indicated that it would have 'genuine emancipated slaves'. It played the city for two weeks. The London Aquarium afternoon show ended in November. A Jarrett and Palmer *Cabin* troupe was in Leeds in November, mounting an afternoon performance for 'country visitors' and the Princess's Theatre in London continued with that other Jarrett troupe. By mid-December one of their troupes was playing Dublin for two weeks. Jarrett and Palmer troupes had revived *Uncle Tom's Cabin* and added a new element: African Americans.[16]

A showman who presented *Cabin* in an unlicensed theatre in Nottingham – 'showing the company of negroes in slave life and in their vocal capabilities' – was fined in January 1879 despite his claim that it was not a theatrical performance. As well as these melodramatic performances there were talks and concerts that utilized *Uncle Tom's Cabin* in one form or another. And always Stowe's book.

John Holmes Grover brought black Americans to the British Isles in 1879. The *Belfast News-Letter* of 27 January named some of the 'host of real negroes' including Mr T. Griffin, Miss M. Grant (octoroon), Kate Essaucius (quadroon), Annie Moore (negress) and Emma Levison (mulatto). Jarrett and Palmer's troupe played Glasgow at this time.[17]

It was now almost essential for *Cabin* shows to include people of African descent.

In Newcastle in March 1879 white members of a troupe refused to go on stage due to financial uncertainty, for the show had not attracted capacity audiences. The Saturday night audience was numerous, and the black members of the cast were prepared to perform, but after disturbances and some mayhem customers were informed that the show would not go ahead and were refunded the ticket prices.[18]

Grover, an American actor, was with a troupe led by Charles Hermann in Chester and Liverpool in the summer of 1881 and the pair moved into theatrical management, appearing in Grover's adaptation of *Uncle Tom's Cabin* at the Prince of Wales Theatre, Chester in September 1881. C.A. Morgan's Tom was 'quietly impressive' and other black parts were played by Miss and Mrs Harmer with Topsy played by Lizzie King.[19] Grover worked in other plays, notably in *I.O.U.*, sometimes playing several parts, including blacks. He apparently returned to America but left an *I.O.U.* company in England, which included 'Thos. Griffin (African)' who had been with him in Belfast in January 1879. It opened in Blackpool in November 1881.

By the time it was in Preston in December, Grover was back in it, but the play was not doing well.[20] In March 1882 Grover presented *Uncle Tom's Cabin* in Cork (Ireland), and Barrow-in-Furness. He blacked up to play Tom but 5-year-old 'Little Baby French' was genuine, she played Topsy. There were other blacks in this *Cabin* troupe. It moved on to perform a dozen times in Glasgow's Theatre Royal. It was in Hartlepool then Darlington into April, when it was noted that 'the *artistes* consist almost wholly of coloured people'. In Liverpool from 4 September it proclaimed it was a 'Celebrated Troupe of Freed Slaves, Negroes, Quadroons, Octoroons, & c' and that Grover played Tom. Weeks later in West Bromwich some principal parts were played by blacks.[21] Charles Hermann seems to have taken over the leadership of this troupe, which toured Britain for many years.

Cabin shows with blacks have been identified at Spennymoor, a mining town near Durham, where Joseph Jones played Tom in April 1886. Several were in London in August 1889, performing at the Elephant and Castle Theatre. *Cabin* actors appearing there included William Peters and a man named Burnett, for their names were mentioned after they had scuffled in a nearby pub. James Traviss worked for a *Cabin* show in Barnsley in late 1890 when he met Mary Haveron. The couple moved to Doncaster as man and wife, where they were apprehended by the police, an event headed 'The Barnsley Abduction'. She was 15 years old, the daughter of a coal miner.

The format of *Cabin* performances can be seen in an advertisement in the *Bristol Mercury* at the beginning of 1891. It had been as successful as any pantomime, earning 'thunders of applause' and 'roars of laughter'. Several songs were included but the dramatic story was 'not sacrificed to an entertainment of song and dance'. The show moved off on 10 January due to prior bookings. Versions were presented in church halls and in the Yorkshire village of Moor Monkton's schoolroom on 6 January 1891 when a York string band assisted in presenting tableaux and songs 'in character' enabled funds to be gathered for the church. The *Cabin* derivative *Eva* was presented by a choir at the Wesleyan chapel in Oswestry in early March and in a Dundee church some days later.[22]

A professional presentation was mounted at the Comedy Theatre, Manchester that month. The inmates of Ecclesall workhouse in Sheffield were able to see 'a lantern entertainment' of *Cabin*: it was 'highly enjoyed'. Hermann's troupe had moved on from Manchester and was at the Theatre Royal in Middlesbrough in June 1891. It was playing Stourbridge in early November 1891 when Hermann was injured in an accident which severed arteries in his hand. *Cabin* and *The Octoroon* were in the programme of the troupe at Huddersfield's Theatre Royal in June. That black roles were still taken by whites in black face can be seen in a summary of the Huddersfield performers, for J.W. Griffen was described as the 'coloured champion banjo player of the world', being one of 'several other genuine coloured artists'.[23]

James W. Griffin (*sic*) an American musician has been traced in the British census of 1891 and in 1901. He and his wife Harriet were lodging at 96 Peel Hall Street in Preston when the enumerator noted that they were both aged 34 and born in America. Ten years later they were at 17 Market Street in Tamworth and he was six years older whilst Harriet was still aged 34. She was also said to have been born in Derby. They had married in Stroud in 1877, and she seems to have been born in that Gloucestershire town in 1851.

Harrington's 'Great American Combination' presenting *Cabin* and *The Octoroon* advertised in the *Era* in February 1892, when it was in Ashton (Manchester). 'The Largest Troupe of Real Negroes and Freed Slaves Travelling this Country' the show included singers, dancers, a chorus and instrumentalists. George Walmer was still playing Tom and Nellie Shannon was Topsy, and they moved on to Bradford. Harrington did not have a monopoly for the *Era* reported Chard and Newsome had been at Warrington in January where an 'exhibition by trained dogs is by no means an insignificant feature' and they had moved to Blackburn where the plantation scene had 'speciality artistes' indicating black performers. This 'Anglo-American Combination' presented *Cabin* all week at Bacup in eastern Lancashire, 'to moderate houses' and next were seen on the east coast at Goole. Harrington's Bootle appearances drew 'capital houses'. Hermann's troupe claimed to be the sole company authorized by Mrs Stowe, and its appearance at Glasgow's Royal Princess's Theatre was noted as including thirty 'American negroes' and two St Bernard dogs and a donkey. The performance was greeted by a large audience with frequent applause. Nellie Sheffield was Topsy and Tom was played by G. Guilfoyle, and Harriet Guilfoyle played Eva.

A new five-act play *Deborah* at central London's Avenue Theatre in February 1892, was 'a tale of misery, depression and horror' and could not attract a West End audience. It was a spin-off from *Uncle Tom's Cabin*, and the *Era* noted that slavery-based dramas were played out and *Cabin* attracted provincial audiences chiefly because of the songs and 'breakdowns' (dances) and circus acts.

Edward Irons was working in an *Uncle Tom's Cabin* show in Aberdare in South Wales in January 1892. Harrington's troupe was in Middlesbrough at the end of February 1892.

Hermann was running three *Cabin* troupes. Opening in Skipton on 7 March 1892 was his troupe A with thirty blacks, two dogs and two donkeys; troupe B with fifteen blacks, one dog and one donkey was then in South Wales and the third troupe (again fifteen blacks, one dog and one donkey) was in England's south-west. The Skipton opening was packed. Both the show and Walmer were praised in Paisley, Scotland, in mid-March. They moved on to Greenock.[24]

If the advertising was truthful then sixty black performers worked in these four *Cabin* shows around Britain in 1892. Hermann's *Cabin* was in Blackpool when the *Era* (19 March) noted the 'real Negroes, who give plantation songs and dances'. They criss-crossed Britain with Harrington in Oldham in late March, then Warrington and Keighley, and Hermann went back in Doncaster. Harrington announced in the *Era* that his 'troupe of Negroes' was not one 'of niggers by aid of burnt cork and black wigs'.

In mid-April 1892 Hermann's troupe played Manchester's Queen's Theatre. 'This touching recital of negro slavery never fails to attract', the troupe having 'real live negroes and the bloodhounds as bloodthirsty, apparently, as one could wish' and the old story of Eva and Topsy 'seems to be perfectly new at each successive representation'. Harrington advertised in the *Era* that 'Every Coloured Part in these Plays is played by a Coloured

Person.' There was a *Cabin* show in Warrington in early April 1892, one in St Helens and another in Yarmouth. The agricultural show in the village of Marsden in western Yorkshire had a fairground atmosphere and crowds watched *Uncle Tom's Cabin* performed by a travelling theatre troupe next to the New Inn. George Walmer and Nellie Shannon were still with Harrington, playing Lowestoft on the east coast in May 1892, whilst far to the west in Truro Hermann included 'the Louisiana Troubadour Quartette' and the 'Darktown Brigade Band' for their three days at the Public Rooms.[25] Versions of *Uncle Tom's Cabin* had been presented in most urban areas in late nineteenth-century England.

As the summer drew closer *Cabin* shows were in Leamington, Windsor, Manchester, Stockport, Brighton, and in Birmingham where Walmer was praised ('himself a negro and an admirable actor to boot'), the audience reacting with 'unrestrained merriment' and tears. The show included part-singing and 'unadorned plantation dancing'. Walmer's performance was singled out when *Cabin* played Weymouth. Hermann's thirty blacks were in Greenwich, London for a week from 18 July 1892 (Tom was played by W.H. Porter) having presented their seven scenes in Halifax and in Liverpool's Shakespeare Theatre (it now had the smallest donkey on the stage and four St Bernard dogs were featured in the snow-storm scene, possibly because bloodhounds were less docile on stage). Harrington's troupe was praised in Plymouth at the beginning of July, its presentation of *The Octoroon* including 'step dances, banjo playing, and other specialities.... by the coloured members of the company' which the audience wanted to be repeated.[26]

At the end of July Harrington's troupe played a week at the Grand in Islington, London with 'plantation songs, dances, glees, hymns, banjo and bone solos'. Nearby the Parkhurst Theatre in Holloway had a *Cabin* show. Playing Quimbo was John Karala (*sic*); Porter played Tom. Sambo and Jumbo were played by Joe Holley and W. Cisco. Harrington moved to Leamington and was to open in Cardiff on 8 August, then went to Merthyr Tydfil. Friday and Saturday evenings had *Cabin* presentations. Walmer and Nellie Shannon were in Dumfries, Scotland, in September, part of a 'numerous contingent of coloured people of both sexes' in Harrington's Cabin which included 'plantation singing ... marked by taste and feeling'. One might question the taste and feeling of Hermann's publicity which still claimed the dogs were worth a fortune and that the donkey was still the smallest on stage. But their October 1892 presentation in Darlington was followed at the Theatre Royal by the reputable D'Oyly Carte Company presenting *The Mikado* and

Iolanthe, light operas by Gilbert and Sullivan.[27] In the half-century since Stowe's novel had taken the world by storm *Uncle Tom's Cabin* was a standard feature in British theatres albeit modified and adapted.

Travelling around the country by train, staying in hotels, working alongside veterans in theatres, these performers not only saw more of the country than most Britons, but had a steady influence on the locals on and off the stage. There were friendships, marriages, and children.

Cabin moved on to Stockton and played Wigan in late December 1892. Theatrical troupes were used to moving from town to town, week after week, only happy to fill in vacant weeks (often announced in the *Era* inviting managers to make contact), but the cast of Hermann's *Cabin* show must have been pleased when they were playing the Princess's Theatre in London for some weeks in November 1892, despite the Wednesday matinees. Then they played the Star Theatre, Wolverhampton in late December. Their first visit to Swansea was in March 1893, when reduced prices were arranged for children on a Saturday morning. The troupe was scheduled to visit the island of Guernsey in May, for five performances. Harrington added a third presentation, the play *The White Slave* in mid-1893 when they were playing in Jarrow.[28]

A show at London's Earl's Court entertainment centre included a log hut or cabin in which Celestine MacLaney or McLauney would sit, pretending to be Uncle Tom and exhibiting shackles alleged to be from his time as a slave, and sell knick-knacks. He died in mid-1894 and an inquest revealed that he was homeless, but had many friends in London and California. He was addicted to drink. Aged in his sixties, his death from heart disease was natural.[29]

Cabin was taken up by Moore and Burgess's minstrels at St James's Hall in central London. They were a very professional black-face minstrel troupe. Major London newspapers praised it, and the *Penny Illustrated Paper* noted the songs by leading lyricist George R. Sims included one that 'should be soon hummed all round the town'. Hermann's troupe moved to play Ipswich, where Tom was played by W.H. Porter. The banjo solos were of 'high merit'. In late May they were at the Britannia in Hoxton, London.[30]

Charles Otter was with Hermann's *Cabin* troupe in Spennymoor near Durham city in early 1896. Scheduled for a week there, Otter was taken ill and died, leaving a widow and having a burial that was not attended by *Cabin* colleagues for the show had moved on. Born in New Jersey, Otter had been in Britain since the mid-1870s. In early 1897 Josh A. Hybert advertised in the *Era* for 'coloured people with suitable specialities, coloured man for baggage, fit-up, & c' stating 'all must be strictly sober and respectable'. Applicants were to contact him care of the post office in Wells, Somerset. In Portsmouth in January, Hybert's *Cabin* included the Louisiana Quartet in plantation songs and dances. In July, in Weston super Mare, Hybert was seeking males and females who could sing for his *Cabin* show's 'long tour' due to start at the end of August. Generally active in England's south-west, Hybert's troupe did play Dover in March 1897, for just two nights at the town hall. Then it played two nights in nearby Maidstone. Tom was played by N. Harris, Topsy by Miss Power, and Sambo and Jumbo by Messrs Moning and Albert.[31]

Hybert's next *Cabin* tour was to start in August 1897, and his advertisement in the *Era* on 19 June sought male and female coloured vocalists and a 'gent[leman]' to play Tom who had to be a good bass singer. Eva had to be able to sing, have a minimum age of 11 and look younger. And a pianist-director was required too. Hybert advertised for engagements with some success, appearing at Oxford for two nights in October then two at the town hall in Luton, for his *Cabin* worked halls in small towns such as Biggleswade for the night of 19 October, but it continued for several years and always employed black men and women.

Harriet Beecher Stowe would not have recognized Sambo and Jumbo, or Quimbo, who were mutations from her novel. They, the dogs, the singers and dancers, banjo players and so on were appreciated by the audiences around the British Isles. Stowe died in 1896, aged 85, having written thirty books. When President Abraham Lincoln met Stowe in 1862 he is reported to have said 'So you're the little woman who wrote the book that started this great war.'

Cabin shows had taken African Americans to Hartlepool and Darlington, Preston and Barrow-in-Furness, Stourbridge and Oswestry, Bacup, Merthyr Tydfil, Halifax, Spennymoor, Wigan and Wolverhampton, Ipswich, Dover and Maidstone, Truro, Dumfries, Skipton, Keighley, Oxford, Luton and Biggleswade, Paisley and Greenock, Warrington, Yarmouth, as well as cities – London, Manchester, Bradford and Liverpool among others. Men and women of African descent born in Britain or the West Indies appeared in *Cabin* shows too. These groups of entertainers would have been 'often stared at and followed by idle boys and girls on the streets' as the Fisk Jubilee Singers reported in the 1870s.

We will examine black women in Victorian times after studying what contemporaries considered to be a major social problem, the abuse of alcohol. Male and female temperance speakers, black and white, were to be found all around the British Isles.

Chapter 11

The Temperance Movement

Nelson Countee was not the only black American who was active in the British temperance movement. Indeed, anti-drinking speakers had long been associated with anti-slavery activists. We have seen that in 1852 the *Temperance Chronicle* recommended that alleged fugitive slaves should 'be required to produce introductory certificates from well-known friends of the anti-slavery cause'.[1]

A black man took to the platform provided in Lechlade on 29 January 1852 at a temperance meeting. James Walker of London (but lately of nearby Faringdon, Berkshire) spoke of his years of alcoholism, living in a pigsty, breaking his bones when intoxicated and having one failed marriage until he took the pledge. Walker had an impact for over twenty people joined the temperance society afterwards.[2] Nothing is known on Joseph Woodhouse who spoke at a temperance meeting in a church school house in Shankill, Belfast on 30 June 1856.[3] John Anderson was active in temperance circles, addressing the Band of Hope Union in London's Bloomsbury in October 1861, saying shoeless Britons were the result of boozing. He spoke in east London's Stratford at the Temperance Hall on 4 December 1861.[4] William Lindsey, 'a coloured man, and recently a slave' addressed a meeting of the British and Foreign Freed-Men's Aid Society in Waterloo Street, Stepney, in 1866.[5] He was said to have reached Liverpool in late 1865, having escaped from North Carolina in 1859 and eventually studying at Oberlin in Ohio. The audience in Chesterfield's temperance hall collected over three pounds for him.[6]

With temperance publications and halls supporting anti-slavery we need to examine temperance. It never had the national impact of America's thirteen years of prohibition which started in 1920, but had numerous supporters in Victorian Britain. Father Theobald Mathew in Ireland had one quarter of the population take his pledge in the 1840s. The sale of alcohol on Sundays was widely seen as an affront to the Christian God, and laws were passed including a partial ban in the whole of Scotland and by 1848 in England and Wales. One group able to purchase booze on Sundays were travellers: this legislation was often flouted. There were riots for it was noted that those with their own cellars could indulge at home.

Towns had temperance halls where uplifting talks were given, and tea and coffee supplied. Thomas Cook's international travel business started with a Leicester temperance society's railway excursion. By 1880 there were over two hundred journals as well as numerous tracts and hundreds of books being published on temperance in Britain. These efforts had started as a movement to improve social conditions, and it does not take too much of a leap to see such thinking involved British anti-slavery abolitionists. Nonconformist Christians who made a substantial contribution in anti-slavery efforts were anti-alcohol by faith.

As their facilities expanded with wider literacy, village halls had small libraries. There would have been slavery narratives in many of them. Lord Shaftesbury who was involved in black uplift projects became president of the People's Café Company in 1874. Towns had commercial cocoa rooms, with Robert Lockhart expanding from Liverpool and Newcastle to London where he had twenty-three by 1884. Alcohol sales fell; tea, coffee and cocoa sales boomed.

In 1868 an American organization, the Independent (sometimes International) Order of Good Templars came to Britain. It had uniforms, titles, badges, and rituals: rather like Freemasonry. The treatment of blacks in America led to a split. In 1877 Wells Brown, a member of the Order of Good Templars, told a British audience of the split between the British and American branches because of the latter's colour-bar. That helps explain post-1877 African American temperance speakers, but what of the earlier ones?

Perhaps these speakers found that their anti-slavery hosts held firm opinions on alcohol, and were stimulated to do so themselves? Many British and Irish abolitionists were Nonconformists with temperance beliefs. African-American Christians were generally Nonconformists (Crummell is an obvious exception). Black people knew the African slave trade had been awash with alcohol, the supply of rum and other spirits to Africans helping break up those societies, and leading to the sale of men, women and children in order to obtain the products of distilleries. To oppose it was almost natural once the economics of the Atlantic slave trade were understood.

Temperance aims in America had been linked to the struggle for black emancipation. Along with attainments in religion and intellectual culture, high moral worth and dignity would be admired by the larger society. Set an example by the free people of colour, steady habits would influence the soon-to-be-free slaves, whose capacity for freedom and its responsibilities should not tolerate drunkenness. 'Negro leaders invariably linked abstinence with abolition, holding that to keep sober was to strike a blow at slavery. Among Negroes, as among whites, a supporter of abolition was likely to be a supporter of temperance'. Self-improvement would follow the taking of full responsibility for actions.

Both Garnet and Wells Brown had been active in American temperance circles before reaching Britain. We have seen that William Wells Brown was back in Britain in 1877. In Derby in August 1877 he made a lengthy speech on temperance as a member of the Order of Good Templars. He told the audience of the split between the British and American branches because of the latter's colour-bar. Coloured American Templars were now affiliated to the English Grand Lodge.[7] Brown addressed meetings in more than thirty locations, and left from Liverpool on 30 August.

Jefferson Davis, Confederate president, had a black coachman, William Andrew Jackson. He was in Sheffield in early January 1863, at the Temperance Hall.[8] On 3 and 5 February Jackson spoke at meetings 'crammed to excess' in Aberdare in south Wales.[9] Jackson was in Leeds on 24 March 1863, saying that he had been in England since 5 November. The Princess Theatre was crowded.[10] In 1863 Jackson lived at 17 Hanover Street in Walworth, (near Peckham High Street in south London). He had been giving an open-air talk in nearby Lewisham when a drunk demolished the table Jackson was standing on. The magistrate said public streets were not the proper place for lectures but drunkenness was no excuse and the accused was fined ten shillings and costs. Jackson refused to ask for costs as his intention had been to make an example of the man.[11] This is not John Andrew Jackson from South Carolina who is detailed elsewhere.

In Newport on the Welsh-English border another fugitive spoke at a town hall meeting in mid-1863. He was Francis 'Tedric' (*sic* – Fedric) from Kentucky who was married to an English woman and ran a lodging house in Manchester. His *Life and Sufferings* had been published in Birmingham in 1859 and a second book was published in London in 1863.[12] He had been in Sheffield in late 1860, supported by testimonials from 'a number of gentlemen' including the mayor. He gave two lectures. His plans were to establish a temperance hotel.[13] He addressed a crowded meeting in Edinburgh in early 1861, and in Dundee he suggested that teetotalism would aid the ending of slavery, and later attended a prayer meeting. In his fifties, he had been a fugitive slave for about five years. A collection was made in Broughty Ferry near Dundee at the end of March to assist Fedric to establish a business in Bristol.[14]

In 1877 Broughty Ferry's Congregational church hosted 'an escaped slave' named Anderson who was a student of divinity. There was a collection at the end of the meeting.[15]

American female temperance campaigners came to Britain. As in the days of slavery, they spoke of horrors for African Americans. Ida B. Wells was born in Mississippi in the last months of American slavery and challenged Southern racism in Memphis in the 1880s. She moved from teaching to journalism on the newspaper *Free Speech* and became entrenched in her opposition to Southern ways after three friends were murdered by a Memphis mob in 1892. Her newspaper office was then destroyed, but fortunately she was absent. She started to work for the *New York Age*, and took her anti-lynching campaign to England. She had met Catherine Impey an English woman who edited *Anti-Caste*, which had the support of Quakers, temperance advocates and humanitarians. Impey invited Wells to England and she reached Liverpool in mid-April 1893.

Impey lived in Street in Somerset. A small shoe- and boot-producing town, Street was much influenced by Quakers, and Impey was one. As a temperance campaigner she had travelled in America in 1878 where her observations of black people led her to focus attention on what she called caste. She was aware that the Templars split over black membership, and she had stayed with William Wells Brown in Boston at that time. Impey fought racial prejudice in a very English way: through publications and by supporting speakers.

One early African-American visitor was Benjamin Tanner, a future bishop in the African Methodist Episcopal (AME) Church. He spent two weeks in Street in 1881, when in England for a Methodist conference (which also involved African-American churchman Daniel Payne. Payne had visited Britain in 1867[16]). There were thirty-four 'gentlemen of colour' attending that conference, of which twenty-eight represented the AME Church. One was Alexander H. Clark. A black Canadian, Revd J.O. Banyon, was also noted. Payne spoke on the relationship between Methodism and the temperance movement.[17]

Impey got to know J.E. Celestine Edwards a London student born in Dominica in the British West Indies in 1858 who had settled in Scotland in the late 1880s, moving to Hackney in London in 1891. A medical student, temperance lecturer and Christian evangelist, Edwards was to be firmly linked to the Impey sisters. He read the literature on American slavery and wrote a study of the Canadian Bishop Hawkins with facts and quotations. His *From Slavery to a Bishopric, or the Life of Bishop Walter Hawkins of the British Methodist Episcopal Church of Canada* was published by John Kensit in London in 1891. Hawkins had arrived in Liverpool in the spring of 1891.[18] Both Hawkins and Edwards died in 1894.

The Salvation Army was teetotal. An African American who worked in Sheffield's steel works moved to Rotherham where he was involved with the Salvation Army, and settled down with his wife and her four children. The upkeep of those children upset him and he threw some scissors. Gilbert Lennison's wife took him to court on a charge of assault at the beginning of December 1880.[19] The Bridgwater, Somerset Salvation Army's parade on 22 June 1881 had the new banner carried by 'a man of colour'.[20] These parades were often attacked, and an incident in Notting Hill, London in July 1882 led to three men being accused of attacking Captain William Ley. One of the witnesses was Joseph Roker who had carried the flag, and said that he had also been attacked. His assailant was sent to prison for one month.[21] Yet another black Salvationist was Thomas Joshua Darkin who lived in Colchester where he was known as the 'Hallelujah Darkie', selling copies of *War Cry*.[22] He was found guilty of assaulting a woman at the Salvation Army's centre, and sent to prison for twelve months with hard labour.[23] Many newspapers reported this. There was some animosity towards the Salvationists. One commentator noted with disdain that in Scarborough in 1882 a black man danced and played the tambourine in front of his marching colleagues, which had led to a woman being thrown by her horse. Such 'music hall and circus type' publicity in the streets should be stopped.[24] In Worksop in mid-1886 Harriet Walker married a black Salvationist officer, John Rogers from Sheffield.[25] In August 1887 an escaped slave named Smith was the lecturer at the Salvation Army's barracks in the coal-exporting port of Blyth: he was a labourer on the new railway there.[26]

The Salvation Army's activities involved Agnes Foster and her family. Websites note that she had been instrumental in establishing the Salvation Army in Jamaica in the 1880s after forty years in England, and suggest that she had been taken to England as a slave. The British census of 1851, 1861, 1871 and 1881 recorded her as born in Jamaica, now the wife of a farmer named John Foster, with four Yorkshire-born children. The London archives of the Salvation Army located Agnes Foster and her daughter Jane (aged 25, a 'teacher of music') at 8 Vernon Avenue in Barton, Eccles (Manchester). She joined the new Salvation Army in Eccles and became an officer, based in South Shields into 1883. She went to Jamaica soon after and although unauthorized, she founded the Army's work in Kingston in 1887. Officially adopted by 1888, the first edition of Kingston's *War Cry* in 1888 noted that one of her daughters was an officer of the Salvation Army in England. The 1891 census lists her as an 'evangelist' visiting a house in Gate Street, Swinton (Eccles). The 1901 census located her in Bristol, a widow aged 74 living at 56 North Hill, Bedminster. The Jamaica *Gleaner* of 25 October 1902 noted that she was living with a daughter in Eccles. She died in Eccles, aged 87, on 18 March 1910.

Agnes Bizzett Foster spent most of her adult life in England. Acknowledged as 'Mother Foster' by Salvationists in Jamaica, her activities in Britain deserve investigation. This is a black British family and the lives of her children may reveal more about Victorian times and could detail American Salvationists. The Salvation Army was in favour of temperance, and still is, one of the survivors of the era of Victorian anti-drinking organizations.

Like those fugitive slaves, Ida B. Wells told the unpalatable truth about life in the U.S.A. and stimulated social and financial support. The eighteenth annual meeting of the National British Women's Temperance Association in London on 9 May 1894 heard her speak to an audience of approaching 500, when the president said that no crime could justify such retribution, which was duly reported in the *Liverpool Mercury* on the same page as its report on parliamentary activities.[27]

Lady Henry Somerset who inherited a house that was 3 miles (5 km) from its front gate, met African-American women other than Wells, notably Amanda Smith who was a temperance lecturer and Christian evangelist who worked in India for ten years. The pair were in Truro in late January 1894 at a meeting crammed to suffocation. Smith had already appeared in Redruth. She stayed there, and spoke at the Methodist church on her life (born in slavery in 1837, twice widowed). This was her second visit to England.[28] She had been noted speaking to a temperance group in Leeds in November 1878, to Quakers in Darlington and at another Christian event in Romsey (Hampshire) in August 1879, and when on her way back from India she spoke three times in Liverpool in 1881.[29] In 1894 she moved to Bristol and spoke at Clevedon when she was described as an African, the meeting was 'overflowing'. She went on to Cardiff.[30] She spoke at a crowded temperance meeting in Bury St Edmunds in Suffolk at the end of February. Smith's 255-page autobiography was published in London in 1894. It had an introduction by Bishop James Thorburn of India. The women's temperance movement had its annual celebrations in London the following year, at Lady Somerset's home in Reigate where she had established the Duxhurst Colony for Inebriate Women, and at a service at Westminster Abbey at the end of July 1895. Amanda Smith sang to the gathering at Exeter Hall, and a newspaper report noted that there were other 'foreign and coloured delegates'.[31]

Hallie Quinn Brown also lectured and sang, presenting British audiences with stories about her people. In Dundee in February 1896 she spoke on 'Women and the Drink Question' at the Gilfillan Memorial Church, at nearby Broughty Ferry she gave a 'dramatic and humorous recital' on 18 February, and later her talk was on 'Negro Education' at a Congregational church, which she ended by singing 'Steal Away'. Born in 1850 she had been educated at and currently worked as professor of rhetoric at Wilberforce University in Ohio, and had worked at Booker Washington's Tuskegee Institute in Alabama. The *Era* reported that her dramatic and musical recital found great favour. She recited at a gathering for the United Temperance Council in Glasgow on 22 April, and was still in Dundee in October, met with a spell of illness, then was back on stage in mid-November. Proceeds of these concerts were for the education of African Americans. She was in Perth at the end of January 1897 and in Aberdeen in March 1897.[32]

Pioneer Fisk singer Isaac Dickerson cycled around Palestine and then worked as a temperance lecturer and Christian minister in Plumstead, London from the mid-1890s. He died in Plumstead in 1900.[33] The 1891 census finds him a visitor at 7, Bruce Grove, Tottenham (London) the home of the octogenarian widow of pioneer meteorologist and Christian, Luke Howard.

And there were cheats. In 1893 John Downes earned a living as a tragedian (dramatic actor), elocutionist and journalist in England. He was 27, living at 13 Halliford Street, Islington. He knew Lillian Anderson who had been an actress, and when visiting her to discuss articles on Christianity he had written for magazines, he had taken four blank cheques. Three had been presented and the fourth was in his possession when he was arrested in the summer of 1893. Downes was a correspondent of the African American *Freeman* of the U.S.A., and he had copies of begging letters addressed to well-known charitable Britons. He was given bail. He was described as a 'mulatto actor'. The name used on those cheques was that of a Londoner who had discussed Downes's idea of producing a magazine supporting temperance. Downes pleaded guilty at the Old Bailey on 16 October to deception and fraud (£8 10s from one man, 10s from another – the ex-actress was not named) so was sent to prison for twelve months with hard labour.[34] Downes played in *Hypatia* which had opened at London's Haymarket on 2 January 1893 but his name was not included in the listing published in the *Morning Post* on 3 January. Downes probably played the part of a slave or a Nubian in the market scene set in ancient Egypt. *Hypatia* failed to have the impact of Beerbohm Tree's next production, Oscar Wilde's new play *A Woman of No Importance*.

One individual who linked experience of slavery, flight to Canada, military service in the Civil War, and time as an engine driver, to become a delegate to the British Wesleyan Conference in Liverpool in 1896 was also a temperance lecturer. John Henry Hector's story may have been muddled by journalists, who certainly confused the African Methodist Episcopal Church (AME) with the African Methodist Episcopal Zion Church (AMEZ), an easy error. He was noted as a coloured minister 'said to be an eloquent speaker and preacher' who was certified as a representative at the conference.[35] In the temperance movement he was 'popularly known as the "Black Knight"'. 'Left an orphan in early life, he passed several years of hardship. Later on he fought in some of the battles of the great Civil War, having been five times wounded. Subsequently, as a railway engine driver, he had many a perilous experience'.[36] In March 1899 he was at the Wrexham Temperance Union, saying he planned to go to Australia and New Zealand after that year's Wesleyan Conference. The newspaper of that coal-mining town described him 'as black as coal fresh from the mine' and said he had been born of escaped slave parents in Canada. He was still in that district, at Threapworth on 6 May 1899.[37]

Both the AME and AMEZ churches were black-led, and had congregations in Canada. African Americans fought during the Civil War in regiments under white officers and many were used as labourers. Capture by Confederates or a Confederate victory would mean slavery. He served as a bandsman in a Rhode Island regiment and ended the war in New Orleans.

In his years in 1890s Britain Hector lectured on slavery, on the American Civil War, and temperance. In 1896 an Isle of Man newspaper noted his presence in Castleton. He was in Hull in late 1896. In February and September 1897 he appeared in Lincoln and in December 1897 in Aylesbury, where he gave two talks for the Congregational Total Abstinence Society. In May 1898 he lectured on slavery at the Miners' Hall in Sunderland and was billed as the 'well-known temperance lecturer' when he spoke at the Corn Exchange in Beverley, East Yorkshire to 'crowded audiences'. He was again in Hull in November 1898 when the *Hull Daily Mail* said he was 'the Black

Knight of the temperance movement' and 'a negro of fine physique'. He spent some time in Belfast where he was described as 'famous'. In March 1899 he was at the Wrexham Temperance Union, saying he planned to go to Australia and New Zealand after that year's Wesleyan Conference. The newspaper of that coal-mining town said that he had been born of escaped slave parents in Canada. He was still in that district, at Threapworth on 6 May 1899. In August 1899 Hector was the speaker at the Trades Hall, Belmont Street, Aberdeen. He lectured on his life and American slavery according to the Tyneside evening paper in September 1899.[38]

Chapter 12

Women

Zilpha Elaw and Ellen Craft, Hallie Quinn Brown, Ida B. Wells and Amanda Smith have been noted among the African Americans in Britain. Contemporary reports seldom detail or even name black or white female partners, as with Julia Garnet and Mary Wells Watkins. Others including Cassie Stevens, Sarah J. Martin, Mary and Laura Harlan, are also overshadowed by male relatives. Esther 'Hettie' Johnson is known due to her work as an actress which was in the public eye, and research by family historians. There were others, of course.

A fashionable audience attended a recital by Elizabeth Taylor Greenfield at London's Hanover Square Rooms on 30 May 1853. The critic of the *Morning Chronicle* thought that she had 'some feeling for singing pathetic ballads, but nothing more, and nothing else'. A soprano with a powerful and wide range, she was untrained ('perfectly uncultivated'). If she worked hard and trained it was unlikely that audiences would attend her recitals 'because she was a woman of colour'.[1] Elizabeth Taylor Greenfield had been born in Mississippi around 1824 and was freed from slavery as an infant. This visit to Britain was her first and lasted into 1854. She had, as the *Morning Chronicle* noted, the patronage of the Duchess of Sutherland. *The Times* reported on 1 June 1853 that this 'coloured lady (from America) … does not greatly shine' yet she had an 'extraordinary voice' with the lower notes being 'almost masculine'. The *Nottinghamshire Guardian* (2 June) reported 'a very distinguished company was present' at the concert; *Lloyd's Weekly* (5 June) headed its review with 'The Black Swan' and sourly noted 'even the spirit of May-fair [*sic*] cannot create genius'. Her second London recital was on 15 June at Exeter Hall, a public hall closely linked with anti-slavery meetings. On 23 July she was at Stafford House (the London home of the Sutherlands) with tickets at a guinea each for this recital by the 'Negro vocalist'.[2] It was reviewed in the *Illustrated London News*.

She gave a recital as the Black Swan in Dublin on 9 August with a violinist from the East Indies named De La Valaderes.[3] They were still in Dublin on 17 August. 'Home Sweet Home' was a major item in her programmes. She gave two recitals in the Corn Exchange, Preston (19 and 21 September 1853), performed in York and Leeds two months later and was in Edinburgh on 5 December. Other announcements listed titled women supporters, used 'Black Swan' and declared her to be an American vocalist. In late 1853 she presented two recitals in Lincoln, one being judged 'delightful'.[4]

Opportunities seem to have diminished for an advertisement appeared in *The Times* on 24 April 1854 stating 'the Negro Vocalist' was available for both public and private engagements. In early May 1854 she sang 'some of her national songs' at Buckingham Palace for Queen Victoria, accompanied by Sir George Smart.[5] Smart was 'one of the most influential musicians of his time'. The Duchess was a famed wealthy hostess who supported the anti-slavery movement. Stowe joined with the Duchess in supporting Elizabeth Greenfield.

Stowe abridged the novel and readings were given including by her associate the 'mulatto' Mary Webb around England in 1856.[6] At Stafford House on 28 July 1856 a reading from *The Christian Slave* (based on *Uncle Tom's Cabin*) was presented by Mrs Mary E. Webb 'a mulatto, the daughter of a fugitive slave' who had given readings in Massachusetts and was trying to repeat that in England. This high society event had tickets costing half a guinea (more than a week's income for millions in Britain). She was pictured at Stafford House in the *Illustrated London News*. From Philadelphia according to a London poster, she was born in Massachusetts in 1828, her mother having escaped from Virginia.[7] She and her husband Frank knew Harriet Beecher Stowe who had given them an introduction to Lady Hatherton (daughter of the Duke of Northumberland) dated 24 May 1856.[8] The *Daily News* reported that there was 'not much to strike the observer' but the second part showed Mary Webb's dramatic power with 'a mixture of solemnity and pathos quite indescribable' and the hall was nearly filled although high society's summertime retreat, abroad or to the country, had started.[9]

She moved on to Birmingham. She was in Lancaster on 12 August: 'Mrs. Webb has we believe been patronised by several members of the aristocracy but for ourselves we cannot say that we were in all respects pleased with the entertainment' for in her reading of *Uncle Tom's Cabin* she failed to distinguish between all the different characters. The evening was interesting. She was expected in Sheffield in late September.[10] Frank Webb wrote *The Garies and their Friends* which Routledge published in London in 1857, a pioneering novel with Lord Brougham's introduction and Stowe's preface.[11] The *Morning Post* (6 October 1857) review was two columns long. The Webbs settled in Jamaica where the climate was thought to have been good for her tuberculosis, and Frank Webb worked for the Post Office, a position obtained through the Duke of Argyll.[12] The duke's wife was one of Victoria's daughters.

Not everyone admired the Duchess of Sutherland, for the Sutherland estates in Scotland had been cleared of crofters and their families so that sheep could be raised; the inhabitants went into exile. Their treatment was contrasted to Uncle Tom and his colleagues by *Lloyd's Weekly Newspaper* of 5 October 1856.

On 14 October 1859 a meeting at the Countess of Huntingdon's Connexion's Spa Fields Chapel in London heard American anti-slavery activist Revd Samuel May of Syracuse, New York, update the audience on anti-slavery activities in America. Listening were Sarah Parker Remond, and Ellen and William Craft: Remond had been lodging with the Crafts.[13] We have noted Remond's brother, Charles, in Britain and Ireland in the 1840s.

London's *Daily News* of 6 December 1859 reported that Frederick Douglass was in Halifax where he remarked that his freedom had been purchased by Britons and that he was pleased that, as a runaway slave, he had such people to run amongst. Other newspapers noted this. On 22 December he attended a meeting of the Leeds Young Men's Anti-Slavery Society along with 'Miss Remond, a free-born coloured lady' who also addressed the gathering.[14] Sarah Remond had reached England at the beginning of 1859.

Remond was an excellent public speaker, and found much support among women's reform activists. Sponsored by the American Anti-Slavery Society she spoke on slavery. She told the story of Samuel Green in Maryland who had been condemned to prison for ten years for possessing a copy of *Uncle Tom's Cabin*, in 1857.[15] Most of the people in her British audiences knew *Cabin* of course. As with Eileen Craft, there was a double attraction: a female speaker with an African ancestry. Remond also talked about sexual exploitation, mentioning that 'they could not protect themselves from the licentiousness which met them on every hand' and the 'degradation that a woman could not mention.'[16]

With all these arrivals we need to consider official British and American attitudes to foreigners. The modern mind may well be surprised to learn that there were no immigration restrictions in Victorian Britain. An act of 1836 required the captain of a ship to hand over a list of non-British passengers, and failing to do so or to produce a passport would lead to a nominal fine, for which just three clerks were employed. Even the activities of immigrants such as the verbose revolutionary Karl Marx and another London refugee,

Felice Orsini who came close to assassinating the Emperor of France, made no difference. An Aliens Act was finally passed in 1905. Other countries were different, and from 1856 the United States required arriving passengers to produce a passport. For Americans of African descent the legal decision of 1857, the Dred Scott case, stated that they could not be American citizens. Some were able to obtain local passports or official documentation, notably in Massachusetts. With no immigration controls in Britain, the absence of a passport would only affect the traveller when returning to the U.S.A., and when seeking to travel on from Britain to continental Europe.

Sarah Remond, who had been joined in London in late 1859 by her sister Caroline, wanted to travel to France, and the US legation in London refused to endorse her passport (she had a state department one, issued in 1858), telling her that she was not an American citizen. She informed the British press and the matter became a cause célèbre.[17] *The Times* printed her letter to the US legation dated 12 December, the official reply of 14 December, and her acknowledgement which pointed out that she and others like her had been burdened with taxation, and quoted from her passport which stated that she was a citizen. Remond also told the press that her sister Caroline, and friends, with first-class tickets from Boston to Liverpool on the *Europa*, were not allowed to sit with white passengers. The *Europa* was a Cunard steamer. *The Times* headed the quoted documents 'Disabilities of American Persons of Colour'. Caroline Putnam's husband Joseph was a civil rights leader in Boston.

Sarah Remond continued her public speaking, following immensely successful meetings in Warrington near the Cheshire–Lancashire border within days of her arrival in England. The level of support led to the creation of the Warrington Anti-Slavery Society by local abolitionist and temperance advocate William Robson, with assistance from William Powell.[18] She had gone to Dublin in May 1859, where she impressed Richard Webb.[19] Remond studied in London at Bedford College in Bloomsbury, and continued to move in anti-slavery and women's rights circles. The 1861 census found her visiting the Robsons in Bewset Road, Warrington (she was a 'ladies college student' aged 34, born in America). She lived out the Civil War years in Britain and went to Italy where she qualified in medicine, married an Italian, and died in Rome in 1894. She travelled with a British passport, for she had become a naturalized British citizen in 1865. The documents are in Britain's National Archives.[20] The two pages of copper-plate handwriting form the 'memorial' or official application. Her address was given as Aubrey House, Notting Hill, in London.

This was the grand home of Peter Alfred Taylor and his wife Clementia. He was a radical philanthropist and his wife was active in promoting female suffrage. Both were anti-slavery, and from 1862 were active in the new Emancipation Society which published Remond's *The Negroes and Anglo-Africans as Freedmen and Soldiers* in 1864. In 1862 Taylor became Member of Parliament for Leicester, and held the seat until 1884. The Taylors hosted Italian nationalists Mazzini and Garibaldi. Taylor was one of the first British parliamentarians to publicly support Lincoln and the North in the Civil War. Taylor's wealth came from Courtauld and Taylor, which had silk mills in England: and was to become the world's largest manufacturer of artificial silk (rayon) from 1905. Another of the men who signed Remond's memorial was James Stansfield. A radical and MP for Halifax from 1859 he was strongly supportive of Mazzini and the cause of Italian nationalism. Matthew Davenport Hill was a lawyer and prison reformer; and William Shaen was also a radical lawyer. These men have entries in standard British biographical sources. All seem to have been raised in the Unitarian church tradition.

Clementia Taylor's entry in the *Oxford Dictionary of National Biography* quotes from American writer Louisa May Alcott: 'Her house is open to all, friend and stranger, black and white, rich and poor.' Alcott had been in London in 1865, before she wrote the now-famed novel *Little Women*.[21] She must have met Remond.

Clementia Taylor was one of several women who gathered items to be sent to the destitute ex-slaves in America, as well as collecting money. Her name and address and that of Ellen Craft were listed in the monthly *Freed-Man* published by the British and Foreign Freed-Men's Aid Society from August 1866. The society – small and involving several who had been active in anti-slavery activities – had been formed in 1863. Its American focus was reduced, now having much concern over Jamaica and then the development of a school at Cape Coast (on the Atlantic coast of the Gold Coast, now Ghana).[22]

Remond's file, which recorded that her British citizenship had been granted in September 1865, has these comments: 'an African, born in the U.S. aged 41. A spinster has resided 6 years and intends to reside permanently' to which another official noted 'A Proper Case'. Remond's memorial stated 'The strong prejudice against persons of African descent which is entertained by a large proportion of the inhabitants of the United States and the social disabilities under which such persons consequently suffer have determined your Memorialist under no circumstances to return to reside in America.'

She had been active gathering support for the Freed-Men's Society, donations of £22 3s 0d noted in the September 1865 edition of *Freed-Man*. The December 1865 *Freed-Man* announced she ('a lady of colour') was to lecture in Tottenham, London on 'The Freed-men or Emancipated Negroes' of the Southern states, and in January recorded that Remond had collected hundreds of pounds. Remond had a letter published in the February 1866 edition, and the receipt of £40 was noted in June 1866.

Some African-American female singers toured Britain from late 1882 with the Royal Aquarium presenting Madame Selika, a concert soprano.[23] Marie Selika Smith was born in Mississippi in 1849 and raised in Cincinnati, Ohio before studying music in San Francisco. She married Sampson Williams, had success in the eastern U.S.A. and in 1878 sang at the White House for the president and his guests. With that imprimatur, and a fashion for black female concert singers, Madame Selika had a successful career, retiring from the stage in 1917 after her husband died. She died in New York in 1937. Selika appeared on 14 October 1882 at the St James's Hall in London, at a concert in aid of educating slave children in Cuba, alongside Carlotta Patti whose sister Adelina was an extremely famous singer. Selika was described as 'a Creole lady' whose performance had been 'very favourably received'. The *Era* noted that she was a 'fresh vocalist'.[24]

Mixing with several stalwarts of London's musical world must have aided her progress but the Royal Aquarium venue was more of a circus than a concert hall. It opened at noon for eleven hours, and there were a dozen acts as well as the aquarium and an exhibition of pictures, all for one shilling. Selika appeared at 4.45 and 9.15, each slot being fifteen minutes. Other acts included a 'negro delineator' (white humorist in black face), six performing lions, and an organ recitalist. Changes were made but she continued on the bill, making just one appearance of ten minutes by the end of December 1882.[25] The *Morning Post* reviewer commented that most visitors were attracted by the show not by the tanks of fish, praised Nala Dalamanti for her 'surprising' skills as a snake charmer, and of Madame Selika wrote that she was 'a singer possessing an excellent voice, which she uses to advantage'.[26] She was also praised some days later in the *Era*, which was most welcome as that weekly was the main entertainment publication in Britain. The Indian snake charmer had a lengthy review, her handling of a cobra some thirteen feet long (over 4 metres) and how the stage was covered with reptiles was noted, as were the legs of a female trapeze artist. Selika was 'a vocalist of considerable ability', possessing 'considerable fluency of execution' and her singing was well received.

She sang to an orchestral accompaniment. Farini's 'missing link' was absent from the performance but there were performing dogs and musical clowns. There was no mention of her colour in the advertising or reviews after 'Creole' had been used.

The black press in America reported on the successes and experiences of kinfolk in Europe, using reports from migrants and press cuttings. The *New York Globe* of 3 March 1883 reported on Selika, advising that there was a legion of contestants seeking to be heard in London. Her St James's Hall debut had been 'highly successful'. There was no mention of the weeks at the Royal Aquarium. She and her husband had gone to Scotland, Germany and Belgium. They had been aided by the Bohee brothers who 'are now considered permanent London institutions'. Sampson Williams also sang at his wife's concerts, had taken lessons with her tutor Signor Mazzoni, and they had been to France too. They returned to Europe in the late 1880s. An appearance before Queen Victoria (October 1883) has not been confirmed. What is certain is that following Elizabeth Greenfield in the 1850s then the Fisks, from the 1880s there were few years when British audiences were unable to hear African-American females singing. Matilda Sissieretta Jones (1869-1933) toured from the late 1880s through the 1890s, first as Matilda Joyner then as Madame Sissieretta Jones the 'Black Patti'. Flora Batson Bergen (1864-1906) completed three global tours and is alleged to have appeared before Victoria. The vogue ended in the 1890s.

The Bohee brothers were two black banjo players who spent much time in Britain. Born in St John, New Brunswick, Canada and raised in Boston, Massachusetts they inspired many Britons and achieved a professional status which was greatly admired. They worked with African-American women and toured widely.

James Douglas Bohee (born 1844) and George (1856) moved to Boston by 1860. With whites they formed the Bohee Minstrels and from 1878 toured with Haverly's Minstrels along with leading African-American performers, reaching London in 1881. Jack Haverly had sixty-five black performers in his troupe. The London critic of *Entr'acte* (6 August 1881) could see no major difference between Haverly's white minstrels of 1880 and Haverly's coloured minstrels: and ignored the banjo band. The show returned to America in mid-1882. In 1883 the brothers opened a banjo studio in central London. Their claim to have taught royalty and to have entertained the Prince and Princess of Wales was stated in the programme on sale at Manchester's Free Trade Hall in May 1889. George Bernard Shaw currently a music critic in London, wrote in March 1890 having seen the

Bohees at the International Hall that 'if it be true that the Prince of Wales banjoizes, then I protest against his succession to the throne'.

The Bohees and their troupe travelled all over Britain, week after week. *Era* noted they were with Sam Hague in Liverpool's St James's Hall, Lime Street in January 1889, and guests at a ball honouring the First Volunteer Battalion of the Leicester Regiment in Leicester at the end of January, moving to perform at the Lyceum in Stafford in February.[27] Patronage by British royalty enabled them to be billed as 'the Royal Bohee Brothers' when with their 'coloured concert company and orchestral band' they appeared at the Albert Hall in Sheffield for six days from 25 February. There were three matinees too. The city's newspaper thought it was 'a very superior entertainment' and the banjo playing which filled the third and final part was 'delightful'. Colleagues included Madame Lennard Charles (singer), Amy Beight (*sic* – her name was Height) was the comedian, Josie Rivers was a singing humorist and Corlene Cushman was a soprano who sang 'Beautiful Isle'. The *Era* named Madame Esmeralda, Mr W. Sykes and Mr Ike Jones.[28] Audiences were numerous so the booking was extended by a week and the *Sheffield Independent* again praised them. 'Almost entirely composed of men and women of colour' with the banjo-playing brothers the strongest point. James D. Bohee's version of 'Home, Sweet Home' was a 'revelation' for 'exquisite music' could be obtained from the banjo as played by the brothers. 'To hear them both in a duet is to realise that those who have taken up the banjo and made it fashionable are not by any means as foolish as they seemed.' The brothers played at a charitable evening too, one on the banjo and one at the piano.[29]

They played the Victoria Hall in Huddersfield for the week beginning 11 March, where they were stated to have twenty star artistes in the show. As in Sheffield the first section was a comic entertainment involving Webster Sykes, and Esmeralda sang 'Sweet Chiming Bells'. The middle section involved Lennard and Height, the latter singing the amusing 'Hush, little Baby' and Sykes singing and dancing. Bass C.H. Chivers was praised for his rendition of 'Rocked in the Cradle of the Deep' (a song from 1839) and the third part was the brothers and their 'brilliant' playing, costumed and dancing as well as playing.[30] The troupe opened at the Coliseum in Leeds on 25 March when the fashion for banjo playing and the skills of the brothers were noted, along with the jolly songs and dancing. They moved to Barnsley where James was taken ill during a performance; George Bohee's song, dance and banjo solo were noted.[31] The Bohees played St James's Hall, Liverpool in April, for three weeks during which time a trotting race, held in nearby Aintree, included a number of horses named after showmen: Bohee, Proctor, and Hague.³² On 6 May they opened at the Free Trade Hall in Manchester, and were in Belfast in mid-June and then moved south to Dublin into mid-July. The show retained the three-act format. More names emerge: a comic interlude from Richard Parker, a ballad by Fred Walson, Charles Watson danced and sang, and the Black Swan Trio made up of Cushman, Rivers and Jones. The show was modified, with a new sketch of plantation life called 'Uncle Jasper's Holiday' with Nadine Gilbert.³³

James Bohee, giving the London address of 44 Leicester Square, advertised in the *Era* on 13 July for a harpist, a cornet player, musicians for the orchestra, and 'coloured ladies and gentlemen for the chorus'. Applications had to be by letter, for he was in Southport, Lancashire dealing with a court case. Nelly Shannon (surely the Topsy of those *Cabin* shows?) and Mary Ewen 'coloured ladies' had been in the Bohee chorus singing in Liverpool and Southport. They sued him for two weeks' money (£2 10*s* and £3) for they had been discharged without wages or notice. The court heard that they had been seen on Southport's promenade walking with white 'mashers' (well-dressed chaps) in the afternoon and were reprimanded. They were in a pub one evening, with white males, and had been dismissed for the troupe's rule – 'necessary for the good reputation of the company' – was that coloured ladies should not appear in public places with white men. Shannon and Ewen said they did not know of that rule. The judge thought young women should not go to pubs or walk about at night: they had been properly dismissed. Costs were awarded to James Bohee.³⁴

A 'young female coloured servant' was sought for a public business, apparently the King's Head Hotel in Tiviot Dale, Stockport, in 1891.³⁵ Other than Mary Ann McCam we know very little about black (and white) female servants.

Martha Ricks or Rick from Liberia presented a hand-made quilt to Queen Victoria at Windsor, reported in the press in 1892.³⁶ She arrived in Liverpool on the *Calabar* from Monrovia on 11 July, went to the shipping company's office and told Alfred Jones, the company's owner, of her mission. Having gone from America to Liberia with her father when a child she had saved for fifty years and had come to England to present Victoria with a quilt. She was described as a little woman aged 76, and the quilt showed coffee berries that were green, then ripening and in full fruit, on a white satin base. She had not seen her twelve brothers and sisters since leaving America. Jones used his contacts so the quilt and the old lady – also named as Martha Anne Rix – could meet Queen Victoria. The *London Standard* thought she was a shrewd old lady to get interviewed so promptly.

Provincial papers reported her quest, noting she had travelled 3,500 miles (4,900 km). She had travelled with President Roberts's US-born widow Jane Rose Roberts, and soon contacted Edward Wilmot Blyden a Caribbean-born Liberian who was often in London. The *Pall Mall Gazette* published an interview with her, with an illustration. Mrs Roberts said 'she is full of spirits' and the pilgrim told of her meeting the queen and her family on 16 July. Blyden and his wife, daughter and granddaughter had gone with her by train to Windsor with Mrs Roberts and some friends. Advised that the monarch did not shake hands, Martha Ricks said the queen 'really shook hands with me'. She was shown round part of the castle and presented her quilt to an equerry whose task was to pass it to the queen. She planned to stay in England for some weeks, leaving before the cold weather came. On 21 July she and Blyden were lunch guests of the Lord Mayor of London at Mansion House.[37] The *Graphic* published a sketch of the ladies meeting the royals in its issue of 23 July, entitled 'A latter-day pilgrim'.

She attended a meeting of the Salvation Army and greeted founder William Booth, the *Pall Mall Gazette* indicated Mrs Roberts was there (and confused the two ladies). On 29 July she and Blyden were guests at the International Horticultural Exhibition. Back in Liverpool on 5 August a garden party at Alfred Jones's mansion had considerable numbers of the Liverpool merchants who traded with Africa and used his ships. Ricks and the four Blydens were there. Mrs Ricks was to sail for Monrovia the next day. She stayed with Jones over the weekend, and met more 'uninvited' visitors. Blyden's wife and daughter sailed with her to Africa. She had received numerous gifts and the crowd at the dockside had to be managed by police.[38]

Another American visitor to the Impeys in Street was Georgina Simpson who was there from 23 April to 2 June 1897. She was to be an early African-American female who received a doctorate (in Chicago). Almost immediately she was followed by the young poet Paul Dunbar, who stayed with the Impey sisters between 12 and 24 July 1897. Dunbar dedicated his *Lyrics of Love and Laughter* (1903) to Catherine Impey. Simpson twice returned to Street in the 1900s.

Simpson, Ricks, the dancers with Bohee, the nameless servant in Stockport, the prima donnas, Amanda Smith, Sarah Remond and her friend Ellen Craft represent several strands in the lives of female black Victorians, showing we can no longer regard the Fisk Singers in isolation. There were numerous individuals who entertained the British, again, revealing a range of places and activities.

Chapter 13

Elusive Individuals

Tracing African Americans in Victorian Britain has uncovered many different aspects of their lives. They told of beatings, physical exploitation, and the dangers of escape which British audiences could contrast to the new lives made in Canada and now in Britain. Those sorrows and tribulations were at odds with the humour found in minstrel shows and theatrical productions, and the *joie de vivre* of dance routines. We might conclude that British audiences for minstrelsy were never the same people as those who attended meetings in chapels and town halls to hear black lecturers. But copies of the slavery narratives and leaflets must have reached many corners of the kingdom, and distinction in experiences would not have been complete. Those seeking financial and other assistance from the larger society may have emphasized the poverty of most black Americans, and the search for education certainly stressed their illiteracy: but many Britons were illiterate too. Contemporary sources have shown some evidence of self-reliance, of independent lives, and achievements outside a freed slave existence and a quest for alms.

Josephine and Clarissa Brown, teaching in England in 1854, have been noted. A little earlier William Craft had taught carpentering and cabinet making in Ockham, Surrey and his wife Ellen taught domestic crafts there. They were offered positions as superintendent and matron.[1] Later their house in Hammersmith provided guest accommodation, and William Craft established a school in Africa. He had sufficient income to pay for his children's school fees. Joseph Freeman – the foundry labourer – and his six children are known to us because his 1875 gravestone in Essex states that he had been 'once a slave in New Orleans'.[2] Another labourer was James Johnson, whose *Life of the Late James Johnson (Coloured Evangelist) an Escaped Slave from the Southern States of America: 40 Years resident in Oldham, England* was printed in Oldham in 1914, the year he died. Published by his daughter, it enabled his earlier work in local foundries to be uncovered. She died in 1938.

The three adult children of Isaac Cisco included George Washington Cisco who was working as a cotton spinner in Bolton in 1911. He married in 1920 and died in 1935, thirty years after his African-American father, and also in Bolton where the family had lived from 1883. His unusual surname was useful in the search, unlike John Brown whose *Slave Life in Georgia* was published in London in 1855. Brown settled in Dorset in the 1860s. He worked as a herbalist in Taunton where in mid-1865 he claimed an unpaid bill.[3] His advertisement in the *Sherborne Mercury* on 30 October 1866, and both 22 January and 29 January 1867 stressed he was a black man, the 'celebrated American herbalist' offering pills and tinctures for the stomach, liver, coughs and the eyes. He was based in Durngate Street, Dorchester: the town's 1865 *Kelly's Directory* states that he was a medical botanist.[4]

Some individuals were very much in the public eye but tracing them – and obtaining evidence of their identities – can be tricky. James Johnson worked in 'Chuckey Harris's boxing tent', as a pugilist in fairs. Fairground workers are difficult to identify. Lion tamers were often dark skinned but the exotic nature of their roles led to claims of distant origins. The *Morning Chronicle* (5 January 1858) reported that on 2 January 'Macommo, the negro' had been attacked by a lioness. *The Times* of 6 January 1862 reported Macomo (*sic*) the 'African lion tamer' working with Manders' menagerie in Norwich had again been attacked by a lion. He was mentioned in the press in July 1870 when the touring circus was in Newbury. He now performed with lions and tigers, and had injured his fingers when the pistol used in his act was accidentally discharged.[5] The circus went to Southampton where Maccomo's act was described as 'truly astounding'.[6] Sources on circus and other entertainments suggest he was a West Indian sailor named Arthur Williams who turned to circus work in London. When he was in Bath the 1861 census listed him as Martinia Maccomo, unmarried, aged 25, born in Angola.[7] He died in 1871. 'The lion hunter' Maccomo's gravestone was paid for by showman William Manders.

In 1870 Charles Wood 'a man of colour from South America' (which usually meant the southern U.S.A.) was working with Day's menagerie in Walsall when a bear attacked him.[8] The 1861 census indicates that an American named William Williams was a lion-tamer. He was listed in St Helens, aged 50. In view of the employment of blacks in this line of work, we might assume Williams was of African descent.[9] Yet another lion-tamer was Richard Jorgnis who worked as Dacona at the Aquarium in Shoreditch, London at the beginning of 1880.[10] The watchman responsible for the animals and property there was brought to court in mid-April 1882 charged with causing malicious injury to a lioness, worth £1,000. The witnesses included 'a man of colour' John Humphreys who said he was Alicamousa, a lion-tamer. The watchman was working under notice of dismissal, and seems to have poisoned the lioness.[11] Alicamousa, according to his own testimony, was born in Kingstown in St Vincent in the West Indies in December 1859 and toured in menageries from the 1870s. He was in Scotland by the 1890s.[12]

Blacks working as wild animal 'trainers' were such a part of circus practice that Pinder's Royal Circus, based in Perth, Scotland in May 1896, advertised for a 'young man, colour no object, to perform with two lions' every night.[13] In Tyrone, Ireland a circus sought a man to work with performing animals 'Coloured Man Preferred'. In 1895 Bostock's menagerie then in Pontypool sought a 'Respectable Young Coloured Man' as an animal performer. They were also seeking a youth to box with Bostock's kangaroo in Scotland.[14] Sedgwick's Menagerie was in Pontypridd in late May 1895 when an advertisement in the *Era* stated they wanted a lion-tamer: 'coloured man preferred' to work 'untameable lion', and asked Fred Lee to make contact.[15]

In 1887 a London showman attracted attention to his newly-opened menagerie by having a brass band and also a black man playing a trumpet and banging a gong.[16] Posters and press releases told of a troupe of circus elephants which appeared in the Christmas 1893 show at Covent Garden. 'Eph' Thompson, the elephant trainer, was praised when reviews were listed. A 'handsome man of colour' Thompson was said to have been born in Philadelphia in 1860 and was well-known through Europe from the mid-1880s (his son was born in Russia in 1888).[17] He had two elephants hold a wire on which a female performed. Possibly born in Michigan (in Ypsilanti) or Canada, and probably named Moses, his 1909 grave at Brookwood, Woking states he was '"Eph" Thompson'. He died in the German hospital in Alexandria, Egypt on 17 April 1909. His widow Jessie inherited £6,549.

All of these individuals had forged an independent life. Some of those who fought in the boxing ring, usually bare-fist lengthy bouts which attracted gamblers and the demi-monde, later managed touring shows. Retirement to a settled life as a pub owner was common. Bare-knuckle boxing attracted promoters, gamblers and young men who were prepared to spend hours battling an opponent, the winner receiving the equivalent of a year's income. Again, the claims and publicity of these prize-fighters makes identification difficult.

James 'Jemmy' Wharton is supposed to have been born in Morocco in 1813. He went to sea and in 1833 settled in London where he was billed as 'Jemmy the Black' and fought William 'Bendigo' Thompson in 1837. Undefeated he died from tuberculosis in Liverpool in 1856. John Perry is said to have been born in Nova Scotia (Canada) and also in Dublin. He was transported to Australia in 1847. Fame came to 'the Ebony Phenomenon', Virginia-born James 'Jemmy' Robinson in 1846 who died from cholera in 1849, aged 20. His brother George was a boxer too. Thomas Welsh claimed to be an American, and was known to British boxing fans as 'Young Sambo'. The brutality of the sport is evidenced by his 1845 victory over Bill Jordan in a battle that lasted nearly four hours. He then ran a boxing troupe and was a leading member of the boxing fraternity in London.

The tales – tall or true, we may never know – about boxers include much conflicting evidence, as with Robert Travers who said he had been born in America in 1832. Others suggest he was born in Falmouth and raised in Truro. His father sold crockery in Truro into the 1840s. Bob Travers was active in the 1850s and remained within the boxing fraternity, who frequented his London pub. Eight men organized a prize fight (boxing match) at Bentley near Ipswich in Suffolk and five went on trial in July 1856. Robert Travers aged 24 'man of colour' faced a charge of aiding and abetting. 'The scene was rendered somewhat novel by a man of colour from London attending as a short-hand writer for a sporting paper'. Illegal but popular, such events were held in remote places. Two accused, London publicans, had hired a train to take people to Bentley, doubling its population that day. The crowd was not unruly. The prize money was £100. The defence argued that as the match had been on private ground there could be no serious charge and thus no aiding and abetting. The men had been held in custody but were released on bail for trial at the assizes.[18] They were found guilty but lightly punished.

One month later Travers 'the black' fought Job Cobbley for over three hours, and was described as 'the best man of colour that has been seen in the ring since the days of Young Sambo'. Young Sambo was in attendance at the brutal contest, held in Kent before 2,000 people who travelled there by boat. Travers was the favourite but lost the match.[19] He married and had five children and was last noted in 1904. Young Sambo had demonstrated his skills, sparring at a Leicester Square, London gymnasium in 1851 and in Manchester in December that year.[20] He was also to be seen, as with the Travers vs Cobbley bout, as an assistant or second.[21] That 'man of colour' from a London newspaper suggests blacks participated in other ways.

Plantaganet Green was a teacher of boxing accused of abusing a music teacher named William Ridley in 1877. Green's wife and Ridley's son had been seen together, causing Green to be annoyed but that did not permit him to abuse Ridley or 'invade' his house. A police inspector testified that he had known Green for several years and that he was a peaceable man. The boxer was fined one pound plus costs.[22] Green had been mentioned in the London press in 1869 when he participated in a display of boxing.[23] And in 1874 when he had protected a policeman who was being attacked outside the World's End pub in Chelsea. He was the first to interfere, and prevented two attackers from kicking the officer as he lay on the ground. The report from Clerkenwell court said that Green ('a powerful negro') described himself as an artist 'but his real occupation seemed to be that of a prize-fighter'. His 'general demeanour in the witness-box, and the various slang prize-fighter's expressions used by him in giving his evidence, caused considerable amusement in court'.[24]

We have to guess what was in the mind of the whites who challenged boxing-booth blacks in fairgrounds. Standing outside the booth in view of the public, or being at matches where crowds were in their hundreds, made these sportsmen highly visible and the locations were scattered around the kingdom. Black boxers form a separate stratum in Victorian times.

Banjo playing was associated with America. A pioneer American show in Liverpool in 1842 had Joel Sweeney, a black-face performer, sing and play the banjo. He met with success and toured to London. He was one of the first white Americans to take up the banjo, an instrument so little known that a review of the Virginia Minstrels (which Sweeney joined) in Manchester explained it was 'a rude guitar'. Soon American songs with lines such as 'I'm off to Alabama with a banjo on my knee' were performed to Britons.[25] Four men, the 'Ethiopian Entertainers' singing and playing violin, banjo, tambourine and castanets appeared in London in May 1844.[26] Blacked-up minstrels had a banjo player to offer the British public.[27] Banjo players also performed in the streets, and crowds gathered allowing 'the light-fingered tribe [to] carry on their avocations most successfully' so the Southampton police were ordered to prevent this. Buckinghamshire publicans had grown fed up with one white pair in Aylesbury.[28] Banjo player Samuel Thompson was described as a 'troublesome darkey' after a court appearance in Nottingham in late March 1879. He had been ejected after he refused to leave a pub when his offer to play the banjo was turned down. The banjo and two windows were broken. Thompson went to prison for two months.[29]

Other African Americans, following the ending of slavery in the U.S.A., brought their banjos to Britain. We have noted that in 1878 the London *Morning Post* suggested that the novelty of black actors and actresses made an *Uncle Tom's Cabin* performance interesting. 'Several special artists are to be found in the negro ranks' and the *Post* named the Louisiana Troubadour Quartet and the dancing Slidell children, and praised the excellent banjo playing of Horace Weston.[30] The harmonies of the singers were simple but appealing and 'wonderfully well in tune'.[31] Weston was born in Connecticut in 1825 and died in New York in May 1890.

We have noted James and George Bohee, whose banjo playing and stage performances employed other black people. James died in 1897 and left £43 to his brother. Ira Aldridge, who died touring in Poland in 1867, is listed in English probate records as leaving an estate valued at under £10,000 – a very large sum for that time. He had become a British citizen in 1863 to enable him to pass on title in properties he planned to purchase near Hamlet Road in Upper Norwood. There was sufficient capital for two daughters to be educated in a Belgian convent school but his widow's inexperience in business matters led to the loss of property and the melting down of medals for the gold.[32] Thomas Pinckney's widow left £1,043 to her brother, a London surgeon. Marion Thrift left £4,297 in 1907. Dr Rice left over £3,000 to his daughter when he died in 1935, and George Cisco left £391 to his widow in 1935.

Those with sufficient funds paid for the private education of their children, as with the Aldridge sisters, Sydney Crummell in Warminster, and the Craft children in 1860s London. Perhaps there are surviving school photographs? The children of black Americans – and other visible minorities – are somewhat elusive and we have to guess what impact they had on other youngsters. America was not prepared for black-white marriages of course and the experiences of what was then termed 'mixed-race' British-born children would be a fascinating area of research into the black Atlantic world. Their lives in Britain had to reflect Victorian views on race but insufficient numbers of individuals have been identified to come to conclusions that are statistically valid. It is probable that the lives of most black people in Victorian Britain were little different to the lives of whites.

Some of our ideas have to be changed if not abandoned. The black presence was not restricted to ports although black sailors and their families were to be found there. Theatrical entertainers travelled around the nation, as did lecturers on slavery and temperance. Performances at the Aquarium in Westminster and small provincial theatres are at odds with employment in the private homes of members of high society, as with Mary Webb in London in the 1850s. These individuals were not isolated. They worked alongside stage hands, other performers, theatre managers, and musicians, as well as mixing with members of high society and lowlifes. Christian beliefs took them into the homes of fellow believers, and although it remains uncertain where touring lecturers were accommodated, the homes of local people must have provided rest and shelter. These informal contacts like those of school children are probably not documented. Sharing railway carriages, taking sustenance in coffee shops and cocoa rooms (and pubs), discussing publicity with local printers, also placed black people in close proximity to whites. Sarah Remond's associates in her successful application to become a British citizen are at odds with Nelly Shannon and Mary Ewen the 'coloured ladies' employed by Bohee who were all too public in their associations with whites in 1889. Informal marriages included Ira Aldridge and James Bohee, as well as Gustavus Adolphus Nero Rodman Fraser.

There were links which lack an obvious cause, as with Morgan Smith the actor and Ellen Craft. There is no evidence of any 'black community' outside some of Britain's ports. Work on British ships for black sailors was at low status levels, 'servants, stewards, cooks and cabin boys'.[33] Low and uncertain incomes do not encourage friendships which would probably cease when work on a ship was found. Sailors bonded on voyages, not just on the streets of Cardiff, Liverpool, Glasgow, London and Southampton. Kathy Chater has raised serious doubts about earlier historians identifying black communities in pre-Victorian Britain, and warns of using American experience to understand the British black presence.[34]

That presents a mirror to this work, for we know little about what American blacks in Victorian Britain thought of life in the kingdom. The understandable cut-off date of 1865 is an American calendar and did not apply in Britain, for black refugees and settlers did not rush back across the Atlantic when the civil war ended and slavery was abolished. There were also fresh arrivals as we have seen. It would be fascinating to discover what the Craft children thought of America, what motivated Dr Powell to return to Liverpool, and why Thomas Lewis Johnson settled in late 1890s England (and became a British citizen). Sarah Remond's self-exile, British citizenship, and life in Italy raise several questions. That individuals are somewhat elusive despite their achievements and publications taunts the researcher, for the mists that obscure their lives in Britain cover others such as Nelly Shannon and Mary Ewen, Sydney Crummell, Rose and Minnie Avery or Avon, and Thomas Pinckney. Some individuals are paradoxes, being both well-known and elusive as with Harriet Jacobs and her months in England, and the legends linking Joseph Henson to Uncle Tom.

Similar difficulties appear when examining the evidence of black Victorians with Caribbean or African roots, but those raised in the British West Indies were more likely to have attended school and attained a level of literacy similar to the British and Irish. As we have noted with Dr Horton, education in colonial Sierra Leone could be of a high standard and there were other medical doctors trained and active in late nineteenth-century Britain.

Some lives show unexpected achievements, unexpected to those who have failed to consider the vibrant black strand in Victorian history. This is seen in the short life of a Barbados-born graduate of Aberdeen University. Dr Christopher James Davis had also studied in London and was working at St Bartholomew's Hospital when he went to France in 1870 to attend to the wounded in the Franco-Prussian War. At Sedan he attended wounded Bavarians, organized soup for peasants whose property had been destroyed in the fighting, collected financial support in England and caught smallpox back in Sedan and died on 27 November 1870 at Pont Mangy. He was buried in France, aged 28. The grave marker indicates that he worked for that London hospital.[35] The Plymouth Brethren section of British Christianity has been responsible for our knowledge of this black man whose *Grace and Truth and Aids to Believers* went into an eighteenth edition by 1912.

African Americans in London could have met Dr Davis at the hospital, others would have heard of him. More would have read about the three African chiefs and their attendants who toured England in 1895 and met numerous Britons.[36] British-born black people achieved fame in areas out of reach in the United States. The achievements of Robert Branford were uncovered in 2016. Born in Stoke by Nayland in Suffolk in May 1817 he joined the Metropolitan Police in 1838. Branford was promoted to sergeant in 1846, became an inspector in 1851 and superintendent of M-Division (Southwark) in 1856. He retired in 1866 and died in 1869.[37] Samuel Coleridge-Taylor whose father was a medical student from Sierra Leone, was born in London in 1875 and was raised by his mother in Croydon. He attended the Royal College of Music in London for seven years and at the end of the century was being noted for his compositions in the musical and London press. He was influenced, in 1897, by choir leader Frederick Loudin and visiting poet Paul Laurance Dunbar.[38]

It seems that a biography of William Peter Powell would be a useful contribution to this topic, as would a detailed account of Nelson Countee. It is to be hoped that this study will encourage such ventures.

Chapter 14

Postscript

William Ivens Craft, retired coal merchant, died aged 70, in west London in 1926. His children and grandchildren knew about his American ancestry. At this time Coleridge-Taylor's *Hiawatha* was performed for two weeks every summer in central London's Royal Albert Hall – the only composer to receive such treatment (which continued into 1939). Visiting African-American musicians included tenor Roland Hayes, whose concert hall recitals were popular and might be seen as paving the way for Paul Robeson in the 1930s.

African Americans knew that between 40,000 and 50,000 Canadians had fought against the Confederacy and many believed that Queen Victoria had made an offer to purchase the enslaved Americans and then liberate them, which had been rejected by the South.[1] Choir leader and world traveller Frederick Loudin was in Britain in 1900 when he wrote to journalist John Edward Bruce about the reported feelings in America over the new war in South Africa, suggesting a cause was that the British had refused to allow Boers to enslave Africans. Before praising the British sentiment towards Coleridge-Taylor whose complete *Hiawatha* had just been premiered at London's Albert Hall, Loudin wrote: 'I need not tell you what Britain has been to us. This country has passed resolutions at large and influential meetings condemning lynching,' he added.[2]

And the United States? Segregation, legal inequality and violence. On 1 June 1921 a white mob invaded the black community of Tulsa, Oklahoma and destroyed thirty-four blocks, burning churches and homes, killing 300 people. The 'regions of wickedness' had expanded. American settlers had moved into the lands of the Native American, with the land rush of 1889 and Oklahoma's entry as a state in 1907. Tim Madigan's study should be read by those wondering about the differences over 'race' in Britain and America.[3]

Chapter 15

Genealogical Trees do not flourish among Slaves

The men and women who told the British and Irish about slavery in America exhibited determination and diplomacy. They had a legitimacy and authenticity which white co-workers could never claim.[1] Richard Blackett also observed that they were pragmatic when schisms among white abolitionists were common, and they moved between factions. The leaflets, narratives, lectures and public appearances were widespread, numerous and also enabled the Americans to earn a living, which provided some independence for people whose lives in America had been confined and starved of resources.

Fighting oppression was not restricted to African Americans in Britain, for others had similar ambitions, including the Italians who mingled with Sarah Remond at the Taylors in Aubrey House. The Americans also had dreams, those often vague beliefs which sustain the exile. Some settled down in Britain, finding tranquillity and friendships: James Johnson in Oldham, Freeman in Chelmsford. Some had a global vision, a wide focus. Roper considered farming in South Africa; Robert Johnson thought of being a doctor in Africa; the Coppins became missionaries in Cape Town; Crummell was just one who went to Liberia, and several settled in Jamaica. There was William Craft's school in Dahomey. Dreams of a world free from alcoholism, a world strong in the Christian faith, became a moral crusade for some, and had been present in many, from the university-educated Pennington, evangelist Zilpha Elaw and foundry worker James Johnson.

The funds which enabled the Americans to purchase the freedom of their relatives has been seen as part of white patronage, but income from the sale of leaflets and narratives, and wages earned in various occupations, can be overlooked. The impostors were all too aware of the public's willingness and gullibility. Skills such as William Craft's carpentry, Horace Weston's musical talent, Isaiah Powell's work making barrels, Robert Harlan's knowledge of horses, the journalism of William Wells Brown and Elizabeth Greenfield's singing need to be respected as does the labouring of sailors and house servants. We may be sceptical over Lewis the hypnotist and fairground hustlers of any colour, but they survived.

Clarissa and Josephine Brown, the Crafts at Ockham school and William Allen were school teachers whilst John Anderson was the largest (and oldest) pupil at John Pool's village school in Corby in 1861. Thomas Pinckney and Francis Anderson taught in Canada after training in London. Whilst there, Pinckney married a white fellow teacher. They went to England where the 1871 street directory of Southampton records them.

The countless servants and numerous sailors of Victorian times have appeared in these pages when they have been mentioned in the newspapers, a sometimes unfortunate bias that is not resolved easily which is why the Jamaican Mary Ann Styles has been detailed, a London servant for sixty years.

We can only wonder about Jesse Ewing Glasgow of Edinburgh University who died so young, and the lost life of John Glasgow the Lancashire settler sold into slavery in Georgia.

Frederick Douglass commented in his *My Bondage and My Freedom* (1853) that 'genealogical trees do not flourish among slaves'. By presenting even fragments of individuals it is hoped that more will be uncovered on the lives of African Americans in Victorian Britain – who had been born in servitude and lived in freedom.

Chapter 16

What Happened Next?

Ira Aldridge died in Poland in 1867 leaving four children who had been born in England. The illegitimate Ira Daniel migrated to Australia in 1867 and died in Melbourne in 1894. Frederick, born in 1862, died in Scarborough in August 1886. Amanda and Luranah studied music in Belgium and shared a home in London where Luranah died in 1932. Amanda died in 1956, a day short of her ninetieth birthday.

Henry Allen or Jacobs may have been from Virginia but he may have gone back to sea after his frauds led to five years in prison in 1870.

William G. Allen remained in London into the late 1860s but what happened to him and his children has not been discovered.

Francis Anderson trained as a teacher in London 1853-1856 and was sponsored to Maidstone in Ontario, Canada.

John Anderson was sent to Liberia in 1862 but there is no evidence that he settled there. Brode in his *The Odyssey of John Anderson*, pp 120-121 suggests that Anderson, a trained craftsman, may have migrated to Ghana or may have returned to Europe for 'he was not enthusiastic about going to West Africa'.

Rose and Minnie Avery (or Avon) and their father have not been traced after 1857.

Jacob Baltimore appeared as a witness at the Dunlo divorce in 1889 but has then only been traced in Hackney in the 1891 census.

James Bland died in Philadelphia in May 1911. His compositions are still played.

James Douglas Bohee and George Bohee had children outside marriage. James Bohee's 'wife' Matilda Farquhar died in 1940. There are descendants in Australia. George Bohee was in Britain into 1912, and died in New York in 1930. James Joyce mentioned the Bohees in *Ulysses*.

Hallie Quinn Brown died in Wilberforce, Ohio in September 1949, aged 100.

Henry 'Box' Brown returned to America in the 1870s. He died in Toronto in 1897. His widow and their married daughter were living in Pennsylvania in 1920.[1]

John Brown is said to have died in London in 1876.

William Wells Brown spent five years in Britain and Europe, into 1854, returning in the summer of 1877. He died near Boston, Massachusetts in November 1884 where his grave was marked in 2001. His daughter Clarissa (Clara) remained in Britain where her first husband died. Around 1861 she moved to Salford, Manchester to work as a governess. She became an entertainer, married George W. Sylvester in Bradford in 1871 and died in April 1874 in the workhouse in Leeds. She was buried in an unmarked common grave in Beckett Street cemetery.[2] Josephine stayed in America, married, and died from tuberculosis in Massachusetts in January 1874.

Robert Campbell had his family relocate (via England) to Lagos where he died in 1884, a rare 1850s black advocate of African-American migration to Africa who settled in the continent.

Laura Carr toured England in the Fisk Trio in the 1900s.

Lewis Charlton died in Sheffield in March 1888.

Molliston Madison Clark wrote *Tract on American Slavery* (Bradford, 1847). He died in 1872.

James Cooney appears in several postcards of Day's troupe in the 1910s, the clue that triggered a search.[3] The *Morecambe and Heysham Visitor and Lancaster Advertiser* of 9 March 1932 headed its obituary 'Jimmy Cooney's adventurous life'. Valet, sailor, circus clown, boxer and entertainer, and described him as the 'son of slave parents'. He was a theatre commissionaire in Morecambe in the 1920s. He had two children.

Fanny Jackson Coppin died in Philadelphia in January 1913. She and her husband worked in Cape Town 1902-1903, espousing temperance.

Charles Costa or Foster remains untraced after 1862.

(Francis) Nelson Countee's daughter Lucy was born in Aston, Birmingham in 1875 and married Ambrose Day in Leicester in 1901. A photograph of that wedding clearly shows her African descent.[4] Ambrose Day and Lucy Countee Day remained together into 1945 when she died. In 1947 Ambrose married his deceased wife's sister Florence, a widow. She had married William Bott in Hinckley in 1904. She seems to have died in 1962. The sole male child of Countee was Charles William Countee, the 'coloured vocalist' (*Era*, 13 October 1900) in Ashton-under-Lyne where he was on the same variety bill as his nieces Phyllis Mabel and Olga Marion Seville or the Two Countees, a singing act which toured from 1897 into 1914. Phyllis's daughter Pauline Voss was to study at the Royal Academy of Dramatic Art and for many years worked for the long-running radio soap *The Archers*.[5] Charles Countee died aged 38 in 1905.

Ellen and William Craft, and her mother Maria from 1865, were in London until 1869. They left Liverpool on 24 August 1869: Ellen and William, Charles, Ellen, Alfred and baby Mary left Brougham and William Jr to continue their education. William Ivens Craft returned to England in 1881. In September 1912 William Ivens Craft was declared to be a coal agent when his daughter Ellen married Claude Clark in Paddington. A witness to this wedding was Ellen Craft Crum, William's sister. She had married Dr William D. Crum, one of a handful of black doctors in Charleston, South Carolina and he had been US Minister to Liberia in 1910. It was in their home that her father, the escaped slave, died in 1900. Her mother had died in Georgia in 1891. Ellen Crum rushed back to South Carolina after the wedding, for her doctor husband was about to die (a malady from Liberia, it is believed). The son of that London marriage died in Hounslow in 1984.

William Ivens Craft died in Hounslow in 1926. His baby sister died very early.

Charles Estlin Phillips Craft had a long life and died in America in 1938. The Atlantic did not stop the families from staying in contact, and American relatives visited in 1972 and the 1980s, and went to Ockham too.[6] British relatives have been to Boston and Macon.

Alexander Crummell died in Philadelphia in September 1898. His widow Jennie, along with the wife of his son Sydney, and a daughter probably Frances who had been born in Bath in June 1849, attended the funeral in New York.

Paul Daniels studied in Colwyn Bay, North Wales until 1899 when he returned to South Carolina where he assisted at and then headed the Jenkins Orphanage in Charleston. He died in December 1961.

William Howard Day returned to America in 1863 and settled in Harrisburg, Pennsylvania where he died in December 1900.

Isaac Dickerson died in Plumstead, south-east London in early 1900. He had lived there for ten years, and preached around London.

George Dixon wrote or allowed his name to appear as the author of *A Treatise on Boxing* of 1893. He died in New York in 1909.

David Dorr returned to America and ran to freedom in Ohio where he wrote his *A Colored Man Round the World* in 1858. He was injured in the

Civil War, and seems to have died in 1872. His book was rediscovered after more than a century.

Frederick Douglass died in Rochester, New York in February 1895, a highly-respected person. His years in Britain have been understated in this book as he would have overshadowed the others, and he has been well-documented by other historians. David Blight's biography will be published by Yale in 2018.

Paul Dunbar died from tuberculosis in Dayton, Ohio in February 1906. Part of his fame among Britons is his influence on London-born composer Samuel Coleridge-Taylor, dated incorrectly to 1896 by the composer's first biographer.

Alexander Duval had a difficult time in 1850s England and his fate is unknown but a return to his wife Mary and daughter in New Bedford, Massachusetts seems likely.

Zilpha Elaw (Mrs Ralph Shum) died in London in 1873.

Francis Fedric and his wife are being researched. His *Slave Life in Virginia and Kentucky: Fifty Years of Slavery* was published in London in 1863 (and apparently again in Liverpool in 1869) with a preface by a Wolverhampton vicar.

Gustavus Adolphus Nero Rodman Fraser mentioned in the British press in 1885-1886 is untraced after the 1891 census. His career in America has been researched.[7]

Charles Freeman of Barrow-in-Furness 1880 is untraced.

Joseph Freeman died in Chelmsford in November 1875. His six children have not been traced.

Henry Highland Garnet died in Liberia in February 1882. His wife Juliet had died and he remarried.

Jesse Ewing Glasgow died in Edinburgh in December 1860.

John Glasgow's fate is unknown.

Moses Grandy's activities in Britain after his narrative was published are unknown except in 1861 when he was in Cambridge.

Jacob D. Green's *Narrative of the Life of J.D. Green, a Runaway Slave, from Kentucky containing an Account of his Three Escapes* was published in Huddersfield in 1864. Its forty pages end when he reached Canada in 1848. He has not been traced.

Elizabeth Taylor Greenfield died in Philadelphia in March 1876.

Banjo maestro James Warren Griffin seems to have died in Newcastle in the winter of 1902-1903.

William Anderson Hall was in Cardiff in 1862 and may have returned to Canada.

Robert J. Harlan died in 1897. He supported migration within the U.S.A. and thousands went west to Kansas. He was based in Cincinnati. Where his daughter is buried is untraced.

Walter Hawkins returned to Chatham, Ontario where he died in July 1894. Celestine Edwards's biography has been republished.

John Henry 'the Black Knight' Hector's life was detailed in the British press in 1896-1899. He returned to America where he died in 1914.

Amy Height from Boston, Massachusetts who was at a Sheffield theatre in 1889 had some British appearances noted in the *Stage* from 1883 into 1913. She died in London in March 1913, aged 46.

Josiah Henson died in Canada in 1883, respected perhaps for wrong reasons. He was a symbol as well as a man.

John Andrew Jackson and his wife Julia, who spent the 1850s in Britain, are the subject of research by Susanna Ashton.

Harriet Ann Jacobs (Linda Brent) died in Washington, DC in March 1897. In 2008 the University of North Carolina Press published 103 documents relating to her.

John Jacobs the brother of Harriet Jacobs lived in England with a British wife into the 1860s. He was an activist and a sailor. He died in 1875.

Daniel Jenkins died in Charleston, South Carolina in 1937. His orphanage now deals with the elderly. His son Edmund attended the Royal Academy of Music in London 1914-1921. A daughter born in Wigan, Lancashire in 1906 was raised there and retained a Lancashire accent in the 1980s after sixty years in America.

Esther Ann 'Hettie' Johnson married black actor Jack Kavala in 1901 (who worked in a *Cabin* show in London in August 1892 and at the Shakespeare Theatre in August 1893). Kavala's real name was Edward John Gillon. The couple moved out of the entertainment business. She died in Fareham in 1973, aged 102.[8]

Frank Johnson returned to Philadelphia in 1838 after a year in Britain, introduced European-style promenade concerts to Americans, and died in Philadelphia in April 1844.

James Johnson and his wife Charity and daughter Charlotte seem to have settled in Liverpool through the 1850s.

James Alfred Johnson died in Oldham, Lancashire in 1914, aged 66. His daughter Alice died in Oldham in 1938.

Lewis Johnson went away with his French employer in the late 1850s.

Robert M. Johnson spent nearly ten years in Britain but we do not know if he went to practise medicine in Africa or Kentucky after he qualified.

Thomas Lewis Johnson and his wife Sarah lived in Bournemouth into the 1920s. He died there in 1921 and his widow in 1928. Copies of his *Twenty-Eight Years a Slave* were far from rare in the town's used bookshops in the 1980s when veterans still recalled him.

William Henry Jones died in Chatham, Ontario in 1874.[9]

Josephine who reached Liverpool in February 1856 is untraced.

John Kendrick may have taken his name from other black pugilists named Kendrick. His 1854 death registration has not been located.

Billy Kersands kept performing in the black-face tradition, and danced and entertained in the minstrel manner. He died in New Mexico in 1915.

Thomas M. Kinnaird returned to Toronto.

Edmund Kelly (Edmond Kelley) returned to New Bedford, Massachusetts in 1853 then settled in Philadelphia. His *A Family Redeemed from Bondage* had been published in New Bedford in 1851. An active and respected New England church leader he died in 1894.

William James Lathom, the racetrack tipster of Merseyside seems to have died in West Derby, Liverpool, in the summer of 1906, aged 71.

Mattie Lawrence lived in Croydon with her husband from 1890. Henry Thrift died in 1905, aged 46, and she died in February 1907. They were buried in Queen's Road cemetery. They had two daughters Gladys and Amy. Amy married a soldier from New Zealand and died in 1931; a son lived in New Zealand. Gladys also married, and died in 1954.

Henry E. Lewis the mesmerist died in London in 1857.

Frederick Loudin spent months in a sanatorium in Scotland, returned to Ohio where he owned a shoe factory, and died in 1904 just days before his London-born friend Samuel Coleridge-Taylor reached Washington, sponsored by Loudin and his associates. He visited Harriet the widow in Ravenna, Ohio.

Mary Ann McCam lived in North Shields until she died in 1893. She was buried in Preston Village cemetery in North Shields. No children have been identified.

Millie and Christine McKoy died in North Carolina in October 1912.

Joseph Manna's origins are obscure but we know he died in prison in Scotland in the winter of 1869-1870.

George Marshall returned to America in late 1855, apparently with the manuscript of a book. He had been in Australia.

John Sella Martin died in August 1876 in New Orleans.

John Miller's testimony in Hinckley in 1889 was his last known public appearance.

William Mitchell admitted his falsehoods in a letter written in Ramsgate, Kent in March 1864 and published in the *Anti-Slavery Reporter* of May. He is believed to have died before 1880.

Paulus Moort was active in education in Liberia and his wife Mary supported Marcus Garvey's Universal Negro Improvement Association in 1920s Liberia.

Reuben Nixon's tricks and lies were noted from 1853 to 1858. Thereafter: silence.

John Sayers Orr died in prison in British Guiana in 1857.

Henry Parker died in Bristol in late 1905, aged 80. We do not know why unverifiable claims were made that he had escaped slavery in Florida.

Daniel A. Payne became a bishop and highly respected elder of the AME Church. He opposed American migration to Africa. He died in November 1893.

Nathaniel Paul died in Albany, New York in 1839.

James Pennington died in Florida in October 1870.

Nicholson Darlington Pickett disappeared after the court case of 1891.

Thomas Pinckney of South Carolina had worked four years in Liberia before being sent to Chatham, Ontario (Canada) where he ran a school for black refugees. Married to Elizabeth King, an English Canadian in 1860, the couple soon left and settled in Southampton, England.[10] They made a home at 14 Avenue Road. The 1871 census indicates he was not employed as a minister and they had a 12-year-old general servant. This census says he was born in Pennsylvania and was a naturalized British subject. The 1881 census states he had been born in Charleston. Both indicate that his wife had been born in Ashford, Kent. He died aged 70 in December 1887 and his widow in March 1889, aged 72.

Maggie Porter of the first Fisk touring choir outlived her colleagues. She died in Detroit in 1942, aged 89. She vowed never to set foot in the South again – breaking it to return to Nashville in 1931 to celebrate the sixtieth anniversary of the choir setting off.

Isaiah Powell returned to England and was listed at a boarding in 53 Saxony Road, West Derby in the 1901 census which recorded that he was a cooper and unmarried. He was living in Prescot Street, West Derby in Liverpool when Dr William Powell Jr was with him when he died on 7 June 1902. The death registration states he was a journeyman cooper (self-employed barrel maker). William remained in Liverpool, moving to a nursing home in Kirkdale where he died in April 1916, aged 81.[11] Their father was last noted in 1879 when in San Francisco but that was probably the namesake son who had moved to California. He was still in New York in 1873. Philip Foner's request in 1978 that 'the existence of William P. Powell be acknowledged' remains valid.[12]

Caroline Remond Putnam visited her sister in England in 1859. She died in 1908.

Charles Lenox Remond died in Massachusetts in December 1873.

Sarah Parker Remond was in England from 1859, became a British citizen in 1865, and went to Italy where she qualified in medicine. She died in Rome in 1894. A memorial plaque was only mounted in 2013, for Remond was registered under her Italian husband's name which was unknown to researchers for decades.

Dr George Rice died in February 1935, aged 86. His daughter Mary Lucinda Rice ran a private school at the 50 Egmont Road house in Sutton, and died in 1967, aged 85. She never married. The house clearer was of African descent and rescued family photographs.

Martha Ann Ricks' portrait photograph taken in London ('The Queen's Liberian Visitor') and a sketch are in the National Portrait Gallery, London. She died in Liberia in 1901. Kyra Hicks wrote *Martha Ann's Quilt for Queen Victoria* in 2012.

Jane Rose Roberts lived in London until her death in January 1914, aged 95. She is buried in an unmarked grave in Streatham cemetery, Garratt Lane. Descendants of her sister, living in Pittsburgh, plan to mark the plot.

In 1867 Annie Roper sailed on the *Atlanta* to Australia, to work as a governess. Annie married Thomas Edward Donehue in 1871. He died in 1886: she died in 1927 and that line continues.[13]

Thomas Rutling died in Harrogate, Yorkshire in April 1915. He wrote *Tom, an Autobiography with Revised Negro Melodies*. In 2014 a plaque was placed on his home in Valley Drive, Harrogate.

Felix Scott the Liverpool-based boxer was still active in the 1900s. He was born in the Bahamas. There may be a link to the unlicensed peddler of Worcester of 1886.

Ella Sheppard, another Fisk pioneer, died in 1914. She was a friend of Frederick Douglass in his old age.

John Simons, the cook ill-treated in Charleston, is not traced after 1843.

Edward Simpson the sailor recaptured near Cardiff in 1843 vanished.

Georgina Simpson worked as a teacher, received a PhD in German studies in 1921, and was a professor at Howard University in Washington, DC where she died in 1944.

Amanda Smith died in Florida in February 1915.

Henry Smith who stole from his employer in Wolverhampton in 1857 is untraced.

James Caesar Anthony Smith broke away from Henry 'Box' Brown in mid-1851.

James McCune Smith left Britain by 1839 and died on Long Island in 1865. Classified as black in the US census of 1850 he was white in 1860, a definition which continued to be applied to his widow and children.

Samuel Morgan Smith and his wife Mary are being investigated by Aldridge biographer Bernth Lindfors. Smith was buried in the General Cemetery, Sheffield. Their son died on the Isle of Man in 1870.

Peter Thomas Stanford married Beatrice Mabel Stickley in 1888 and left Birmingham in 1895 to investigate lynching in America. His *The Tragedy of the Negro in America* was published in Boston in 1897. He remained there and died in Cambridge, Massachusetts in May 1909.

Cassie Stevens may have remained in England.

Dugald Sutherland's last known public appearance was at the Old Bailey in late 1857.

Benjamin Tanner became a bishop in 1888. He died in Washington, DC in January 1923. His son Henry Ossawa Tanner (1859-1937) settled in France in 1891 where his paintings, generally on Christian themes, were respected.

John Taylor was noted in Rotherham in 1843.

Frederick Bruce Thomas died in Turkey in 1928. Descendants live in France where lingerie-designer Chantal Thomass (*sic* – the double S enables French speakers to pronounce the name in the American manner) has a fashionable shop in Paris.

'Eph' Thompson died in Egypt in 1909 and was buried in Brookwood cemetery in Surrey. His British family continues a century later.

Samuel Thompson and his banjo have not been traced after 1879.

Robert 'Bob' Travers the pugilist was in Sevenoaks, Kent in 1871 and seems to have been living in England in 1904 but his fate is untraced.

Carlos Trower's great-grandson is investigating his ancestor.

Charles Thomas Walker died in Augusta, Georgia in July 1921 and was buried close to his church which thrives. A local school carries his name.

Cassandra Walmer and her father continued in theatrical work. He died in Rowley Regis, Staffordshire in March 1897. She was in Cardiff in

January 1906, went to New Zealand in mid-1907, and married in Brixton (London) in June 1911. She and her husband went to Australia in 1928.[14]

Samuel Ringgold Ward left England for Jamaica in 1855 where he died in 1866.

Booker T. Washington died at his Alabama college in November 1915. A daughter was educated in Germany. From 1895 he was widely seen as African-America's spokesman. His birthplace in the western uplands of Virginia was declared a national monument in 1956, a century after his birth.

James Watkins stayed in England after his wife Mary returned to America. He was in Baltimore, Maryland when the US census was taken in 1880. The fate of the children is not known.

William Watson whose claims led to allegations of fraud in 1856-1858 has not been traced after that.

Mary Webb died in Jamaica in June 1859 and her husband, Frank, in Texas in May 1894. They had moved to Jamaica in 1858. He had a family with a Jamaican woman but returned to America on his own in 1869. His novel *The Garies* was rediscovered in the late 1960s.

Stella Weims died in Jamaica in 1855 after four years with the Garnets in Britain.

Ida B. Wells died in Chicago in March 1931. Her autobiography was published in 1972.

Horace Weston toured Europe, and died in New York in May 1890.

'Blind Tom' Wiggins died near New York in June 1908.

Charles Williams and his shackles have not been traced after 1858.

John Williams and his family went to Canada.

William Williams who mixed with the roughs of Dundee in the 1860s is untraced and seems unlikely to be the firewood seller of West Hartlepool, 1878.

The Wilmington choir may have posed for photographs but one likely group image has not been positively identified.

Joseph 'Black Joe' Wilson of Belfast who died in December 1887 has an unknown burial place.

Alfred Thomas Wood's activities after his prison sentence in Hull in 1853 have not been traced.

Joseph Woodhouse remains an enigma.

Frederick Wright's life after his trial in Fife in 1867 included prison, but after that we have nothing.

Notes

Introduction

1. Howard Dobson, foreword, *Give Me Your Tired, Your Poor...? Voluntary Black Migration to the United States* (New York: Schomburg Center, 1986), p.5.
2. Sylviane A. Diouf, *Dreams of Africa in Alabama: The Slave Ship* Clotilda *and the Story of the Last Africans brought to America* (New York: Oxford University Press, 2007).
3. Eugene D. Genovese, *Roll, Jordan, Roll: The World the Slaves Made* (London: Andre Deutsch, 1975), p.648.
4. Genovese, *Roll, Jordan, Roll*, p.657.
5. Benjamin Quarles, *Black Abolitionists* (New York: Oxford University Press, 1969), p.136.
6. Bernth Lindfors, *Ira Aldridge: The Early Years 1807-1833* (University of Rochester Press, 2011); *Ira Aldridge: The Vagabond Years 1833-1852* (University of Rochester Press, 2011); *Ira Aldridge: Performing Shakespeare in Europe, 1852-1855* (University of Rochester Press, 2013).
7. Ezra Greenspan, *William Wells Brown: An African American Life* (New York: Norton, 2014).
8. Richard J.M. Blackett, *Building an Antislavery Wall: Black Americans in the Atlantic Abolitionist Movement 1830-1860* (Baton Rouge: Louisiana State University Press, 1983); Richard J.M. Blackett, *Beating Against the Barriers: Biographical Essays in Nineteenth-Century Afro-American History* (Baton Rouge: Louisiana State University Press, 1986).
9. Yale University Press published volumes of his papers; his autobiographical writings are easy to find; and there are numerous studies. David Blight's study is scheduled for 2018.
10. Jeffrey Ruggles, *The Unboxing of Henry Brown* (Richmond: Library of Virginia, 2003).
11. The National Archives, Kew (London) HO 1/123/4809.
12. The birth of Charles William Countee was registered in Warwick in early 1867. Nelson Countee's name came to my attention from reports in Leicester newspapers of 1870.

13. Black entertainers in Continental Europe from the 1890s are documented in Rainer Lotz, *Black People: Entertainers of African Descent in Europe, and Germany* (Bonn: Birgit Lotz Verlag, 1997).

14. Nicole King, '"A Colored Woman in Another Country Pleading for Justice in Her Own": Ida B. Wells in Great Britain', Gretchen Holbrook Gerzina (ed.), *Black Victorians/Black Victoriana* (New Brunswick NJ: Rutgers University Press, 2003), pp.88-109.

15. C. Peter Ripley (ed.), *The Black Abolitionist Papers. Vol. 1: The British Isles, 1830-1865* (Chapel Hill: University of North Carolina Press, 1985), p.62.

16. Peter Fryer, *Staying Power: the History of Black People in Britain* (London: Pluto Press, 1984), p.435. The narrative had appeared in parts earlier, and its sexual candour was a problem for publishers. A British edition appeared in 1862 and the book was reviewed in the anti-slavery press of England. See www.docsouth.unc.edu/fpm/jacobs.

17. *Morecambe and Heysham Visitor* and *Lancaster Advertiser*, 9 March 1932, p.6. My thanks to John Rogan, Lancashire County Libraries, Morecambe.

18. *Portsmouth Times*, 12 July 1856, p.5.

19. *Bristol Mercury*, 27 October 1885.

20. The National Archives, census 2 April 1871, RG 10/3288, Short Street, Leicester.

21. *Sheffield Independent*, 25 May 1850, p.6; *Roscommon Messenger*, 1 June 1850, pp.1, 2; *Dumfries and Galloway Standard*, 4 September 1850 and 16 October 1850; he died in Blackheath, London, *Dumfries and Galloway Standard*, 30 September 1857, p.4 and registration of death 10 July 1857 gave his age as 39. *Aberdeen Free Press*, 2 March 1855, p.4 has his forenames.

22. www.search.connectinghistories.org.uk Esther Ann Johnson; thanks to Helen Franklin and Stephen Bourne.

23. T.W.E. Roche, *The Key in the Lock: Immigration Control in England from 1066 to the Present Day* (London: John Murray, 1969), p.61.

24. Roche, *The Key in the Lock*, p.62.

Chapter 1

1. Moses Roper, *Narrative of my Escape from Slavery* (London: Darton, Harvey, and Darton, 1838; repr. Mineola, NY: Dover Publications, 2014), p.37 from *Narrative of the Adventures and Escape of Moses Roper from American Slavery* (Berwick upon Tweed, 1848). The first edition was 1837. There were ten editions by 1856. Roper, *Narrative*, pp.48-49, 52; the 1848 edition is the source on Roper's British venues. *See* docsouth.uncedu/neh/roper/roperhtm.

2. *Aberdeen Journal*, 8 July 1846 quoting the *Dumfries Courier.*

3. *Luton Times*, 25 August 1860, p.4.

NOTES

4. *West Surrey Times* (Guildford), 13 October 1855, p.4.
5. I am indebted to Professor L. David Roper for access to http://www.roperld. com/RoperMoses.htm and to The National Archives, Kew, RG 9/1025 census Merthyr Tydfil, 1861.
6. Email to Jeffrey Green from Rita Hughes in Australia, 22 March 2015. She never met her great grandmother who died when she was a child.
7. Freebmd Newport quarter ending September 1883 11a 313; El Karey had studied at Regent's Park College in London, worked for the Palestine Christian Union Mission, and was based in Nablus. Isabel Burton in 1875/1876 noted his wife was an 'English lady' but this could not have been Alice Roper. Family legends suggest their daughter married a doctor and remained in Palestine/ Egypt.
8. 'A Colored Lecturer Dead', *New York Times*, 17 April 1891, p.1.
9. Zilpha Elaw, *Memoirs of the Life, Religious Experience, and Ministerial Travels and Labours of Mrs. Zilpha Elaw, an American Female of Colour* (London: 1846), p.74.
10. *Kendal Mercury*, 24 July 1847, p. 3; *Kendal Mercury*, 14 August 1847, p.3.
11. My thanks to David Killingray.
12. Elaw, *Memoirs*, pp.4, 139, 144-145. A search of freebmd.co.uk uncovered the marriage. The book is on line at archive.org/details/MinisterialTravels. The *Kentish Mercury* of 20 August 1864 reported this 'lady of colour' had given two sermons at the Bethel Chapel on 13 August.
13. Elaw, *Memoirs*, pp.139, 144-145.
14. Elaw, *Memoirs*, p.8.
15. *The Times* (London), 3 June 1840, p.5.
16. National Portrait Gallery, London.
17. *Standard* (London), 23 September 1841; *The Times* (London), 23 September 1841, p.4.
18. *Standard* (London), 26 August 1840; *Morning Post* (London), 29 August 1840; *Freeman's Journal* (Dublin), 7 November 1840.
19. *The Times* (London), 14 May 1842, p.10 noted L'Instant of Haiti; *The Times* (London), 22 June 1842, p.9 noted the presence of numerous women.
20. *The Times* (London), 22 June 1843, p.3.
21. *Caledonian Mercury* (Edinburgh), 30 June 1851 quoting the *Kelso Chronicle*.
22. Harriet Ann Jacobs, *Incidents in the Life of a Slave Girl* (1861) pp.276-278, on www.docsouth.unc.edu/fpn/jacobs.
23. Information from Lesley Russell in Australia using family papers. See page 131 of www.jeffreygreen.co.uk.
24. www.twmuseums.org.uk/slavery/online-exhibition/mary-ann-macham. Thanks to Sean Creighton.
25. Tynemouth marriage registration quarter ending September 1841, ref. 25.367.

26. *Cornwall Royal Gazette* (Truro), 4 September 1846; *Sheffield and Rotherham Independent* (Sheffield) 12 September 1846, p.8; *Bradford and Wakefield Observer* (Bradford), 17 September 1846, p.5.
27. Frederick Douglass, *My Bondage and My Freedom* chapter 24 and pp.374-375.
28. *The Times* (London), 8 April 1847.
29. www.bulldozia.com Jim Crow in Britain 1847; *The Times* (London), 6 April 1847; three letters on 13 April and one from Douglass in the U.S.A. on 14 April 1847.
30. *West Briton*, 14 March 1861.
31. *Exeter and Plymouth Gazette*, 5 March 1853 p.8 noted the 'large and respectable' audience for Brown in Launceston. He lectured in the Isle of Wight in 1855 (*Isle of Wight Observer*, 31 March 1855, p.3); *New Georgia Encyclopedia* on line. *See* jeffreygreen.co.uk/133.
32. *Plymouth and Devonport Weekly Journal* (Plymouth) 17 April 1851 reported Brown's speech mentioning Glasgow at the Guildhall, Plymouth, 9 April 1851.
33. *Western Gazette*, 8 May 1868, p.7; *Western Gazette*, 23 June 1865, p.5; *Dorset County Chronicle*, 23 March 1865, p.8.
34. My thanks to Ed Bristow, Dorset History Centre.
35. *Bristol Mercury*, 21 April 1855; *Isle of Wight Observer* (Ryde), 7 June 1856; *Western Gazette*, 11 March 1865, p.3; *York Herald*, 1 January 1853, p.6.
36. *Sussex Advertiser*, 28 February 1854, p.6.
37. Ladies's Society for the Aid of Fugitive Slaves in England, 1857 report. Wilson Anti-Slavery Collection, John Rylands University Library, University of Manchester, Box 11 No. 1.
38. Information from Geoffrey Gillon whose illustrations are on findagrave ref. 50858108.

Chapter 2

1. *Liverpool Mercury*, 13 December 1850.
2. *York Herald* (York), 29 March 1851, p.6.
3. *Leeds Mercury* (Leeds), 12 April 1851; *Hampshire Advertiser* (Southampton), 26 April 1851, *Preston Guardian* (Preston), 26 April 1851 and *Lloyds Weekly Newspaper* (London), 27 April 1851. The 1851 census lists them as 'fugitive slave' with 26-year-old William as a cabinet maker and Ellen aged 24 as 'wife of Wm Craft fugitive slave'. Fugitive slave is underlined. Thanks to Howard Rye.
4. *Leeds Mercury* (Leeds), 12 April 1851; *Hampshire Advertiser* (Southampton), 26 April 1851.
5. *Bristol Mercury* (Bristol), 12 April 1851.
6. *Aberdeen Journal*, 12 February 1852.
7. *Freed-Man* (London), December 1865, pp.110-111. Many thanks to Sean Creighton.

NOTES

8. 'Letters to Antislavery Workers and Agencies, Part Five', *Journal of Negro History*, Vol. 10, No. 3 (July 1925) pp.446-447 has their letter dated Ockham School, 29 November 1851 which says 'Through the aid of Mr. Estlin, and some other kind friends, we have been able to settle at the above school'; William Craft, *Running a Thousand Miles for Freedom* of 1860 commented 'It was principally through the extreme kindness of Mr. Estlin, the Right Hon. Lady Noel Byron, Miss Harriet Martineau, Mrs. Reid, Miss Sturch, and a few other good friends, that my wife and myself were able to spend a short time at a school in this country.'

9. *Bristol Mercury* (Bristol), 30 August 1851, quoting from the *Morning Advertiser* (London). *See also Newcastle Courant* (Newcastle), 10 October 1851.

10. Access to All Saint's Church, Ockham courtesy Mary Watson; Craft, *Running a Thousand Miles*, p.84.

11. *Bristol Mercury* (Bristol), 4 October 1851.

12. Announcement in *Liverpool Mercury* (Liverpool), 5 November 1852 'at Ackham [*sic*], Surrey'; his letter from Ockham dated 10 November 1852 is in 'Letters to Antislavery Workers and Agencies, Part Five', *Journal of Negro History*, Vol. 10, No. 3 (July 1925), pp. 447-448.

13. The baptism register at All Saints, Ockham records the baptism of Charles Estlin Phillips Craft on 2 January 1853, with his parents described as 'fugitive slaves'. On 26 April 1863 both Stephen Brougham Dennoce Craft and his sister Alice Isabella Ellen Craft were baptised at All Saints, Ockham, their parents being 'of London'. An American relative visited this church in 1980.

14. *Anti-Slavery Reporter* (London), January 1854, p.124. It was to be combined with William's 'former trade of cabinet-making'.

15. *Berrow's Worcester Journal*, 19 April 1856, p.5; *Leeds Mercury*, 23 October 1856; *Glasgow Herald*, 3 November 1856; *Newcastle Courant*, 7 November 1856.

16. *Huddersfield Chronicle*, 8 November 1856, p.5.

17. *Bradford Observer*, 13 November 1856, p.5.

18. *Manchester Times*, 6 December 1856.

19. *Hampshire Telegraph* (Portsmouth), 29 August 1857.

20. *Bristol Mercury*, 21 June 1851.

21. *The Times* (London), 2 May 1851, p.4.

22. David F. Dorr, *A Colored Man Round the World* (Ohio: 1858; Ann Arbor: University of Michigan Press, 1999), pp.13, 20.

23. *Nottinghamshire Guardian*, 26 June 1851, p.2.

24. *Liverpool Mercury* (Liverpool), 1 April 1851; *Lloyd's Weekly Newspaper* (London), 15 June 1851. Anderson's letter from London 21 April 1851 is in 'Letters to Antislavery Workers and Agencies, Part Five', *Journal of Negro History*, Vol. 10, No. 3 (July 1925).

25. *Anti-Slavery Advocate* (London), 1 September 1859, p.266.
26. *Anti-Slavery Advocate* (London), 2 July 1860 carries an advert.
27. *Leeds Mercury*, 26 March 1862.
28. *Bristol Mercury*, 12 April 1862.
29. *The Times* (London), 31 August 1863, p. 7; *The Times* (London), 4 September 1863, p.7.
30. *Freed-Man* (London), December 1865, p.110.
31. *Freed-Man* (London), December 1865, p.111. This was copied by the *Newcastle Courant* of 15 December 1865, p.2.
32. *The Times* (London), 8 August 1845, p.8.
33. *The Times* (London), 15 January 1856, p.9; *Daily News* (London), 15 January 1856; *Liverpool Mercury*, 16 January 1856; *Morning Post* (London), 16 January 1856, p.6.
34. *Era* (London), 13 October 1867.
35. *Rochdale Pilot*, 9 November 1867.
36. *Era* (London), 25 March 1882.
37. *Freed-Man* (London), July 1866, p.284; *Freed-Man* (London), January 1867, p.83; *Freed-Man* (London), April 1867, p.137.
38. Wilson Anti-Slavery Collection, John Rylands Library, University of Manchester has dated the town hall event to 1840.
39. *Freed-Man* (London), June 1866, pp.262, 266.
40. Descendants of William Ivens Craft have a copy of Ellen Craft's letter from 5 Atkinson Place, Brixton Road, 19 August 1869 to Mr Hayden who she hoped would meet them, obtained from the Charles Chapman Collection. This was Lewis Hayden in whose house in Boston (still standing) they had stayed and were married.

Chapter 3

1. www.discoveringbristol.org; www.cwgc.org Edwin Thomas Charles Head; www.sgsts.org.uk/Henry Parker. My thanks to Kathy Chater.
2. *Bury and Norwich Post and Suffolk Herald*, Wednesday, 11 June 1851, noted 'an inquest was held on Friday, touching the death of a little boy of colour, the son of the Rev. Alexander Crummell, of Queen's College, formerly of the United States. It appears that the poor little fellow was playing with a small button from off his boot, and having put it into his mouth, it got into his throat and choked him. Mr Bumpstead made a post-mortem examination and found the button had lodged in the windpipe.' My thanks to Hannah Murray.
3. British census 1861; *Frome Times*, 24 June 1863, p.3; *Salisbury and Winchester Journal*, 27 June 1863, p.8; *Sherborne Mercury*, 30 June 1863, p.3.

4. *The Times*, 4 July 1851 p.5.

5. Josephine Brown, *Biography of an American Bondman, by his Daughter* (Boston MA: R.F. Wallcutt, 1856), pp.74-75. She omitted 'school' from the college's title.

6. 'Letters to Antislavery Workers and Agencies, Part Nine', *Journal of Negro History*, Vol. 10, No. 3 (July 1925), pp.547-548.

7. *Mission to the Fugitive Slaves in Canada*, report August 1856. Wilson Anti-Slavery Collection, John Rylands University Library, University of Manchester, Box 16 No. 12.

8. *Freeman's Journal* (Dublin), 8 February 1851; *Belfast News-Letter* 27 October 1851; *Dundee Courier*, 26 November 1851.

9. The Wilson Anti-Slavery Papers at the John Rylands Library, University of Manchester holds a copy of *How Ann Maria Weims came to be transformed into the 'Boy Joe'* from 1860.

10. *Freeman's Journal* (Dublin), 8 February 1851.

11. *Medical Directory, 1859*, p.667; information from Jill Newmark, National Library of Medicine, Bethesda, Maryland.

12. *Liverpool Mercury* 4 November 1851 and also 7 November 1851 carried Christopher Bushell's advertisements – he was a ship's broker with an office in the Royal Insurance Building, Dale Street, Liverpool; and as Christopher Bushell and Company was in the *Liverpool Mercury*, 7 February 1854.

13. 'Letters to Antislavery Workers and Agencies', *Journal of Negro History*, Vol. 10 No. 3 (July 1925), p.71, taken from the *Liberator*, 22 July 1853.

14. *Manchester Times*, 18 November 1854.

15. *Daily News* (London), 10 September 1851; *Morning Post* (London), 10 September 1851; *Glasgow Herald*, 12 September 1851.

16. *Liverpool Mercury*, 26 April 1853.

17. *Standard* (London), 16 June 1859, p.2; *Derby Mercury*, 22 June 1859. Both quote *Cheltenham Examiner.*

18. James Watkins, *Narrative of the Life of James Watkins etc* (Bolton: 1852), p.vi, letter dated 9 Grinfield Street, Edge Hill, Liverpool, 24 April 1851.

19. *Preston Guardian*, 25 October 1851; *Lancaster Gazette*, 1 May 1852, p.5.

20. Watkins, *Narrative*, p.44.

21. *Sheffield and Rotherham Independent* (Sheffield), 1 April 1854, p.2; www.search.connectinghistories.org shows a Birmingham poster for 14 June 1853.

22. Watkins, *Narrative*, p. 46, letter dated 16 January 1852.

23. *Sheffield and Rotherham Independent* (Sheffield), 24 June 1854, p.6.

24. *Derby Mercury*, 9 April 1856.

25. *Belfast News-Letter*, 19 November 1856.

26. *Huddersfield Chronicle*, 22 June 1861, p.8.

27. *Lancaster Gazette*, 20 July 1861 p.8; 10 August 1861 p.3; 31 August 1861 p.8; *Preston Guardian*, 29 January 1862; *York Herald*, 19 September 1863, p.5.

28. *Bradford Observer*, 12 June 1856, p.5; *Dundee Courier*, 5 September 1855.

29. *Northampton Mercury*, 13 February 1864, p.5; *Nonconformist* (London), 20 June 1864, p.579.

30. *Nonconformist* (London), 29 April 1863, p.324; *Nonconformist* (London), 6 May 1863, p.343; *Nonconformist* (London), 26 June 1863, p.214. My thanks to David Killingray; *Freed-Man* (London), October 1865, pp.60, 64; *Freed-Man* (London), February 1868, p.31.

31. *New York Times* (New York), 17 August 1876.

32. *York Herald*, 23 July 1859, 2 August 1859 and 27 August 1859; *Newcastle Courant*, 1 April 1859; *The Times* (London), 3 June 1859, p.11; *The Times*, 15 September 1859, p.7; *The Times*, 12 October 1859, p.9; *The Times*, 15 September 1860, p.12.

33. *Brighton Gazette*, 25 July 1867; *Brighton Gazette*, 1 August 1867; *Hereford Journal*, 28 July 1866, p.3; *Dundee Courier*, 5 December 1866, p.3; *Dundee Advertiser*, 6 December 1866; *Era* (London), 14 April 1867, p.10; *Edinburgh Evening Courant*, 24 December 1866, p.1; Halle's comment was in the *Orchestra* quoted in the *Hereford Journal*, 13 October 1866, p.7; *Birmingham Daily Press*, 18 September 1866, p.4; *Dublin Evening Mail*, 13 December 1866, p.4 copied the *Scotsman*.

34. *Leamington Spa Courier*, 12 October 1867, p.8; *Leicester Chronicle*, 23 July 1870, p.8; *Leicester Chronicle*, 5 February 1870, p.8; *Leicester Chronicle*, 6 April 1872, p.8.

35. *Wrexham Advertiser*, 18 August 1877, p.6; *Berrow's Worcester Journal*, 13 July 1878, p.3.

36. *Western Mail* (Cardiff), 15 October 1878; *Derby Mercury*, 6 August 1879; *Western Mercury*, 6 August 1879; *Western Mail* (Cardiff), 10 November 1879.

37. *Leicester Chronicle*, 1 October 1881, p.5. Countee is spelled Counter.

38. *Leicester Chronicle*, 5 December 1891, p.6. Stephen Bourne advises that she was born on 20 June 1888 at 106 William Street near St Pancras station (email dated 8 June 2011); *Era* (London), 24 September 1892; George Walmer died 27 March 1897 in Dudley aged 54.

39. *Bristol Mercury*, 17 January 1888.

40. *Pall Mall Gazette* (London), 9 September 1895; *Standard* (London), 9 September 1895, p.2; *Yorkshire Herald* (York), 10 September 1895, p.5; *Daily Telegraph* (London), 9 September 1895.

41. *Baptist* (London), 13 September 1895, p.166; Sir George Williams's letter was in Charleston, South Carolina in 1979 and had been reproduced in Jenkins Orphanage tracts; *Baptist* (London), 11 October 1895.

42. *Charleston Messenger*, 7 May 1898, p.1. Copy held at Charleston County Public Library, courtesy Nicholas Butler.

Chapter 4

1. *Illustrated London News* (London), 27 May 1843 p.21; *Gloucester Echo*, 25 April 1938, p.4.
2. *Wells Journal*, 7 May 1937, p.8; *Sunderland Daily Echo*, 2 May 1939, p.6.
3. *Liverpool Mercury*, 1 April 1842; *Manchester Times*, 10 June 1843; *Dundee Courier*, 9 January 1850, p.1.
4. *Standard* (London), 28 May 1844; *Era* (London), 2 June 1844.
5. *Lloyd's Weekly London Newspaper*, 22 December 1844, advertisement for Cooke's Royal Circus, Poplar.
6. *Era* (London), 13 February 1848, p.1.
7. *Berrow's Worcester Journal*, 19 February 1876, p.5.
8. *Era* (London), 22 November 1857.
9. *Hampshire Advertiser* (Southampton), 17 August 1861, p.3.
10. *Leicester Chronicle*, 16 February 1861, p.4.
11. *Sheffield and Rotherham Independent*, 3 January 1861, p.2.
12. *Bristol Mercury*, 22 January 1876.
13. *Freeman's Journal* (Dublin), 7 February 1876.
14. *Sheffield and Rotherham Independent*, 4 November 1876, p.7.
15. *Northern Echo* (Darlington), 25 July 1890; *Illustrated Police News* (London), 2 August 1890; *New York Times*, 1 January 1907.
16. *Huddersfield Chronicle*, 28 October 1893, p.8.
17. *Preston Guardian*, 24 July 1852. Nineteenth-century copies sell for thousands of dollars.
18. *Examiner* (London), 29 May 1852.
19. *Leeds Mercury*, 4 September 1852.
20. *Jackson's Oxford Journal*, 4 December 1852.
21. *Bradford Observer*, 9 December 1852, p.7.
22. *Reynold's Newspaper* (London), 3 October 1852; *Morning Post* (London), 29 September 1852, p.4; *Reynold's Newspaper* (London), 16 January 1853.
23. Programme, Pavilion Theatre, London, at East London Theatre Archive (www.elta-project.org/browse).
24. *Era* (London), 6 February 1853.
25. *Morning Chronicle* (London), 18 April 1853; *Manchester Times*, 11 May 1853; *Hull Packet*, 11 February 1853, p.1.
26. *Morning Chronicle* (London), 15 November 1852; *Bradford Observer*, 17 February 1853, p.1.
27. *Caledonian Mercury* (Edinburgh), 10 February 1853.
28. *Isle of Wight Observer* (Ryde), 12 February 1853.
29. *Morning Chronicle* (London), 18 April 1853; *Manchester Times*, 11 May 1853; *Glasgow Herald*, 13 June 1853.

30. *The Times* (London), 19 December 1855, p.14.
31. *Leeds Mercury*, 18 December 1855.
32. *Sheffield Independent*, 22 December 1855, p.12; *Isle of Wight Observer* (Ryde), 10 May 1856, p.1.
33. *Hampshire Telegraph* (Portsmouth), 28 January 1860.
34. *Daily News* (London), 29 July 1856; *Newcastle Courant*, 9 August 1856; *York Herald*, 4 February 1860, p.5.
35. Programme, Britannia Theatre, Hoxton (London), at East London Theatre Archive (www.elta-project.org/browse).
36. *Era* (London), 22 November 1857; *Era* (London), 10 October 1858; *Bristol Mercury*, 16 October 1858; *Era* (London), 29 May 1859; *Era* (London), 29 April 1860; *Era* (London), 23 December 1860.
37. *Royal Cornwall Gazette* (Truro), 21 June 1861, p.5.
38. COPAC has *The Life of Josiah Henson, formerly a Slave, as Narrated by himself to S.A. Eliot*, 1851.
39. *Whitstable Times and Herne Bay Herald*, 9 December 1876, p.4.

Chapter 5

1. The conversation in Chester is noted at the beginning of chapter three of Burrows's book.
2. *Nottinghamshire Guardian*, 8 February 1849, p.4 quoting the *Exeter Gazette*; *Era* (London), 11 February 1849.
3. *Liverpool Mercury*, 6 February 1852 quoting the *Manchester Guardian*.
4. *Hull Packet*, 31 December 1852; *Morning Post* (London), 13 January 1853.
5. *Lancaster Gazette*, 15 January 1853, p.2, quoting the *Liverpool Standard*; *Huddersfield Chronicle*, 15 January 1853, p.3; *Leicester Chronicle*, 15 January 1853; *Era* (London), 16 January 1853; *Berrow's Worcester Journal*, 20 January 1853.
6. *Liverpool Mercury*, 6 February 1852 quoting the *Manchester Guardian*.
7. Fisch, *American Slaves in Victorian England*, p.91 quoting the *Banner of Ulster*; Fisch, *American Slaves*, p.93 quoting the *Temperance Chronicle* of April 1852.
8. *Brighton Gazette*, 16 March 1854; *Brighton Gazette*, 4 May 1854 published a letter to Chamerovzow from Nixon in Lewes prison dated 12 April; *Cambridge Independent Press*, 16 September 1854.
9. *Windsor and Eton Express*, 15 April 1854, p.3 reported him as 'Robert Nixon'; *Anti-Slavery Advocate* (London), 1 May 1854, pp.157-159. *Brighton Examiner*, 14 February 1854 and *Windsor and Eton Express*, 15 July 1854. See also *Brighton Herald*, 18 March 1854. *Brighton Gazette*, 20 July 1854, p.3 has Chamerovzow's warning letter.
10. *Portsmouth Times*, 12 July 1856, p.5.

11. *Anti-Slavery Reporter* (London), 2 March 1857, p.57 quoting *Perthshire Advertiser*, 12 February 1857; *Londonderry Standard*, 3 September 1857, p.2.
12. *Bradford Observer*, 15 October 1856, p.5.
13. *Huddersfield Chronicle*, 4 October 1856, p.5; *Berrow's Worcester Journal*, 13 November 1858, p.5; *Berrow's Worcester Journal*, 20 November 1858, p.3; *Standard* (London), 3 December 1858, p.8 quoting the *Cheltenham Chronicle*. *Berrow's Worcester Journal*, 4 December 1858, p.5 reported the drunken incident too. This is not Henry Watson author of a *Narrative* published in the U.S.A. in 1848-1850. He briefly visited England.
14. *Chelmsford Chronicle*, 18 January 1856, p.3.
15. *Leicester Chronicle*, 29 January 1853; *Leicester Mercury* as quoted by *Reynold's Newspaper* (London) 6 February 1853 states £13 with the promises to reach £30 but this may have been a different meeting.
16. *Freeman's Journal* (Dublin), 8 April 1853.
17. *Aberdeen Journal*, 31 March 1852.
18. *Newcastle Courant*, 12 May 1854.
19. *Huddersfield Chronicle*, 2 and 3 February 1855.
20. Record Office for Leicestershire, Leicester and Rutland in Leicester reference DG6/C/136. Thanks to Archivist Jess Jenkins.
21. *Dumfries and Galloway Standard*, 3 March 1852, p.3 noted he was back in Scotland from New Brunswick; he purchased a house in Portsoy, Banffshire (*Elgin Courier*, 29 October 1852, p.3). The *Falkirk Herald*, 16 January 1851, p.1 noted he was from Virginia; the *Elgin Courier*, 22 April 1853, p.3 said he was a native of St John, New Brunswick and 'a free-born subject of the British crown'. A legal statement in the *Aberdeen Free Press*, 2 March 1855, p.4 gave his name as Henry Edward Lewis. *South Eastern Gazette* (Maidstone), 28 July 1857, p.5 reported his death 'in London last week' following three months suffering; *Dumfries and Galloway Standard*, 30 September 1857, p.4. Death registration 15 July 1857.
22. *Morning Post* (London), 26 November 1857, p.7; *The Times* (London), 18 November 1857, p.11; *Morning Post* (London), 9 December 1857, p.7; *The Times* (London), 9 December 1857, p.11; *The Times* (London), 12 January 1858, p.9.
23. *Birmingham Daily Post*, 5 January 1858.
24. *Royal Cornwall Gazette* (Truro), 21 June 1861, p.5; *Oxford Journal*, 23 March 1861, p.8; *Royal Cornwall Gazette* (Truro), 28 June 1861, p.4.
25. William M. Mitchell, *The Under-Ground Railroad* (Manchester: Tweedie, 1860), pp.iii-iv; *Taunton Courier*, 14 January 1863, p.3.
26. *Newry Herald and Down, Armagh and Louth Journal*, 12 April 1862, p.3.
27. *Nottinghamshire Guardian*, 7 November 1862.
28. *Nottinghamshire Guardian*, 16 May 1873, p.5.
29. *The Times* (London), 26 March 1870, p.12; *Reynold's Newspaper* (London), 3 April 1870; *The Times* (London), 12 April 1870, p.11; *Bradford Observer*, 14 April 1870, p.7; *Reynold's Newspaper* (London), 17 April 1870.

30. *Dundee Courier*, 3 February 1886; *Huddersfield Daily Chronicle*, 3 February 1886, p.3.
31. *Belfast News-Letter*, 5 February 1886 also quotes the *North British Daily Mail* and the *Glasgow Herald*; *Dundee Courier*, 4 February 1886.
32. *Freeman's Journal* (Dublin), 5 February 1886; *North-Eastern Daily Gazette* (Middlesbrough), 5 February 1886; *Huddersfield Chronicle*, 6 February 1886, p.3; *Liverpool Mercury*, 6 February 1886; *Northern Echo* (Darlington), 15 February 1886; *Freeman's Journal* (Dublin), 22 February 1886; *Dundee Courier*, 6 February 1886; *Dundee Courier*, 12 February 1886; *Glasgow Herald*, 17 February 1886; *Dundee Courier*, 20 February 1886; *Aberdeen Weekly Journal*, 18 February 1886.
33. *Aberdeen Weekly Journal*, 22 February 1886; *Glasgow Herald*, 22 February 1886; *Glasgow Herald*, 5 February 1886; *Dundee Courier*, 27 February 1886; *Glasgow Herald*, 1 March 1886.
34. *North-Eastern Daily Gazette* (Middlesbrough), 8 March 1886; *York Herald*, 8 March 1886, p.6; *North-Eastern Daily Gazette* (Middlesbrough), 9 March 1886.
35. *Glasgow Herald*, 28 April 1886.
36. *Leeds Mercury*, 16 November 1886; *Birmingham Daily Post*, 17 November 1886; *Glasgow Herald*, 26 November 1886; *Aberdeen Weekly Journal*, 9 November 1886 quoting the *Rochdale Times*; *Dundee Courier*, 9 November 1886.
37. *Glasgow Herald*, 9 November 1886; *Leeds Mercury*, 9 November 1886; *Aberdeen Weekly Journal*, 15 November 1886; *Cheshire Observer* (Chester), 13 November 1886, p.6; *Aberdeen Weekly Journal*, 16 November 1886; *Glasgow Herald*, 16 November 1886; *Manchester Times*, 20 November 1886; *Dundee Courier*, 26 November 1886; *Glasgow Herald*, 26 November 1886; *Aberdeen Weekly Journal*, 9 December 1886; *Liverpool Mercury*, 9 December 1886; *Western Mail* (Cardiff), 9 December 1886; *Nottinghamshire Guardian* (Nottingham), 10 December 1886, p.8; *Blackburn Standard*, 11 December 1886, p.3; *Freeman's Journal* (Dublin), 11 December 1886; *The Times* (London), 25 December 1886, p.7.
38. *Workington Star*, 3 November 1888.
39. Peter Thomas Stanford, *From Bondage to Liberty* (Smethwick: Durose, 1889), p.83; *Freeman's Journal* (Dublin), 11 February 1893.

Chapter 6

1. COPAC has *The Life of Josiah Henson, formerly a Slave, as Narrated by himself to S.A. Eliot*, 1851.
2. *Daily News* (London), 15 July 1851. Lord Kinnaird was present and his family were notable philanthropists and supporters of underdogs; and the meeting was chaired by the Earl of Harrowby, a friend of Lord Shaftesbury – the

philanthropist called Lord Ashley until 1851, who chaired the Ragged School Union's annual meetings. All would have known fugitive slaves in Britain. See *Illustrated London News*, 5 August 1848 and, pp.146-147.

3. *Liberia* (New York: 1928) reproduced on anglicanhistory.org/Africa/lb/missions1.

4. www.uwo.ca/huron/promisedland. The Southampton street directory for 1863 has no entry, the next extant volume (1871) lists him in Millbrook Road near the docks, and those of 1876, 1884 and 1887 list him at Brent Cottage/14 Avenue Road on the corner of Rose Road. The Pinckneys died there.

5. *Preston Guardian*, 1 November 1856.

6. *Christian News* (Glasgow), 6 June 1857.

7. *Sheffield Independent*, 21 January 1860, p.10.

8. *Glasgow Herald*, 27 March 1860.

9. *New Brunswick Courier* (St John). My thanks to Susanna Ashton.

10. *Western Daily Press*, 14 September 1860, p.2.

11. *Cheltenham Chronicle*, 30 July 1861, p.2.

12. *The Times* (London), 16 January 1861, p.10; *The Times*, 27 February 1861, p.12; *The Times*, 25 February 1862, p.5.

13. *The Times* (London), 16 January 1861.

14. *Lloyd's Weekly Newspaper* (London), 23 June 1861; *Belfast News-letter*, 25 June 1861; *Reynold's Newspaper* (London), 7 July 1861.

15. *Morning Chronicle* (London), 3 July 1861; *Daily News* (London), 3 July 1861; *Morning Post* (London), p 3; *Leicester Chronicle*, 6 July 1861, p.2.

16. *Bury and Norwich Post* (Bury St Edmunds), 20 August 1861.

17. Harper Twelvetrees, *The Story of the Life of John Anderson, the Fugitive Slave* (London: William Tweedie, 1863), chapter twelve.

18. *Luton Times and Advertiser*, 28 September 1861, p.4.

19. *North Wales Chronicle* (Bangor), 5 October 1861 states this was 'last week'.

20. *Leeds Mercury*, 12 October 1861; *Essex Standard*, 13 December 1861.

21. *The Times* (London), 17 June 1862, p.14; *The Times* (London), 13 May 1861, p.8; *Reynold's Newspaper* (London), 7 July 1861.

22. www.movinghere.org.uk; *Illustrated London News*, 9 March 1861, p.223.

23. *Dundee Courier and Argus*, 31 December 1862.

24. Wilson Anti-Slavery Collection, John Rylands Library, University of Manchester has dated the town hall event to 1840.

25. *Freed-Man* (London), June 1866, pp.262, 266.

26. *Freed-Man* (London), December 1867, pp.267-268.

27. *Leeds Mercury*, 12 June 1891.

28. *Daily News* (London), 7 January 1859 quoting the *West Sussex Gazette*.

29. www.memorials.inportsmouth.co.uk/southsea/shannon.htm; Maritime Museum of the Atlantic, Halifax, Nova Scotia; pp.2-5. In 2010 a commemorative postage stamp was issued in Canada.

30. *Hampshire Telegraph* (Portsmouth), 27 December 1871.
31. *Glasgow Herald*, 1 August 1855 copying the *Liverpool Albion.*
32. *The Times* (London), 20 March 1856, p.12.
33. *Daily News* (London), 20 March 1856; *Morning Chronicle* (London), 20 March 1856.
34. *Glasgow Herald*, 24 March 1856; *Glasgow Herald*, 9 June 1856; see *Caledonian Mercury* (Edinburgh) 30 June 1855.
35. *Caledonian Mercury* (Edinburgh), 6 February 1857.
36. *Caledonian Mercury* (Edinburgh), 24 March 1856.

Chapter 7

1. *Belfast News-Letter*, 10 September 1873.
2. *Graphic* (London), 3 May 1873; *Daily News* (London), 7 May 1893.
3. *Dundee Courier*, 19 September 1873.
4. *Northern Echo* (Darlington), 10 November 1873.
5. *Daily Gazette* (Middlesbrough), 4 April 1874, p.2.
6. *Western Mail* (Cardiff), 6 June 1874.
7. *Essex Standard* (Colchester), 11 June 1875, p.5.
8. *Manchester Times*, 5 February 1876; *Liverpool Mercury*, 7 February 1876.
9. *Sheffield Independent*, 11 March 1876, p.11.
10. *Jackson's Oxford Journal*, 22 April 1876, p.5.
11. *Belfast News-Letter*, 5 December 1876, p.1.
12. *Liverpool Mercury*, 21 November 1876, p.1.
13. *Berrow's Worcester Journal*, 20 January 1877, p.5; *Royal Cornwall Gazette* (Truro), 20 April 1877, p.4; booklet for Agricultural Hall, Bridgnorth, January 1877 in John Johnson Collection, Bodleian Library, Oxford. It details the singers.
14. *Aberdeen Journal*, 28 August 1877, p.2.
15. *Daily Gazette* (Middlesbrough), 20 August 1877, p.2.
16. *Star* (St Peter Port), 20 September 1877.
17. *Bristol Mercury*, 10 May 1878.
18. *Isle of Man Times* (Douglas), 13 July 1878, p.1; *Hampshire Advertiser* (Southampton), 13 July 1878, p.8.
19. *Star* (St Peter Port), 29 June 1878.
20. *Dundee Courier*, 29 July 1878.
21. *Era* (London), 24 November 1878, p.13; *Y Genedl Cymreig* (Caernarvon), 12 December 1878, p.8; *Era* (London), 5 January 1879.
22. *Isle of Man Times* (Douglas), 20 September 1879, p.5.
23. *Era* (London), 5 October 1879.
24. *Jackson's Oxford Journal*, 8 November 1879; *Ipswich Journal*, 18 November 1879.

25. *Era* (London), 23 November 1879; *Era* (London), 30 November 1879; *Belfast News-Letter*, 19 December 1879. Beverly Tetterton of Wilmington advised that both Giles and Stokes were local names.
26. *Leicester Chronicle*, 17 January 1880, p.7; *Leicester Chronicle*, 31 January 1880, p.7.
27. *Liverpool Mercury*, 4 November 1880, p.1.
28. *Otago Witness* (New Zealand), 13 May 1887, p.28. My thanks to Bill Egan.
29. *Era* (London), 24 October 1891; oldbaileyonline.org.case t18911019-792 19 October 1891.
30. *Sheffield Independent*, 7 March 1891, p.1; *Sheffield Independent*, 9 March 1891, p.1; *Sheffield Independent*, 10 March 1891, p.3.
31. *Sheffield Independent*, 28 March 1890 and 1 April 1890.
32. *North-Eastern Daily Gazette*, 20 June 1890 and 26 June 1890; *Isle of Man Times*, 9 August 1890.
33. E. Azalia Hackley Collection, Detroit Public Library.
34. *Weekly Standard* (Blackburn), 18 March 1899, p.7; *Weekly Standard* (Blackburn), 25 March 1899.
35. *Kentish Independent and County Advertiser* (Woolwich), 17 February 1900.
36. *Yorkshire Herald* (York), 17 November 1893, p.3; *Leeds Mercury*, 11 January 1896; *Leeds Mercury*, 26 February 1895.
37. wcl.govt.nz/heritage/robertbradfordwilliams.
38. *Crisis* (New York), Vol. 3 No. 5 (March 1912) p.188 said he was born in Boston, Massachusetts and was a baritone.
39. *Era* (London), 31 July 1897.

Chapter 8

1. Ruggles, *The Unboxing of Henry Brown*, p. 216 n. 25 advises the only known copy of the 1852 edition is in the New York Public Library.
2. *Liverpool Mercury*, 11 July 1881.
3. *Royal Cornwall Gazette* (Truro), 1 December 1882, p.4; *Royal Cornwall Gazette*, 23 February 1883, p.5.
4. *Derby Mercury*, 27 August 1884.
5. *Bristol Mercury*, 27 October 1885.

Chapter 9

1. *Dundee Courier*, 27 October 1858.
2. *Aberdeen Journal*, 4 July 1860.
3. www.exhibits.library.villanova.edu/institute for colored youth; *Christian Recorder* (Philadelphia), 6 April 1861.

4. *Essex Standard*, 27 January 1865, p.3.
5. *Rochdale Pilot*, 9 November 1867 (my thanks to Bernth Lindfors).
6. *Rochdale Observer*, 9 November 1867.
7. *Medical Directory* 1881, p.675; www.sutton.gov.uk/info/200554/heritage; British census 1881 lists him at the Woolwich Union (workhouse) infirmary and states he was 32 and single. The marriage was registered in the last quarter of 1881 in Woolwich and the bride's birth in Lewisham was in 1849.
8. *Medical Directory*, 1887, p.245. The census of 1881, 1891 and 1901 state he was born in the USA and that of 1901 suggests he had remained an American national. That of 1891 names his wife Florence May Rice aged 41 and their daughter Mary Lucinda Rice aged 8, both born in Plumstead.
9. Oldbaileyonline.org case t18810502-498.
10. *Medical Directory*, 1893, p.282.
11. British census 1861.
12. Oldham Local Studies and Archives have the copy.
13. London-born Amy Barbour-James was not permitted to join her school's netball team, she explained in an interview with Jeffrey Green in 1982. Also born in 1906 of black parents, Olive Harleston recalled her Wigan schooldays and enjoyed a reunion with old school colleagues in 1983.
14. *African Times* (London), 5 June 1899, p.87; memorial stone, Charleston, South Carolina states he was born 9 June 1872 and died 1 December 1961.

Chapter 10

1. *Northampton Mercury*, 30 June 1866; *Era* (London), 1 July 1866; *Era* (London), 4 August 1867.
2. *Coventry Herald*, 21 June 1867.
3. *Shields Daily Gazette*, 13 October 1873.
4. *Liverpool Daily Post*, 31 August 1868; *Liverpool Daily Post*, 3 September 1868. The 1871 census lists the American-born George Grosse (*sic*) aged 23 was living in Wapping, London, with his English wife Emma.
5. *Era* (London), 4 August 1867.
6. *Western Gazette*, 11 March 1865, p.3.
7. *Manchester Times*, 21 December 1853.
8. *Leicester Mercury*, 25 September 1858, p.3.
9. *Leeds Intelligencer*, 31 July 1858, p.9.
10. *Western Times*, 18 December 1852, p.7; *Dublin Evening Mail*, 14 September 1864, p.3.
11. *Suffolk Chronicle*, 28 December 1861, p.10; *South Bucks Free Press*, 29 November 1862, p.8; *Hertfordshire Express*, 5 March 1864, p.3; *Bedfordshire Mercury*, 27 February 1864 p.5 reporting the lecture in

Sandy; *Cambridge Chronicle*, 15 October 1864, p.7; *Bedfordshire Mercury*, 28 January 1865, p.4; *Hertfordshire Express and General Advertiser*, 28 January 1865, p.2.

12. *Leeds Mercury*, 12 April 1859, p.3; *Devizes and Wiltshire Gazette*, 23 February 1865, p.2; *Shoreditch Observer* (London), 24 October 1863, p.3; *Reading Mercury*, 27 May 1865, p.5. *Leicester Mercury*, 31 October 1863, p.5; *Oxford Chronicle*, 17 June 1865, p.7; *Watford Observer*, 29 July 1865, p.1.

13. *Staffordshire Sentinel*, 9 May 1863, p.4; *Bolton Chronicle*, 30 January 1864, p.8; *Gloucester Journal*, 15 April 1865, p.8; *Wrexham Advertiser*, 3 June 1865, p.6; *Fife Herald*, 26 January 1865, p.3; *Stamford Mercury*, 20 October 1871, p.5; *Wrexham Advertiser*, 28 February 1874, p.6.

14. *New York Times*, 21 July 1879.

15. *Morning Post* (London), 2 September 1878, p.2; *Standard* (London), 2 September 1878, p.6.

16. *Freeman's Journal* (Dublin), 3 September 1878; *Daily News* (London), 5 September 1878; *Morning Post* (London), 12 September 1878, p.1; *Standard* (London), 12 September 1878, p.4; *Era* (London), 15 September 1878; *Era* (London), 29 September 1878; *Bristol Mercury*, 30 September 1878; *Bristol Mercury*, 19 October 1878, p.4; *Standard* (London), 6 November 1878, p.3; *Leeds Mercury*, 12 November 1878; *Pall Mall Gazette* (London), 12 November 1878; *Era* (London), 15 December 1878.

17. *Glasgow Herald*, 4 February 1879.

18. *Dundee Courier*, 7 March 1879, p.7.

19. *Era* (London), 6 August 1881; *Era* (London), 10 September 1881.

20. *Era* (London), 24 September 1881, p.8; *Era* (London), 29 October 1881, p.16; *Era* (London), 10 December 1881.

21. *Era* (London), 4 March 1882; *Era* (London), 11 March 1882, p.9; *Northern Echo* (Darlington), 4 April 1882; *Liverpool Mercury*, 4 September 1882, p.1; *Era* (London), 21 October 1882.

22. *North-Eastern Daily Gazette* (Middlesbrough), 29 April 1886; *Morning Post* (London), 7 August 1889, p.6; *Yorkshire Herald* (York), 13 December 1890, p.5; *Bristol Mercury*, 15 December 1890; *Bristol Mercury*, 1 January 1891, p.4; *Yorkshire Herald*, 10 January 1891; *Wrexham Advertiser*, 7 March 1891; *Dundee Courier*, 2 April 1891.

23. *Manchester Times*, 27 March 1891; *Sheffield Independent*, 14 April 1891, p.6; *North-Eastern Daily Gazette* (Middlesbrough), 9 June 1891; *Morning Post* (London), 4 November 1891, p.2; *Huddersfield Daily Chronicle*, 23 June 1891, p.3; *Huddersfield Daily Chronicle*, 14 July 1891, p.3.

24. *Morning Post* (London), 23 February 1892, p.5; *Era* (London), 27 February 1892; *Western Mail* (Cardiff), 11 January 1892; *Era* (London), 27 February 1892; *Era* (London), 5 March 1892; *Era* (London), 12 March 1892; *Glasgow Herald*, 15 March 1892; *Era* (London), 19 March 1892.

25. *Era* (London), 9 April 1892; *Manchester Times*, 15 April 1892; *Era* (London), 16 April 1892; *Era* (London), 16 April 1892; *Era* (London), 23 April 1892; *Huddersfield Chronicle*, 30 April 1892, p.7; *Era* (London), 7 May 1892; *Royal Cornwall Gazette* (Truro), 12 May 1892, p.1.

26. *Birmingham Daily Post*, 7 June 1892; *Era* (London), 23 July 1892; *Era* (London), 9 July 1892; *Liverpool Mercury*, 11 July 1892, p.1; *Era* (London), 23 July 1892 quoting the *Western Independent* of 13 July 1892.

27. *Standard* (London), 25 July 1892, p.4; *Era* (London), 30 July 1892; *Era* (London), 6 August 1892; *Era* (London), 24 September 1892; *Era* (London), 10 October 1892, p.1.

28. *Northern Echo* (Darlington), 19 October 1892; *Era* (London), 31 December 1892; *Morning Post* (London), 2 November 1892, p.2; *Standard* (London), 2 November 1892, p.4; *Morning Post* (London), 19 November 1892; *Era* (London), 31 December 1892; *Western Mail* (Cardiff), 6 March 1893; *Star* (Guernsey), 29 April 1853; *Era* (London), 1 July 1893, p.1.

29. *Morning Post* (London), 23 August 1894, p.7; freebmd lists Celestine McLauney's death registration in Fulham, quarter ending September 1894, entry 1a 180.

30. *Standard* (London), 27 April 1894, p.1; *Penny Illustrated Paper* (London), 28 April 1894; *Ipswich Journal*, 28 April 1894; *Ipswich Journal*, 5 May 1894; *Era* (London), 19 May 1894.

31. *Era* (London), 22 February 1896; *Era* (London), 2 January 1897; *Era* (London), 30 January 1897; *Era* (London), 3 July 1897; *Era* (London), 13 March 1897; *Era* (London), 27 March 1897.

Chapter 11

1. Fisch, *American Slaves*, p.93 quoting the *Temperance Chronicle* of April 1852.

2. *Jackson's Oxford Journal*, 7 February 1852.

3. *Belfast News-Letter*, 1 July 1856.

4. *Leeds Mercury*, 12 October 1861; *Essex Standard*, 13 December 1861.

5. *Freed-Man* (London), April 1866, p.225.

6. *Sheffield Daily Telegraph*, 1 December 1865, p.4; *Sheffield Daily Telegraph*, 2 December 1865, p.10.

7. *Derby Mercury*, 29 August 1877.

8. *Sheffield and Rotherham Independent*, 8 January 1863, p.3.

9. *Daily News* (London), 7 February 1863.

10. *Leeds Mercury*, 25 March 1863; *Leeds Mercury*, 28 March 1863.

11. *Morning Post* (London), 6 October 1863, p.7; *Lloyd's Weekly Register* (London), 11 October 1863; *Reynold's Newspaper* (London), 11 October 1863.

NOTES

12. *Bristol Mercury*, 18 July 1863; Fryer, *Staying Power* notes his *Life and Sufferings of Francis Fedric, while in slavery* (1859) and *Slave Life in Virginia and Kentucky* (1863); freebmd.org.uk does not reveal a marriage in England or Wales.

13. *Sheffield Independent*, 3 November 1860, pp.1, 8; *Sheffield Independent*, 10 November 1860, p.10.

14. *Caledonian Mercury* (Edinburgh), 20 February 1861; *Dundee Courier*, 11 March 186; *Dundee Courier*, 18 March 1861; *Dundee Courier*, 1 April 1861.

15. *Dundee Courier*, 17 August 1877, p.1.

16. *Freed-Man* (London), August 1867, pp.202-204.

17. *The Times* (London), 30 August 1881, p.3; *The Times* (London), 10 September 1881, p.6; *The Times* (London), 13 September 1881, p.4.

18. J.E.C. Edwards, *From Slavery to a Bishopric, or the Life of Bishop Walter Hawkins of the British Methodist Episcopal Church of Canada* (London: Kensit, 1891), pp.27, 169.

19. *Sheffield and Rotherham Independent*, 4 December 1880, p.15.

20. *Bristol Mercury*, 23 June 1881.

21. *Daily News* (London), 17 August 1882.

22. *Essex Standard* (Colchester), 19 August 1882, p.2; *Bury and Norwich Post* (Bury St Edmunds), 22 August 1882, p.6.

23. *Belfast News-Letter*, 3 November 1882; *Birmingham Daily Post*, 3 November 1882; *Daily News* (London), 3 November 1882.

24. *Hull Packet*, 15 June 1883.

25. *Sheffield and Rotherham Independent*, 18 June 1886. The census of 1891 lists him aged 30, born in Jamaica, working as a joiner; that of 1901 states he was 40 and born in the British West Indies, a self-employed cabinet-maker with two sons all living in Devon. The 1911 census confirms he was born in Kingston, Jamaica around 1861 and was living in Salcombe, Devon with his wife Susan Bessie Rogers and their five children. He was a cabinet-maker and upholsterer. The family has connections to Canada. He seems to have died in Devon in the winter of 1914-1915.

26. *Morpeth Herald*, 27 August 1887, p.2.

27. *Liverpool Mercury*, 10 May 1894; *Reynold's Newspaper* (London), 13 May 1894.

28. *Royal Cornwall Gazette* (Truro), 28 December 1893; *Royal Cornwall Gazette* (Truro), 1 February 1894, pp.5, 6.

29. *Leeds Mercury*, 29 October 1878; *Northern Echo* (Darlington), 11 August 1879; *Hampshire Advertiser* (Southampton), 16 August 1879, p.7; *Liverpool Mercury*, 11 July 1881.

30. *Bristol Mercury*, 3 February 1894; *Western Mail* (Cardiff), 13 February 1894.

31. *Royal Cornwall Gazette* (Truro), 1 August 1895, p.6.
32. *Dundee Courier*, 8 February 1896, p.1; *Dundee Courier*, 18 February 1896, p.4; *Dundee Courier*, 26 February 1896, p.3; *Era* (London), 22 February 1896; *Glasgow Herald*, 22 April 1896; *Dundee Courier*, 21 October 1896, p.4; *Dundee Courier*, 19 November 1896, p.4; *Dundee Courier*, 1 February 1897, p.3; *Aberdeen Weekly Journal*, 24 March 1897.
33. *Kentish Independent and County Advertiser* (Woolwich), 17 February 1900.
34. *Lloyd's Weekly Newspaper* (London), 24 September 1893; *Morning Post* (London), 25 September 1893, p.7; *Weekly Standard* (Blackburn), 30 September 1893, p.2; *Lloyd's Weekly Newspaper* (London), 29 October 1893; oldbaileyonline.org ref t18931016-918 16 October 1893; *The Times* (London), 25 October 1893, p.3.
35. *Leeds Mercury*, 23 July 1896; *Sheffield and Rotherham Independent* (Sheffield), 23 July 1896, p.6.
36. *Yorkshire Herald* (York), 12 November 1896, p.6.
37. *Isle of Man Times* (Douglas), 12 January 1897, p.2; *Wrexham Advertiser*, 11 March 1899, p.5; *Wrexham Advertiser*, 13 May 1899, p.8; *Wrexham Advertiser*, 20 May 1899, p.6.
38. *Hull Daily Mail*, 30 November 1896, p.6; *Lincolnshire Echo*, 25 February 1897, p.2; *Lincolnshire Echo*, 27 September 1897, p.3; *Bucks Herald* (Aylesbury), 11 December 1897, p.6; *Sunderland Daily Echo*, 18 May 1898, p.4; *Beverley Echo*, 18 May 1898, p.3; *Hull Daily Mail*, 11 November 1898, p.4; *Belfast Telegraph*, 7 December 1898, p.1; *Isle of Man Times* (Douglas), 12 January 1897, p.2; *Wrexham Advertiser*, 11 March 1899, p.5; *Wrexham Advertiser*, 13 May 1899, p.8; *Wrexham Advertiser*, 20 May 1899, p.6; *Aberdeen Press and Journal*, 28 August 1899, p.4; *Shields Daily Gazette*, 15 September 1899, p.1.

Chapter 12

1. *Morning Chronicle* (London), 1 June 1853.
2. *Morning Post* (London), 18 July 1853, p.1.
3. *Freeman's Journal* (Dublin), 1 August 1853.
4. *Era* (London), 1 January 1854.
5. *Era* (London), 14 May 1854; *see also* 'The Museum of the African American Diva' at funtrivia.com.
6. *Daily News* (London), 29 July 1856; *Newcastle Courant*, 9 August 1856; *York Herald*, 4 February 1860, p.5.
7. *Morning Post* (London), 28 July 1856, p.5; Virginia.edu/uncletom/xianslav/xs for text and illustrations.
8. rootsweb.ancestry.com/1856 uncle tom's cabin; is a study of her husband and his novel of 1857.

9. *Daily News* (London), 29 July 1856. Other newspapers copied this review (*Hampshire Telegraph*, 2 August 1856; *Liverpool Mercury*, 2 August 1856; *Wrexham and Denbighshire Weekly Advertiser*, 2 August 1856).

10. *Berrow's Worcester Journal*, 23 August 1856, p.5; *Lancaster Gazette*, 20 September 1856, p.4; *Sheffield Independent*, 20 September 1856, p.8.

11. *The Times* (London), 12 October 1857, p.5 carried an advert quoting the *Literary Gazette* said it was more remarkable than *Uncle Tom's Cabin*; COPAC indicates it was republished in 1969 in the USA.

12. *Caledonian Mercury* (Edinburgh), 8 March 1858; *Liverpool Mercury*, 9 March 1858.

13. *Anti-Slavery Advocate* (London), 1 September 1859, p.266.

14. *Leeds Mercury*, 24 December 1859.

15. *Manchester Weekly Times*, 17 September 1859.

16. 'Lecture on American Slavery by a Coloured Lady', *Warrington Times*, 29 January 1859.

17. *The Times* (London) 7 January 1860, p.9 headed its report 'Disabilities of American Persons of Colour'.

18. *Warrington Times*, 29 January and 5 February 1859. *See also* Taylor, *British and American Abolitionists*, pp.436-437 for Powell's letter from Field Street, Everton, 21 January 1859: 'Miss Remond is at present in L'pool'.

19. Taylor, *British and American Abolitionists*, p.440 for Webb's letter to May, Dublin 3 May 1859: 'She is really very clever – the most so of all the coloured people I have met, except Douglass, & is a very much more sensible & thoroughgoing person than he.'

20. The National Archives, Kew (London) HO 1/123/4809.

21. *New York Times*, 7 March 1888, obituary.

22. *Freed-Man* (London), December 1866, p.284; *Freed-Man*, January 1867, p.83.

23. *Morning Post* (London), 29 December 1882, p.1.

24. *Daily News* (London), 16 October 1882; *Era* (London), 21 October 1882.

25. *Morning Post* (London), 12 December 1882, p.1; *Pall Mall Gazette* (London), 14 December 1882; *Morning Post* (London), 27 December 1882, p.1.

26. *Morning Post* (London), 28 December 1882, p.6.

27. *Era* (London), 19 January 1889; *Leicester Chronicle*, 2 February 1889, p.5; *Era* (London), 23 February 1889.

28. *Sheffield Independent*, 23 February 1889, p.1; *Sheffield Independent*, 26 February 1889, p 6; *Era* (London), 9 March 1889.

29. *Sheffield Independent*, 5 March 1889, p.6; *Sheffield Independent*, 11 March 1889, p.3.

30. *Huddersfield Daily Chronicle*, 8 March 1889, p.1; *Huddersfield Daily Chronicle*, 12 March 1889, p.3.

31. *Leeds Mercury*, 26 March 1889; *Era* (London), 30 March 1889.

32. *Liverpool Mercury*, 16 April 1889; *Liverpool Mercury*, 22 April 1889; *Liverpool Mercury*, 23 April 1889.

33. *Manchester Times*, 4 May 1889; *Belfast News-Letter*, 17 June 1889; *Freeman's Journal* (Dublin), 25 June 1889, p.4; *Freeman's Journal* (Dublin), 1 July 1889; *Freeman's Journal* (Dublin), 10 July 1889.

34. *Cheshire Observer* (Chester), 20 July 1889, p.3; *Leicester Chronicle*, 20 July 1889, p.3.

35. *Liverpool Mercury*, 8 July 1891, p.4.

36. *The Times* (London), 13 July 1892, p.12; *The Times* (London), 18 July 1892, p.9.

37. *Liverpool Mercury*, 12 July 1892; *Standard* (London), 12 July 1892, pp.4, 7; *Leeds Mercury*, 19 July 1892; *Pall Mall Gazette* (London), 19 July 1892; *Standard* (London), 22 July 1892, p.5; *North-Eastern Daily Gazette* (Middlesbrough), 23 July 1892.

38. *Daily News* (London), 26 July 1892; *Pall Mall Gazette* (London), 26 July 1892; *Era* (London), 6 August 1892; *Liverpool Mercury*, 6 August 1892; *Pall Mall Gazette* (London), 6 August 1892; *Liverpool Mercury*, 8 August 1892; *Yorkshire Herald* (York), 10 August 1892, p.6; I am indebted to Kyra E. Hicks, authority on black quilt makers, author of *Black Threads* (2003) and the novel *Martha Ann's Quilt for Queen Victoria* (2007).

Chapter 13

1. 'Letters to Antislavery Workers and Agencies, Part Five', *Journal of Negro History*, Vol. 10, No. 3 (July 1925) pp.446-447 has their letter dated Ockham School, 29 November 1851 which says 'Through the aid of Mr. Estlin, and some other kind friends, we have been able to settle at the above school'; William Craft, *Running a Thousand Miles for Freedom* of 1860 commented 'It was principally through the extreme kindness of Mr. Estlin, the Right Hon. Lady Noel Byron, Miss Harriet Martineau, Mrs. Reid, Miss Sturch, and a few other good friends, that my wife and myself were able to spend a short time at a school in this country.'

2. I remain indebted to Geoffrey Gillon who told me of the grave.

3. *Western Gazette*, 23 June 1865, p.5.

4. My thanks to Ed Bristow, Dorset History Centre.

5. *Morning Post* (London), 27 July 1870, p.3.

6. *Hampshire Advertiser* (Southampton), 30 July 1870, p.5.

7. British Fairground Ancestors, 1861: Showmen in members.shaw.ca/pauline777.

8. *Birmingham Daily Post*, 28 September 1870; *Dundee Courier*, 29 September 1870; *Bristol Mercury*, 1 October 1870.

9. British Fairground Ancestors, 1861: Showmen in members.shaw.ca/pauline777.

10. *Lloyd's Weekly Newspaper* (London), 18 January 1880.

11. *The Times* (London), 17 April 1882, p.12.

12. svgancestry.com
13. *Era* (London), 2 May 1896.
14. *Era* (London), 16 March 1895; *Era* (London), 20 April 1895.
15. *Era* (London), 1 June 1895.
16. *Morning Post* (London), 4 May 1887, p.8.
17. Thompson's application for a US passport, Rostov, July 1895; Leo Thompson's application, Leipzig, December 1908. Library of Congress courtesy Rainer Lotz. Thompson died in Egypt in 1909 and his son in England in 1920. Both are buried in Brookwood cemetery, Surrey and descendants live in England. *See also* ypsigleanings.aadl.org.
18. *Ipswich Journal*, 19 July 1856. See also: *Morning Chronicle* (London), 17 July 1856; *Morning Post* (London), 1 August 1856, p.7; *Ipswich Journal*, 2 August 1856.
19. *Freeman's Journal* (Dublin), 21 August 1856 quoting the *Morning Advertiser* (London). Boxing historians study an aspect of entertainment, and there are images of Travers who is thought to have been born in Virginia in 1836 (or London in 1832) and moved to Britain with his parents. In August 1863 he fought in Oxfordshire. Kevin Smith, *Black Genesis. The History of the Black Prizefighter 1760-1870* (New York: iUniverse, 2003) pp.146-160 says he stated he was raised in Truro, Cornwall where his father sold crockery. He married a Manchester woman and had five children. He ran The Sun and 13 Cantons which if that pub is the London one, it was built in 1882. Smith thinks Travers was alive in 1904. The obvious errors in British place names make Smith an unreliable source.
20. *Era* (London), 12 January 1851; *Era* (London), 20 April 1851; *Era* (London), 8 June 1851; *Era* (London), 14 December 1851.
21. *Reynold's Newspaper* (London), 16 February 1851; *Lloyd's Weekly Newspaper* (London), 15 February 1852; Smith, *Black Genesis*, p.149.
22. *The Times* (London), 25 August 1877, p.11.
23. *Morning Post* (London), 20 March 1869, p.6.
24. *The Times* (London), 19 November 1874, p.11; *Morning Post* (London), 9 October 1874, p.7.
25. *Liverpool Mercury*, 1 April 1842; *Manchester Times*, 10 June 1843; *Dundee Courier*, 9 January 1850, p.1.
26. *Standard* (London), 28 May 1844; *Era* (London), 2 June 1844.
27. *Lloyd's Weekly London Newspaper*, 22 December 1844, advertisement for Cooke's Royal Circus, Poplar.
28. *Hampshire Telegraph* (Portsmouth), 25 August 1849; *Jackson's Oxford Journal*, 14 July 1849.
29. *Nottinghamshire Guardian*, 28 March 1879.
30. *Morning Post* (London), 2 September 1878, p.2.
31. *Standard* (London), 2 September 1878, p.6.

32. Herbert Marshall and Mildred Stock, *Ira Aldridge: The Negro Tragedian* (Carbondale: Southern Illinois University Press, 1968), pp.291, 292, 295, 299-300.

33. Ray Costello, *Black Salt: Seafarers of African Descent on British Ships* (Liverpool University Press, 2012), p.107.

34. Kathleen Chater, *Untold Histories: Black People in England and Wales during the Period of the British Slave Trade, c.1660-1807* (Manchester University Press, 2009), pp.38-67 especially p.85.

35. *Aberdeen Weekly Journal*, 9 February 1894 quoting from *Cassell's History of the Franco-Prussian War*, volume 10; *Roll of Graduates* (Aberdeen, 1890); Brethren Archive online shows the cemetery and grave at Fond de Givonne near Sedan.

36. Neil Parsons, *King Khama, Emperor Joe, and the Great White Queen. Victorian Britain through African Eyes* (University of Chicago Press, 1998).

37. My thanks to Stephen Bourne who traced Branford from a reference in Clive Emsley, *The Great British Bobby: A History of British Policing from 1829 to the Present* (London: Quercus, 2009) and rev. ed. (2010). Emsley described Branford as 'half-caste'. His source was Timothy Cavanagh, *Scotland Yard Past and Present. Experiences of Thirty-Seven Years* (London: Chatto and Windus, 1893): 'not an educated man: but what to my idea was of much greater importance, he possessed a thorough knowledge of police matters in general. I should say he was about the only half-caste superintendent officer the Met ever had.'

38. Jeffrey Green, *Samuel Coleridge-Taylor, a Musical Life* (London: Pickering and Chatto, 2011), pp.41-43, 44, 97, 98, 104.

Chapter 14

1. Gerald Horne, *Negro Comrades of the Crown: African Americans and the British Empire fight the U.S. before Emancipation* (New York University Press, 2012), p.192.

2. Adelaide Cromwell Hill and Martin Kilson, *Apropos of Africa: Sentiments of American Negro Leaders on Africa from the 1800s to the 1950s* (London: Cass, 1969), pp.123, 124.

3. Tim Madigan, *The Burning: Massacre, Destruction, and the Tulsa Race Riot of 1921* (New York: St Martin's Griffin, 2001).

Chapter 15

1. Blackett, *Building an Antislavery Wall*, p.195.

Chapter 16

1. My thanks to Kathy Chater.
2. My thanks to Lynda Kitching of the Friends of Beckett Street Cemetery, Leeds.
3. Jeffrey Green, *Black Edwardians: Black People in Britain 1901-1911* (London: Frank Cass, 1998), pp.100-101.
4. My thanks to Mark Rollason, family historian, e mails July 2014.
5. My thanks to Elizabeth Stacey whose grandmother was Nelson Countee's daughter Mary Ann Amelia Seville.
6. Members of the Craft family in Charleston, South Carolina and in southern England, combined with Mary Watson of Ockham, helped unravel this complex and warming family history.
7. Malton A. McLaurin, 'Divine Convictions: The Tale of an African American Trickster in Victorian Britain', *Gateway Heritage*, Vol. 15 No. 3 (Winter 1994-1995), p.5.
8. www.search.connectinghistories.org.ukEsther Ann Johnson; thanks to Helen Franklin and Stephen Bourne.
9. E mail to Jeffrey Green from Hilary Dawson in Toronto, 21 November 2015.
10. www.uwo.ca/huron/promisedland. The Southampton street directory for 1863 has no entry, the next extant volume (1871) lists him in Millbrook Road near the docks, and those of 1876, 1884 and 1887 list him at Brent Cottage/14 Avenue Road on the corner of Rose Road. The Pinckneys died there.
11. Jill L. Newmark, 'Face to Face with History', www.archives.gov/publications/prologue/2009 has a photograph from August 1863 of William Powell in uniform; C. Peter Ripley (ed.), *Black Abolitionist Papers*, Vol. 5, No. 1 (Chapel Hill, North Carolina: University of North Carolina Press, 1992), p.235; Ripley (ed.), *Black Abolitionist Papers*, No. 12, p.237. My thanks to Bernth Lindfors. Death registrations, West Derby district. Other information: courtesy Kathy Chater and Jill Newmark.
12. Philip S. Foner, *Essays in Afro-American History* (Philadelphia: Temple University Press, 1978), p.107.
13. E mail to Jeffrey Green from Rita Hughes in Australia, 22 March 2015. She never met her great grandmother who died when she was a child.
14. My thanks to Howard Rye.

Further Reading

The Fisk Jubilee Singers have an excellent historian in Andrew Ward whose *Dark Midnight When I Rise* (2000) uses the reports sent from Europe by choir members. Although making only a vacation visit to Europe in 1870, Jeremiah G. Hamilton's life (Shane White, *Prince of Darkness*, 2015) – 'Wall Street's first black millionaire' – shows that nineteenth-century African-Americans included remarkable individuals whose lives outside stereotypes have been overlooked. The Mississippi-born waiter-turned-hotelier Frederick Thomas, who made a fortune in imperial Russia and spent weeks working in London in 1895, also has a recent biography (Alexandrov, *The Black Russian*, 2013). Descendants of Hamilton live in Switzerland, of Thomas in France.

Booker T. Washington first visited England in 1897, commenting that 'The English colonial system brings each year hundreds of representatives of all races and colors from every part of the world to London': Louis R. Harlan, *Booker T. Washington: The Making of a Black Leader, 1856-1901* (New York, Oxford University Press, 1972), p.241, a fine account of a slave child who rose to be a leader of his people. Another who struggled for an education is Mamie Garvin Fields who wrote *Lemon Swamp and Other Places: A Carolina Memoir* (1983). She was born in 1888.

The deaths and rioting initiated by white Americans destroying lives, property, churches and hopes can be seen in Leon Prather's *We Have Taken a City* (1984), an account of the destruction of black Wilmington, North Carolina in a vicious affirmation of white supremacy in 1898.

The following books provide more background:

Baptist, Edward E., *The Half Has Never Been Told: Slavery and the Making of American Capitalism* (New York, Basic Books, 2014)

Chater, Kathleen, *Untold Histories: Black People in England and Wales during the Period of the British Slave Trade, c. 1660-1807* (Manchester University Press, 2009)

Dabydeen, David, and Edwards, Paul (eds), *Black Writers in Britain 1760-1890* (Edinburgh University Press, 1991)

Flanders, Judith, *The Victorian City: Everyday Life in Dickens' London* (London, Atlantic Books, 2012)

FURTHER READING

Hattersley, Roy, *Blood and Fire: William and Catherine Booth and their Salvation Army* (London, Little, Brown, 1999)

Marsh, Jan (ed.), *Black Victorians: Black People in British Art, 1800-1900* (Aldershot: Lund Humphries, 2005)

Stevens, Mark, *Broadmoor Revealed: Victorian Crime and the Lunatic Asylum* (Barnsley, Pen & Sword Social History, 2013)

Winder, Robert, *Bloody Foreigners: The Story of Immigration to Britain* (London, Little, Brown, 2004)

Bibliography

Primary Sources

Ajayi, J.F.A., *Christian Missions in Nigeria 1841–1891: The Making of a New Elite* (Evanston IL, Northwestern University Press, 1965)

Alexandrov, Vladimir, *The Black Russian* (London, Head of Zeus, 2013)

Alpern, Stanley B., *Amazons of Black Sparta: The Women Warriors of Dahomey* (London, Hurst, 1998)

Anthony, Barry, *Murder, Mayhem and Music Hall: The Dark Side of Victorian London* (London, Tauris, 2015)

Blackett, Richard J.M., *Building an Antislavery Wall: Black Americans in the Atlantic Abolitionist Movement, 1830–1860* (Baton Rouge, LA, Louisiana State University Press, 1983)

Blackett, Richard J.M., *Beating Against the Barriers: Biographical Essays in Nineteenth-Century Afro-American History* (Baton Rouge, Louisiana State University Press, 1986)

Brendon, Piers, *Thomas Cook: 150 Years of Popular Tourism* (London, Secker and Warburg, 1991)

Bressey, Caroline, *Empire, Race and the Politics of Anti-Caste* (London, Bloomsbury, 2013)

Brode, Patrick, *The Odyssey of John Anderson* (Toronto, Osgoode Society, 1989)

Brooks, Tim, *Lost Sounds: Blacks and the Birth of the Recording Industry, 1890–1919* (Urbana, University of Illinois Press, 2004)

Burnett, John, *England Eats Out 1830–Present* (Harlow, Pearson, 2004)

Collicott, Sylvia L., *Connections: Haringey, Local-National-World Links* (London, Haringey Community Information Service, 1986)

Colman, Terry, *Passage to America: A History of Emigrants from Great Britain and Ireland to America in the mid-Nineteenth Century* (London, Hutchinson, 1972)

Dickerson, Vanessa D., *Dark Victorians* (University of Illinois Press, 2008)

Draper, Christopher and Lawson-Reay, John, *Scandal at Congo House: William Hughes and the African Institute, Colwyn Bay* (Lanrwst, Gwasg Carreg Gwalch, 2012)

Duster, Alfreda M., *Crusade for Justice: The Autobiography of Ida B. Wells* (Chicago, University of Chicago Press, 1972)

BIBLIOGRAPHY

Elkin, Robert, *Royal Philharmonic* (London, Rider, 1946), p.11

Farrison, William Edward, *William Wells Brown, Author and Reformer* (University of Chicago Press, 1969)

Fisch, Audrey, *American Slaves in Victorian England* (Cambridge University Press, 2000)

Flavell, Julie, *When London was Capital of America* (New Haven, Yale University Press, 2010)

Foner, Philip S., *Essays in Afro-American History* (Philadelphia, Temple University Press, 1978)

Fryer, Peter, *Staying Power: The History of Black People in Britain* (London, Pluto, 1984)

Fyfe, Christopher, *A History of Sierra Leone* (London, Oxford University Press, 1962)

Fyfe, Christopher, *Africanus Horton 1835–1883: West African Scientist and Patriot* (New York, Oxford University Press, 1972)

Genovese, Eugene D., *Roll, Jordan, Roll: The World the Slaves Made* (London, Andre Deutsch, 1975)

Gerzina, Gretchen Holbrook (ed.), *Black Victorians, Black Victoriana* (New Brunswick, NJ, Rutgers University Press, 2003)

Green, Jeffrey, *Edmund Thornton Jenkins: the Life and Times of an American Black Composer, 1894–1926* (Westport, Connecticut, Greenwood Press, 1982)

Green, Jeffrey, *Black Edwardians: Black People in Britain 1901–1914* (London, Frank Cass, 1998)

Green, Jeffrey, 'Minstrelsy' in David Dabydeen, John Gilmore and Cecily Jones (eds), *The Oxford Companion to Black British History* (Oxford University Press, 2007), pp.299–301

Greenspan, Ezra, *William Wells Brown: An African-American Life* (New York, Norton, 2014)

Hattersley, Roy, *Blood & Fire: William and Catherine Booth and their Salvation Army* (London, Little, Brown, 1999)

Hendrick, George and Willene, *The Creole Mutiny: A Tale of Revolt aboard a Slave Ship* (Chicago, Ivan Dee, 2003)

Horne, Gerald, *Negro Comrades of the Crown: African Americans and the British Empire Fight the U.S. before Emancipation* (New York University Press, 2012)

Horn, Pamela, *The Victorian and Edwardian Schoolchild* (Gloucester, Alan Sutton, 1989)

Jefferson, Paul (ed.), *The Travels of William Wells Brown* (Edinburgh University Press, 1991)

Jenkins, Paul (ed.), *The Recovery of the West African Past: African Pastors and African History in the Nineteenth Century* (Basel, Basler Afrika Bibliographier, 2000)

Johnson, James, *The Life of the Late James Johnson (coloured evangelist)* (Oldham, 1914)

Johnson, Thomas L., *Twenty-Eight Years a Slave* (Bournemouth, Mate, 1908)

Law, Robin, *Ouidah: The Social History of a West African Slaving 'Port' 1727–1892* (Oxford, James Currey, 2004)

Lee, Maureen D., *Sissieretta Jones, 'The Greatest Singer of her Race', 1868–1933* (Columbia, SC, University of South Carolina Press, 2012)

Lindfors, Bernth (ed.), *Ira Aldridge: The African Roscius* (Rochester, New York, University of Rochester Press, 2007)

Lindfors, Bernth, *Ira Aldridge: The Vagabond Years, 1833–1852* (Rochester, New York, University of Rochester Press, 2011)

Longmate, Norman, *The Waterdrinkers: A History of Temperance* (London, Hamish Hamilton, 1968)

Martell, Joanne, *Millie-Christine: Fearfully and Wonderfully Made* (Winston-Salem, NC, John F. Blair, 2000)

Moses, Wilson Jeremiah, *Alexander Crummell: A Study of Civilization and Discontent* (New York, Oxford University Press, 1989)

O'Connell, Deidre, *The Ballad of Blind Tom* (New York, Overlook Duckworth, 2009)

Okokon, Susan, *Black Londoners 1880–1990* (Stroud, Sutton Publishing, 1998)

Quarles, Benjamin, *Black Abolitionists* (New York, Oxford University Press, 1969)

Reynolds, Harry, *Minstrel Memories: The Story of Burnt Cork Minstrelsy in Great Britain from 1836 to 1927* (London, Alston Rivers, 1928)

Ripley, C. Peter (ed.), *The Black Abolitionist Papers. Vol 1: The British Isles, 1830–1865* (Chapel Hill, University of North Carolina Press, 1985)

Roche, T.W.E., *The Key in the Lock: A History of Immigration Control in England from 1066 to the Present Day* (London, John Murray, 1969)

Ruck, Calvin W., *The Black Battalion 1916–1920: Canada's Best Kept Military Secret* (Halifax, Nimbus Publishing, 1987)

Ruggles, Jeffrey, *The Unboxing of Henry Brown* (Richmond, Library of Virginia, 2003)

Shaw, George Bernard, *London Music in 1888–89 [sic] as Heard by Corno di Bassetto (later known as Bernard Shaw)* (London, Constable, 1937)

Smith, Kevin R., *Black Genesis: The History of the Black Prizefighter 1760–1870* (New York, iUniverse, 2003)

Southern, Eileen, *The Music of Black Americans: A History. Third Edition* (New York, Norton, 1997)

Stratmann, Linda, *Cruel Deeds and Dreadful Calamities: The Illustrated Police News 1864–1938* (London, British Library, 2011)

Taylor, Clare, *British and American Abolitionists: An Episode in Transatlantic Understanding* (Edinburgh University Press, 1974)

Temperley, Howard, *British Antislavery 1833–1870* (London, Longman, 1972)

Toll, Robert C., *Blacking Up: The Minstrel Show in Nineteenth-Century America* (New York, Oxford University Press, 1974)

Turnbull, Richard, *Shaftesbury: The Great Reformer* (Oxford, Lion, 2010)

Visram, Rozina, *Ayahs, Lascars and Princes: The Story of Indians in Britain 1700–1947* (London, Pluto Press, 1986)

Ward, Andrew, *Dark Midnight when I Rise: The Story of the Fisk Jubilee Singers* (New York, HarperCollins Amistad, 2001)

Waters, Hazel, *Racism on the Victorian Stage* (Cambridge University Press, 2007)

Whyte, Iain, *'Send Back the Money!' The Free Church of Scotland and American Slavery* (Cambridge, James Clarke and Co., 2012)

Winder, Robert, *Bloody Foreigners: The Story of Immigration to Britain* (London, Little, Brown, 2004)

Winks, Robin W., *The Blacks in Canada* (New Haven, Yale University Press, 1971)

Winter, Alison, *Mesmerized: Powers of Mind in Victorian Britain* (University of Chicago Press, 1998)

Wood, Marcus, *Blind Memory: Visual Representations of Slavery in England and America 1780–1865* (Manchester University Press, 2000)

Wright, Philip, *Knibb, 'the Notorious' Slaves' Missionary 1803–1845* (London, Sidgwick and Jackson, 1973)

Other Sources

'In Retrospect: Black Prima Donnas of the Nineteenth Century', *Black Perspective in Music* (New York), Vol. 7 No. 1 (Spring 1979)

'Letters to Antislavery Workers and Agencies, Part Five', *Journal of Negro History*, Vol. 10, No. 3 (July 1925)

Bourne, Stephen, 'Amy Height (1866–1913)', *BASA Newsletter* (London), 58, January 2011

Erlmann, Veit, '"A Feeling of Prejudice": Orpheus M. McAdoo and the Virginia Jubilee Singers in South Africa 1890–1898', *Journal of Southern African Studies*, Vol. 14 No. 3 (April 1988)

Gardner, Eric, '"A Gentleman of Superior Cultivation and Refinement": Recovering the Biography of Frank J. Webb', *African American Review*, Vol. 35, No. 2 (Summer 2001), pp.297-308

Green, Jeffrey, '"Beef Pie with a Suet Crust": A Black Childhood in Wigan (1906–1920)', *New Community*, Vol. XI, No. 3 (Spring 1984), pp.291–298

Green, Jeffrey, 'An American Band in London, 1914' *Musical Traditions 9* (Autumn 1991) cover and pp. 12–17

Hamer, Philip M., 'Great Britain, the United States, and the Negro Seamen Acts, 1822–1848', *Journal of Southern History*, Vol. 1 No. 1 (February 1935), pp. 3–28

Hamer, Philip M., 'British Consuls and the Negro Seamen Acts, 1850–1860', *Journal of Southern History*, Vol. 1, No. 2 (May 1935), pp.138–168

Hill, Robert A., 'King Menelik's Nephew: Prince Thomas Mackarooroo, aka Prince Ludwig Menelik of Abyssinia', *Small Axe 26* (June 2008)

Howard, Ron, 'Carlos Trower, the African Blondin', *BASA Newsletter 62* (London) March 2012, pp.7–10.

Kates, Susan, 'The Embodied Rhetoric of Hallie Quinn Brown', *College English*, Vol. 59, No. 1 (January 1997)

McLaurin, Malton A., 'Divine Convictions: The Tale of an African American Trickster in Victorian Britain', *Gateway Heritage*, Vol. 15 No. 3 (Winter 1994–1995)

Norris, William, 'Additional Light on S. Morgan Smith', *Black American Literature Forum*, Vol. 20 No. 1/2 (1986)

Olney, James, '"I Was Born": Slave Narratives, Their Status as Autobiography, and as Literature', *Callaloo*, No. 20 (Winter 1984)

Oxford Dictionary of National Biography for William Brougham, Henry Box Brown, Isaac Brown, Ellen and William Craft, John Bishop Estlin, Mary Anne Estlin, Charles Hastings, Africanus Beale Horton, William Henry Lane, Millie and Christine McCoy, James Samuel Risien Russell, Peter Thomas Stanford, the Duchess of Sutherland, and Egbert Austin Williams

Rye, Howard, 'The Jenkins' Orphanage Bands in Britain', *Storyville* (Chigwell, Essex), No. 130 (June 1987)

Southern, Eileen, 'Frank Johnson of Philadelphia and His Promenade Concerts', *Black Perspective in Music*, Vol. 5 No. 1 (Spring 1977), pp.7–11

Index

INDEX